Powerful Partnering

With Words I Never Learned in Medical School

E.L. Hollenberg, M.D.

Xulon
PRESS

Xulon Press
11350 Random Hill Center
Suite 800
Fairfax, VA 22030
(703) 279-6511
XulonPress.com

Dedication

To all those who want to...

Become partners,

Striving for the best,

Climbing higher, stronger, better.

May this book help you in your quest.

I am writing this book to create a positive perspective of the medical profession. Virtually every profession is under attack, with persons maligned and serious criticisms being leveled. Medicine as a profession has often been criticized in recent years, blamed for the problems existing in the healthcare delivery systems. The blame game is an exercise in futility and negativism.

It is true that, as a profession, we have in many ways abdicated our leadership role in maintaining a high commitment to serving people's medical needs. It is time for us to redefine and assert our proper values, championing the qualities and processes that make for excellence. This cannot be done by political processes alone, but will require strength of character and spiritual power.

The great majority of physicians already exhibit character traits of excellence. They are, for the most part, committed to the welfare of their patients. They continue in spite of the highly erosive and frustrating forces thrust upon the profession by legislators, entrepreneurs and governmental bureaucrats. Almost all physicians feel victims of poor planning, flawed processes and burdensome regulations. We desire to retain the sacred elements of excellence in doctor-patient relationships, but we never learned how to do this in our medical school training.

In an address honoring the twentieth anniversary of the American Board of Family Practice, Arnold S. Relman, M.D., addressed this deficiency in our medical training. Dr. Relman, who was the editor-in-chief of the New England Journal of Medicine for a number of years, aptly called his address "What Medical Graduates Need to Know But Don't Learn in Medical School." In part, Dr. Relman said:

> What should doctors know that they don't learn in medical school? The quick answer to that is, "A lot!" Of course, it would be fatuous to deny that medical school teaches you much that you have to know to practice medicine. Without what you learned in medical school you couldn't practice medicine. But the sad fact is that, in their formal curriculum, the best medical schools today don't teach many things doctors really have to understand about the practice of medicine.
>
> First of all, if they can't do anything else, doctors must at least be skillful at talking and relating to patients as human beings. They must understand all the personal, psychological and social factors that go in the problems that patients bring to physicians. I don't know of any medical school—and I've been in and around a lot of them in more than 40 years in medicine—that teaches this skill adequately. Some, to their credit, are beginning to pay attention to the problems and are trying to organize their educational curriculum to deal with it. But many schools seem to believe that it's much more important to students to learn the technological content of medicine and that they will learn how to deal with patients simply by example.
>
> In my judgment, one of the main reasons the medical profession is losing favor with the public is that more and more patients perceive their doctors simply as technicians

and specialists. They don't see us as interested in them as people, and feel that we are not willing to give them the time, attention or emotional support they need.

I am so proud to be part of one of the noblest professions in the world. I am grateful to have known and worked with many professors and physicians who were not only brilliant but also of excellent character. Many patients will attest with pride to the excellence they have observed in the physicians who have attended them. However, only a small portion of the commendable character found in physicians today was formed during their medical training. Many physicians possessed superior character traits before attending medical school—learned in their homes, churches, synagogues, scouting, 4-H or schools.

In cases where students are deficient in character traits when entering medical school, yet truly desirous of serving their patients, they generally are not challenged to grow in these deficient areas. They are, however, smart enough to acquire sufficient knowledge to pass the tests and specialty boards. Many are even in the top of the class. On the contrary, some of those in the lower half of the class struggle through school but make some of the best doctors. Just as wisdom and knowledge often have no connection, getting good grades and having good character are two distinct processes.

Throughout this book I want to show my deepest gratitude to my wife and family, teachers, parents and patients who have helped shape my character and motivate me to strive for success in living, serving and growing. While I have not reached my full potential or the end of my career, I know that my patients who understand our partnership will help me continue to grow, through a deeper comprehension of the words, habitudes and processes in this book.

Acknowledgments

Although many people have contributed their thoughts and time to make this book rise above my solitary efforts, I can only mention a few here. Most of all, I am grateful to my wife, Jean, my partner for 50 years. Not only has she encouraged me, but it is also through her that I began learning, and continue to learn, about partnering. For 15 years she has lived with my preoccupations about this project. Her writing skills and endless hours of proofreading gave me the freedom to create the big picture. She also supplied me with invaluable criticisms, making sure that my words were firmly grounded in reality. When the rough manuscript began coming together, she provided valuable attention to detail, which is difficult for me. Without her life and love, I could not have written about powerful partnering.

Jim Buchan has been a very capable editor-in-chief. He has polished both the structure and substance, and has been a creative sounding board for my ideas. I am grateful for his encouragement and guidance. I especially appreciate his life as a Christian minister, lawyer, author and leader.

Brad Conn, whom I delivered into this world 36 years ago, has been a joy to our family. He has grown into a very proficient and creative illustrator. The paradigms and drawings in this book are his workmanship, as he accurately translated my concepts to paper.

Jodi Barr, my niece, is also a gifted and creative artist, and she is responsible for the cover. She quickly caught the spirit of this book and patiently persisted through our many revisions.

Special thanks to my business consultant, David Scroggins and Brian Shockney, CEO, of Logansport Memorial Hospital. Both read the early manuscript and gave much encouragement to persist in my efforts.

All our children, older grandchildren and closest friends listened, shared and served as a stimulus to concepts that were evolving and growing in my mind. I am grateful for their love and lives, which have given me second and third chances to celebrate the wonder of childhood.

Contents

Prologue

This book is about my discovery of many powerful words that I wish I would have learned in medical school or residency training. Most of us in the practice of medicine are familiar with these words, yet their significance and power often elude us. Our training concentrated mostly on precise definitions of scientific processes and phenomena—the factual, observable and measurable data. Any word that was abstract or difficult to see or measure was set aside and never embraced as important. Over the past 15 years I have been on a quest to examine and define these words, extracting their untapped potency.

My quest began when, as a practicing physician, I repeatedly witnessed principles that had a great influence on the well-being of my patients. I became increasingly concerned by the realization that these "habitudes," as I like to call them, were never adequately addressed in my medical training.

Here are some of the keywords, among others, that unlock powerful processes of growth and well-being:

- ▶ Excellence
- ▶ Success
- ▶ Character
- ▶ Attitude
- ▶ Destiny
- ▶ Commitment
- ▶ Partnering
- ▶ Gratitude
- ▶ Life
- ▶ Process

My medical colleagues and I have been immersed in the white-coat discipline of scientific methods, accumulating a vast store of knowledge in disease and disease processes. This is the tradition of medical integrity that has brought about today's wonderful miracles of preventing and curing diseases. Our scientific vocabulary and factual knowledge are enormous and awesome. Most of my nearly 50 years in the practice of medicine have been spent in the continual pursuit of new scientific knowledge that would benefit my patients. This zeal for up-to-date medical education is shared by most physicians today.

However, we humans are comprised of more than fact, disease, measurable chemistry, or other physical realities that can be understood from a scientific point of view. We have feelings, thoughts, passions, desires, purposes, values, choices, will power, and the freedom to act and respond. All these are abstractions—very difficult to measure and manage. Yet the words listed above, and many others, are vital to the true art of medicine, which is the art of healing. They deal with human behavior, which includes not only medical but also behavioral science.

In medical school we focused almost exclusively on the scientific hard stuff and left the soft stuff to the behavioral scientists. By "hard stuff" I am referring to facts, measurable data, proven studies, direct observation, and objective rather than subjective experience. "Soft stuff," on the other hand, is subjective, intangible, and difficult to measure or prove. Although medical school provided a modicum of exposure to psychology, psychiatry, sociology and human behavior, the curriculum was filled mostly with the necessary understanding of disease, disease processes, and an incredible mass of technology.

This book is about my quest to balance an understanding of the hard stuff and the soft stuff in medicine. As I became aware of my patients' needs and their perceptions of the healthcare delivery systems, there seemed to be a huge cry for physicians to go beyond their scientific disciplines and truly understand and respond to their patients as human beings. The public is yearning, even demanding, that we physicians learn and communicate a paradigm beyond our traditional medical training. They are asking that we display compassion, inspire trust, and help them manage their expectations and conflicts.

My patients desire more choice and participation in their care. This requires a greater understanding of the words that affect not only disease, but human behavior. Such an understanding is fundamental to our aspirations for excellence and partnership in the providing of healthcare.

In this book I will define some words that should determine our relationships as doctors and patients. By understanding these words and word processes, communication can greatly improve. If doctors and patients share this clear understanding of human behavior, they can form a solid partnership. This will come about as physicians and patients gain a common vocabulary and common perceptions. Patients will have a better opportunity for the kind of treatment they deserve when they seek medical care.

In his classic book, *Alice in Wonderland,* author Lewis Carroll has Alice saying, "The meaning of words is not in words but in persons." Dictionaries do not actually define words, they just offer a selection of meanings. Each of us has his own perception of the meaning of a specific word. Understanding each other thus requires a sharing of each other's perceptions of the vocabulary we use. Each word becomes a unit of energy, charged with enormous, magical powers.

Since these words will be explored in more detail in later chapters, I am only presenting them here briefly. Hopefully this will serve as a helpful introduction, laying a foundation for the exciting discussion ahead.

Excellence

What is excellence? Excellence is the highest human standard of behavior, ethic, practice or thing achieved by superiority of character. Excellence is necessary for success. Yet this does not mean perfection, for perfection in human relations is unattainable. Excellence is a standard for which everyone is capable of striving: becoming the best he or she can be. This should be the standard pursued by your physician. However, even though you deserve the best from your doctor, please don't expect perfection.

Excellence: the highest human standard of behavior, ethic, practice or thing achieved by superiority of character.

It is crucial to clarify this most basic of doctor-patient expectations. Many physicians bask in the adulation of patients expecting perfection. But that is an unrealistic expectation—doomed to disappointment. In excellence we have a greater chance for successful human relation, because the science of medicine will always be inexact, unlike mathematics or physics. The human body and mind are highly unpredictable and varied in their responses. Each individual is unique.

Success

What is your definition of success? What is your physician's definition of success? This issue wasn't ever fully explored in my medical training. Physicians differ greatly in their concepts of success, as do most patients.

So how should success be defined? I define it as a journey of striving for excellence in living, serving and growing to our full potential.

Success: a journey of striving for excellence in living, serving and growing to our full potential.

Success in medicine is a long and arduous climb. Reaching for the summit of success takes character, and our character determines how close to the summit we will come. True success means learning the art of living and serving. Our technical training in the prevention and treatment of diseases never prepared us for what it takes to make a life, rather than just make a living. Our ultimate success in living will not be measured by our bank statements or our technical expertise. Instead, it will be determined by our character traits.

Success is never cast in concrete, but is the process of climbing higher, with some plateaus and falls along the way. It is, as Earl Nightingale has pointed out, a "steady realization of a worthy ideal or goal or purpose." The character traits defined in this book will provide you with the power package to ensure reaching the summit of the mountain of excellence and success.

4

This is a journey of both male and female. Although I often use the masculine pronoun "his" in referring to physicians, this is only because the English language doesn't provide a unisex alternative. I am fully aware of the contributions women make to the medical profession, since two of my daughters are physicians, while my wife and two of our other daughters are nurses. My wife and daughters make sure I have no claims to gender superiority or preference when it comes to the practice of medicine.

Character

Character is the stamp of individuality impressed upon a person by nature, education and habits. It is the inner core of one's being. Character is unique, and every person on earth is different from any other. It is not a static condition, but rather a quality that can grow and develop.

In medical school we studied at great length the growth and development of the human body, but rarely did we deal with the processes of character growth. What a tragedy to limit our understanding to the human body and disease, without a real understanding of the unique character of the person.

Character: the stamp of individuality impressed upon a person by nature, education and habits; the inner core of one's being.

What is your definition of character? What is your physician's definition of character? The answer to this question will have profound consequences.

Most medical licensing boards would like to assure the public that all physicians have "good character." However, when I was a member of the Medical Licensing Board of Indiana from 1975-1983, no laws on the books ever defined "good character." And that is actually a good thing, for I will detail later why it would be impossible and imprudent for legislators and lawyers to enact "good character" into law.

There are undoubtedly many good physicians, not needing anyone to spell out what it means to exercise good character. Even if the legislatures or licensing boards tried to codify the requirements of good character, they would surely fail. Though they might come up with some pious-sounding rules, they would be powerless to actually bring about an improvement of character, for it is fundamentally a moral issue, a matter of the heart. Good people don't need the rules, for they will instinctively behave in ethical ways; bad people wouldn't follow the rules, even if they were enacted.

Virtue

Virtue is the culmination of excellent character traits that have been cultivated by the processes of striving for the growth of our thoughts, attitudes, actions and habits of excellence. Much has been written of it in the Holy Bible and books such as William Bennett's wonderful treatise, *The Book of Virtues.*

Virtue: the culmination of excellent character traits that have been cultivated by the processes of striving for the growth of our thoughts, attitudes, actions and habits of excellence.

Virtue is the essence of excellence. Virtues are the epitome of character education and habit. By concentrating on the processes rather than the outcomes, our chances are greater for success and excellence in the virtues we seek. Talking, reading and studying about virtues is not likely to help us actually achieve them unless we understand the process of their development. We should be able to clearly define how to achieve virtue and success by studying the processes—just like understanding the physiology and processes of the normal body.

We are then dealing with the soft stuff—not taught in medical school, but why not! Don't we all deserve a virtuous physician?

Process

By now you've probably figured out that I *love* the word "process." Process is a system of "how to." In a positive sense, a process is a system of ways to advance in growth, expertise, excellence and productivity by continuous improvement over time.

In this book I will be sharing 12 powerful processes that take a lifetime of understanding and effort to improve. Each chapter describes a commitment to a specific process that calls for vastly greater understanding in medicine or almost any other profession or life work.

Process: a system of "how to" advance in growth, expertise, excellence and productivity by continuous improvement over time.

These 12 process words were not a great object of study during my medical training. My present understanding came later than I like to admit in my profession as a family physician. Consequently, during much of my early practice I was only minimally aware of the 12 dynamics of "how to" achieve excellence and success in medicine. Instead, I was taught to diligently study all the scientific specialties (25 or more!), in order to gain knowledge of the diseases in each organ or system of the body and then learn how to treat the diseases.

Of course, this course of study was necessary—but something was missing. We lacked a serious study of the processes of character development, information that is essential for understanding and treating the whole person. This omission was particularly unfortunate since patients are increasingly expecting to be understood. This means more than properly diagnosing the diseases afflicting them; it means understanding their unique personalities.

I have been inspired by many of the paradigms and processes described by Stephen Covey in his very good book, *Seven Habits of Highly Effective People.* In subsequent chapters, I relate my experiences and understanding of some of his principles as applied to the field of medicine. This book is about living and growing, seen from my perspective as a physician, scientist, biologist, businessman, husband, father, grandfather, and member of the family of humankind.

Much of this book was compiled while I was teaching in the Department of Family Practice at the University of Illinois at Peoria. My participation in the residency program for five years, 1987-1992, made me keenly aware of what is being taught in medical school and residencies. Believe me, very little of the vast amount of material presented was the soft stuff described here, and 97% was the hard stuff.

Success and excellence will come about only as we understand the complexities of the processes and try to simplify them for effective living. You, the patient, are a very important part of our continued understanding of all of life, especially the aspects that are nebulous and abstract.

Life

How should "life" be defined? Ask yourself, or anyone, the definition of life and you will likely be met with one of the following reactions:

1. No response ("It's impossible to define life.")
2. A raised eyebrow ("It's too complicated."), or
3. A laugh or smile ("Why even try?").

Life: the expression of movement, structure and processes in the phenomena of creative force, union, growth, birth, growth, struggle (forming identity and independence), growth, embrace (learning interdependence and partnering), growth, maturity, growth, productivity, growth, death and creative force.

As a physician, biologist and would-be philosopher, I want to try and define it simply, because we physicians deal with *living* persons. We are constantly studying how to maintain life. In order to understand the living processes and phenomena of life, we need to have a picture that is universal and panoramic. Here it is:

Definition: Life is the expression of movement, structure and processes in the phenomena of creative force...

union
  growth
  birth
    growth
      struggle (forming identity and independence)
        growth
          embrace (learning interdependence and partnering)
          growth
            maturity
            growth
              productivity
              growth
              death
                creative force

Let me explain these basic phenomena as they occur in most of the forms of life, from the simplest viruses and bacteria to the most complex creation of all, the human being. There are some exceptions, but in general the paradigm below is a useful key to understanding the development of human character.

There is a beginning and end to life. Our destiny is defined as our vision of the end of life's journey. We'll know toward the end of our lives whether or not we've achieved true success. Our destiny will be determined by our character and growth.

Many of us believe that the mysterious power that created all forms of life has a vision for a life even after death. It is beyond the scope of this book to try and explain all the wonders and mysteries that existed from the beginning of the universe, 15 billion years ago. It is impossible for me to explain the significance of our short existence here on earth without a deep conviction that our life is valued and surrounded by powers of love and spiritual nurture.

Life is the expression of structure, movement and processes, as shown by what I call the "Destiny Diagram":

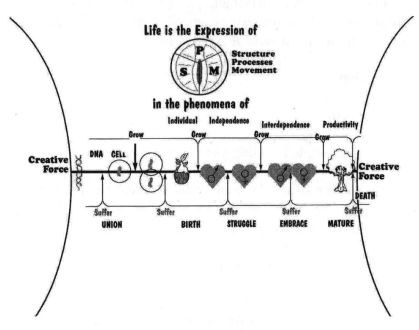

In the beginning, life was created out of a fantastic orderly union of elements. One of the earliest and most primitive "living" structures formed was DNA, deoxyribo-nucleic acid. This DNA became more and more complex with the double helix of proteins which contained the road map and destiny of each species on earth. The DNA for each living thing was encoded with an infinite but predictable variety for the individual of any species.

After this, the creative forces united two DNA individuals of the same species. A result of their union was the birth of a new individual. The phenomenon of struggle and need for independence is especially strong in youth.

However, independence and its freedom will not survive well unless we embrace another person, our kindred species of the opposite sex. This embrace and union is sustained by the supreme goal of interdependence as found in the family.

Partnering

As with many other words used in this book, "partnering" is perceived by people in a variety of ways. It is often vague both in concept and implementation. Whether in the family or the business world, few people understand the process of partnering.

What does it mean to be a "partner"? A partner is a unique person in relationship with one or more persons who are growing toward interdependence and unity of purpose and values.

Partner: a unique person in relationship with one or more persons who are growing toward interdependence and unity of purpose and values.

A healthy family system is a good model of partnering. Family unity helps nurture full maturity and productivity. Each individual in the biological world has a purpose to produce something, to contribute his or her purpose within interdependent relationships.

When productivity and maturity end, there is death. And after death is a mystery subject to each person's vision.

Even more basic to an understanding of character development is a cascade of creative energies. These begin by thought and the power of words (written or spoken or perceived). I call this the thought-to-destiny cascade:

> *Our thoughts coalesce into attitudes...*
> *Our attitudes incline us to our actions...*
> *Our actions, when repeated, create our habits...*
> *Our habits consolidate into our character...*
> *Our character predetermines our destiny.*

This energy cascade will be alluded to in each chapter. If a reader does not understand or accept this premise, he or she may fail to derive any benefit from this book. Our successful vision for the end of life, in my opinion and that of many successful people, is almost assured if we commit ourselves to this process. Processes of living, partnering, and growing in unity all begin with thoughts.

Commitment

What is your definition of commitment? Commitment is the choice of attitudes and actions which sustains steadfast loyalty to persons, principles, values, processes, purposes or things, regardless of circumstances or adversity. Commitment is the central element that holds life together. It is the glue, the cement, that unifies our lives. It is the power that pushes us on our journey up the mountain to the summit of success and excellence.

Commitment: the choice of attitudes and actions which sustains steadfast loyalty to persons, principles, values, processes, purposes or things, regardless of circumstances or adversity.

Our success or failure is in large measure determined by our choices of attitudes, actions and the things to which we commit ourselves. Often our successes are not achieved by short-term goals but by a commitment for the long haul of our journey.

When we entered medical school or marriage, we knew that neither was a short-term commitment. The adversities and stresses encountered while following those life-long commitments were managed and processed with long-term devotion. The challenges were met only by great and deep commitment.

The power sources that center our life commitments are defined and put together by each person. Our commitments define our character as well as our destinies. The words we choose and the thoughts we nurture as our central commitment are the power source to our attitudes.

Attitude

Attitude is our mindset. Our attitude is our tendency to react or respond. Attitude is defined as that changeable, reprogrammable, restructurable, renewable pattern of our thoughts, which makes growth possible. It is the most essential force for choice and change, both of which are determined by our attitudes.

Attitude is about the most crucial thing that can be reckoned with in medicine. Yet very little of my medical training equipped me to deal with this vital area. Most physicians, consequently, understand very little about its formation and relevance to character.

Attitude: that changeable, reprogrammable, restructurable, renewable pattern of our thoughts, which makes growth possible; the powerful, changeable mindset which predetermines our actions, either to react or respond to circumstances and stimuli.

Most of us fear sharing matters of attitude in our human relations. Yet physicians can't help but see positive and negative attitudes in their patients. How can we become partners in helping people keep their relationships growing, unless we learn how to deal with attitudes?

We often observe the effects of winds that we are unable to see, such as when wind blows through the trees or billows the sails of a ship. Attitude is a similar force, having great impact even when it is not clearly seen or understood. Yet it is a force that we must seek to understand. We need a better grasp of the processes of its formation and the ways that our lives are shaped by its dynamics. Like the unseen force of our immune system, we often have no idea how attitude is either protecting us from harm or leaving us open to attack.

Gimper

Gimper is an unusual and interesting word, and it is another word I did not hear in medical school. Charles Swindoll describes a gimper in his book, *Growing Strong in the Seasons of Life*. His definition was expanded from the writings of Dr. M.R. DeHaan and seems to me a fitting conclusion for this introduction to striving for excellence:

Gimper is the name for one who aspires to excel, to be

different. A gimper is committed to the core, thoroughly and unequivocally. His dedication results in rich fruit of determination, excellence and achievement. Setting their sights high, gimpers drive toward goals, absorbed in the passion of quality accomplished at any cost.

Are you a gimper? I hope so, for those with such an exceptional commitment to excellence will get the most out of this book.

In writing this book my first purpose is to clarify my own meaning of words relevant to patient care and healing. My second purpose is to assist both patients and physicians in understanding the art of human relations in the practice of medicine. Many of our patients are hungering to share their humanity, and they want us to share ours. They want us to share not only our scientific understanding, but also to deal with the high standards of human behavior that will help prevent disease and facilitate healing. That is the partnership that will revitalize the practice of medicine today—doctors and patients striving together for excellence.

My Bronze 'Success Coins'

On this book's cover and at the beginning of each chapter, my logo of the "success coin" is illustrated. Perhaps I should explain its significance in my life. One side of the coin shows the 13 C's, as described later. On the other side is my definition of success. I have given away hundreds of these bronze coins as a reminder to the recipients of what the road to success can mean in their lives.

The coin denotes fantastic power, but only if it serves as a catalyst for us all to gain a clearer vision of what success is—and the powerful processes that can assure us of its achievement. Of this I am certain: Without a dynamic growth of our understanding of the 13 C's, we will not find true success in life. It is my cherished hope that you will find this book an adventure toward success in partnering.

Chapter One

Growing in

Creativity

*"You shall be like a tree
Planted by streams of water,
Which yields fruit in season"* (Psalm 1:3).

As you can tell, I like to examine the meaning of words. A word is the written or spoken symbol of the basic unit of energy in thought processes and communication. Words have power! Here is another list of key words that will affect our destiny:

- ▶ Awareness
- ▶ Freedom
- ▶ Think
- ▶ Feel
- ▶ Imagine
- ▶ Desire
- ▶ Purpose
- ▶ Choose
- ▶ Persist

- ▶ Change
- ▶ Grow
- ▶ Work – create
- ▶ Play – create
- ▶ Books
- ▶ Aging
- ▶ Value
- ▶ Act
- ▶ Become response-able

There is perhaps no greater power than creativity. In the biological world, creativity is the underlying unseen force in growth. The various phenomena of physical growth are described in marvelous detail in embryology, anatomy, physiology and all the other sciences we studied in premed and medical school. It was a rich experience to be immersed in the wonders of the human body's growth. The harmony, unity and balance demonstrated in the different organs and systems of the human being are truly awesome.

The processes that hold our 60+ trillion cells together are beginning to be understood through modern science and research. There remain, however, countless mysteries and unanswered questions. The scientific mind is relentlessly pursuing these questions, hoping to relieve human suffering. Our vocabulary in medical training is vast, and new technology has contributed a flood of additional words to our lexicon.

Most of this is a positive trend, but there are also dangers. Technological advances can easily cause us to lose our perspective, forgetting that the human spirit, emotions, feelings, and similar qualities of life are what make us human. We have experimented on monkeys, mice and rats for physical similarities, and this has been necessary and rewarding. However, if we look honestly at the curriculum in medical school and specialty training, we will have to acknowledge that we have just begun to address the need for more emphasis on human character.

This means that we should educate physicians in the processes of social and spiritual growth, in addition to the physical and intellectual. Education in our schools should have more balance, as shown in the following paradigm:

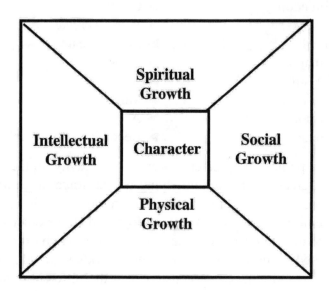

In the middle of this diagram is a space which could well be thought of as our character—our soul or inner being. Education can be defined as the powerful process of stimulating our physical, intellectual, social and spiritual growth, so we can become what we were meant to be. Robert Louis Stevenson stated this long ago: "To be what we are and to become what we were meant to be is our only end in life."

Education: the powerful process of stimulating our physical, intellectual, social and spiritual growth, so we can become what we were meant to be.

It is crucial to understand this chapter before moving on to the remaining ones. The entire book is written to share an understanding of the principles and processes of growth toward success in living. Creative living demands striving for excellence, and this principle is found in all of the biological world. Every living thing is intricately made and beautiful.

The same paradigm of life is applicable to trees and garden plants as well as to humans. Growth of character can be compared to the growth of a tree, starting with the miracle of growth from seeds.

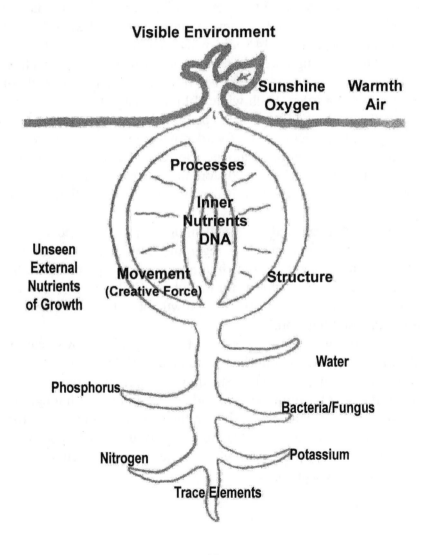

Visible Environment

Sunshine   Warmth
Oxygen   Air

Processes

Inner
Nutrients
DNA

Unseen
External
Nutrients
of Growth

Movement
(Creative Force)

Structure

Water

Phosphorus

Bacteria/Fungus

Nitrogen

Potassium

Trace Elements

For more than 30 years my family and I have planted trees each spring on our small farm. What was once an eroded, poorly farmed corn field is now a young forest. The trees are varieties of pine, oak, walnut and many others. They are 35 to 40 feet high. It has provided great satisfaction to watch them grow, prune them to straightness, and see them become what they were meant to be.

Planted as small seedlings the diameter of a pencil, many of these trees are now eight to ten inches in diameter. Some grew crooked and won't be worth much. Some grew slowly, and others didn't make it at all. About 50 trees out of each acre will some day be grand specimens of worth as they continue to grow. The first harvest of trees will be in about 14 years, when I am 88 years old. I hope to see that day, although there is always some sadness in felling a tree.

Every spring for many years I have also enjoyed the miracle of growth in our garden. Each winter I look through seed catalogues, plan my garden, and visualize the produce just as it is so beautifully portrayed in the pictures. That garden never quite comes to reality as marvelously as in the catalogue. However, we enjoy the process and the fruit of our labor. Food stored in the freezer and in canning jars is delectable. There is a quality of excellence not found in the grocery store.

My six children and 18 grandchildren have provided another great source of understanding regarding the wonders of growth. While the uniqueness of each child is enjoyed, the processes of his or her growth are the same as for the others. Children grow through processes that are similar to the growth of a tree, vegetable or flower, all coming from a seed.

A seed has within it the potential for growth, but growth can be thwarted if it lacks vital nutrients and elements. The preceding picture is a very simplified understanding of the highly complex processes that go on within the seed and its environment. Although the growth of human character is similar, the processes of character formation (creativity and growth) are *infinitely* more complex in the human. They are much more of a wonder than the phenomena in plant life, flowers and trees.

Education: not stuffing our minds with facts, knowledge and technology, but rather discovering, challenging and nurturing our creative imagination with awareness and freedom...

> To think...to feel
> To image, desire...to purpose
> To prioritize...to choose
> To act...to persist
> To become response-able...to change
> To grow into our full potential.

Having already defined education, I now want to succinctly define the *process* of education. In large measure, our character growth is determined by our process of education. Education is not stuffing our minds with facts, knowledge and technology, but rather discovering, challenging and nurturing our creative imagination with awareness and freedom...

> To think...to feel
> To image, desire...to purpose
> To prioritize...to choose
> To act...to persist
> To become response-able...to change
> To grow into our full potential.

The paradigm of character development/growth/creativity begins with self—an individual at any age whose potential is determined by this primordial paradigm:

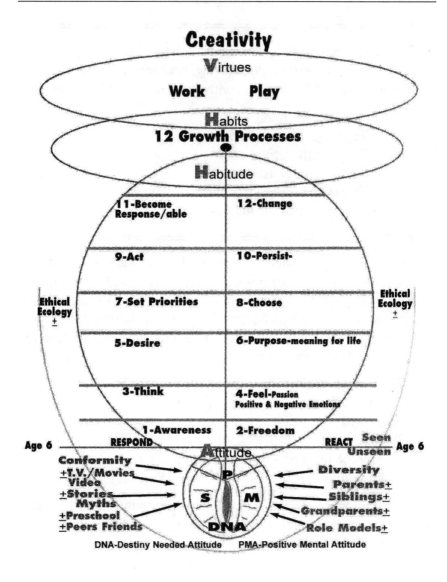

DNA-Destiny Needed Attitude   PMA-Positive Mental Attitude

The DNA in character is what I call a "destiny needed attitude"—a positive attitude. Growth begins with a basic desire and determination to maintain a positive attitude. A decision aspiring to a positive mental attitude is one of life's greatest motivational processes, for it gives us a sense of worth and destiny. As the diagram shows, our DNA combines with structure, processes and movement, forming character with the assistance of 12 essential inner nutrients or microprocesses. These essential inner nutrients for growth, or EINGs, are described below.

EING #1: Awareness

Awareness of mind and inner freedom may seem like abstract concepts, but they are very real. Awareness can be defined as becoming consciously circumspect and cognizant of our self and our circumstances. Another definition is this: The conscious faculty of our brain which is alert and alive with all of our senses tuned to our internal and external environment.

Awareness: becoming consciously circumspect and cognizant of our self and our circumstances; the conscious faculty of our brain which is alert and alive with all of our senses tuned to our internal and external environment.

Thoreau once stated, "A man is alive only to the degree that he is aware." We need to be aware of self—who we are and where we are going. This includes our ideals, purposes and passions. Through our senses we become aware of other persons and of our own circumstances, situations, dangers, needs, longings and aspirations. Most of all, we need to become aware of our relationship to our environment and the divine plan for all of us on the spaceship earth.

Many people lack this needed awareness. However, growth in the other essential inner nutrients is hindered until we become aware of our need to seek liberation from the negative thoughts and feelings that hold us in bondage. Ignorance and sloth are forces that hold us in the bonds of unawareness.

EING #2: Freedom

The second essential inner nutrient for growth (or creativity) is the natural creative force of freedom within the human spirit. This is the quintessential inner nutrient of growth. It liberates us to think, feel, desire, purpose, prioritize, choose, act, persist, become response-able, and change. These are all essential elements of growth.

Freedom: the quintessential inner nutrient of growth that liberates us to think, feel, desire, purpose, prioritize, choose, act, persist, become response-able, and change.

It is my conviction that none of the other nutrients for growth ca n be fully implemented without this foundation of inner freedom. When inner freedom and awareness are combined, a person experiences an ambiance of spirit and mind that goes far beyond the political and social freedom we champion in America. Thomas Jefferson spoke passionately and eloquently when he said, "I swear on the altar of God eternal hostility against any form of tyranny over the mind of man." He recognized that political and social freedom are essential to liberate the mind of man. He was also aware that there are tyrannical forces in the mind of man that must be fought against. Jefferson's work reflected the words of the Great Physician: "You shall know the truth, and the truth shall set you free" (John 8:32).

I am aware that Jefferson struggled with the tyranny of slavery. He never freed his slaves, so his great contribution to political freedom for the whites didn't translate into liberty for the enslaved blacks. We must be grateful, however, for his tremendous passion for political freedom in America.

Inner freedom and awareness go hand in hand. Both are absolutely necessary for the full expression of the 10 other nutrients for growth.

EING #3: Thinking

As shown in the following diagram, thinking encompasses several different kinds of brain activity, including thought, feeling, desire, memory, conscience and special sense perception.

CREATIVE MIND

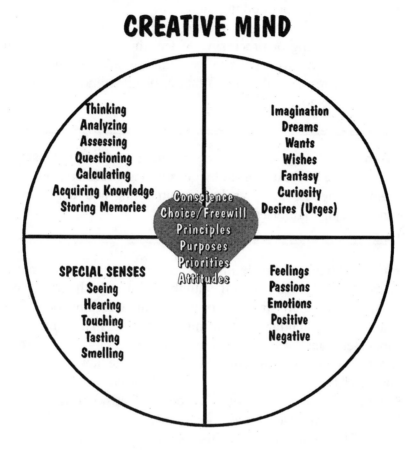

Thinking
Analyzing
Assessing
Questioning
Calculating
Acquiring Knowledge
Storing Memories

Imagination
Dreams
Wants
Wishes
Fantasy
Curiosity
Desires (Urges)

Conscience
Choice/Freewill
Principles
Purposes
Priorities
Attitudes

SPECIAL SENSES
Seeing
Hearing
Touching
Tasting
Smelling

Feelings
Passions
Emotions
Positive
Negative

Thinking may be defined as the faculty of our conscious mind that processes knowledge and experience by questioning, reasoning, problem-solving, assessing, analyzing, computing and compartmentalizing memories. Several types of thinking should be examined.

The first type of thinking is the analytical, informational, cognitive, questioning, objective type of processing information. This is what we did so diligently in medical school. It is the unemotional, scientific way of understanding physical processes. I estimate that 98% of my brain activity during medical education was juggling the millions of scientific facts that were presented. Neurologists call this "left brain" activity—information management. It makes for intellectual growth, but nothing more.

There are positive thoughts and negative thoughts. Positive thinking is the nurturing or processing of any thought that yields harmony, unity and growth. Negative thinking involves processing thoughts that result in the deterioration, disintegration and disharmony of the person.

Thinking: the faculty of our conscious mind that processes knowledge and experience by questioning, reasoning, problem-solving, assessing, analyzing, computing and compartmentalizing memories.

Our 50-100 billion tiny brain cells, called neurons, are a fantastic system, about as awesome as the number of stars in the Milky Way galaxy. In the small structure of the brain, weighing only three pounds, is the potential for performing functions many times more complicated than the largest computer now made by the wizards in computer technology. Most of us don't appreciate how powerful our brain truly is.

Albert Schweitzer was once asked, "What's wrong with the world?" His reply was, "Well, I guess that people just don't think." Louis E. Thayer said it well in his poem,

Think Big
Think big because thought rules our lives
And little thoughts produce the little man.
Build up a mind where only thrives
The true incentive and worthy plan.
See that no weeds shall there abide—
That only flowers and fertile soil shall find.
Grow thoughts to view with honest pride—
To glorify this garden in your mind.

Think big in terms of happiness
For those who walk a bitter path through life
Of self think just a little less

And think of peaceful thoughts that conquer strife
Think big and no worthy deed
Will mar the record which you leave behind;
While joy will spring from every seed
You've planted in that garden of your mind.

EING #4: Feeling

The fourth essential inner nutrient for growth is to feel emotion. Feeling is the faculty of our mind that reacts or responds to stimuli or circumstances with emotions that energize our behaviors and thoughts, either positively or negatively.

Feeling is the part of brain processing that deals with our passions. Becoming aware of our passions is the first step in managing our emotions, both positive and negative.

Adler and Towne in their book, *Looking Out / Looking In,* list 39 positive and 91 negative emotions. Here are only a few of each, although the rich diversity of emotions and huge intellectual capacity is what distinguishes humans from all other creatures.

Positive	Negative
acceptance	anxiety
love	anger
joy	apathy
peace	arrogance
confidence	doubt
freedom	fear
enthusiasm	isolation
gratitude	grief
hope	jealousy
sexiness	greed
romance	loneliness
wonder	self-satisfaction
tenderness	lust

These are examples of normal feelings and emotional brain activities which are often ignored in the educative processes. In medical school we were usually so pressed for acquiring intellectual and cognitive skills that we didn't take sufficient time to process our true feelings. Many medical students and residents are unaware of their feelings and have no one to help them keep balance in their emotional (spiritual and social) growth. Even after graduation and years of medical practice, many physicians continue to increase their intellectual expertise but fail to pay attention to their emotional needs.

Feeling: the faculty of our mind that reacts or responds to stimuli or circumstances with emotions that energize our behaviors and thoughts, either positively or negatively.

Much of this book deals with these emotional "soft words" which are so essential for growth. Our emotions and passions are the inner flame that ignites our thoughts, dreams and fantasies to action.

Arnold Toynbee says of our feelings, "Apathy can only be aroused by enthusiasm. Enthusiasm can only be aroused by an ideal which takes the imagination by storm and an intelligible definite plan for carrying out that ideal into practice."

Thoughts create feelings.
Feelings create thoughts.
That is the pump action of thought and feeling.

EING #5: Desire

Desire is the fifth essential inner nutrient for growth. This brain function is perhaps the most difficult to define. In this section is a cluster of words that represent the highest, most mysterious, and perhaps the most powerful brain activity.

To wish,
to dream,
to fantasize,
to imagine,
to aspire...

...all are part of this brain function. If there is anything in us that relates to our Creator, it is this magnificent quality—the creative imagination. This is the stuff which has built our civilization. The creative imagination is the most powerful force in man's inventiveness and innovation. Desire can be defined as the faculty of our imagination that creates a vision of our aspirations, dreams, wants and wishes for something of value.

Desire: the faculty of our imagination that creates a vision of our aspirations, dreams, wants and wishes for something of value.

There are positive and negative fantasies in our brain. I can't identify the source of this excellent quote that I learned years after graduation: "Whatever we vividly imagine, ardently desire, sincerely believe, and enthusiastically act upon, will inevitably come to pass." Another illustration of this all-important essential in growth is the well-known Disney song:

When You Wish Upon a Star

When you wish upon a star,
Makes no difference who you are.
Anything your heart desires will come to you.

If your heart is in your dreams,
No request is too extreme.
When you wish upon a star as dreamers do.

Fate is kind.
She brings to those who find the
sweet fulfillment of their secret longings.
Like a bolt out of the blue, fate steps in and sees you through.
When you wish upon a star, your dreams come true.

Our children learned this song through *Pinnochio*—long before I did, and several years after I became engaged in medical practice.

In 1956 I studied hypnosis under Dr. Milton Erickson, who was the master of this art. He demonstrated to many physicians the tremendous power of imagination and desire. The following year, hypnosis was recognized by the American Medical Association as a useful, scientifically acceptable tool in the practice of medicine. It still is not taught in many medical schools. Although hypnosis is officially recognized, its enormous powers are relegated by most practicing physicians to "alternative medicine." How sad to relegate such amazing imaginative powers to such low priority and frequency of use.

Negative fantasies, wishes and dreams can be incredibly destructive and evil in our personalities and society. The terrible force of violence and sexual fantasies created in the minds of children is taking its toll on our society.

Evil: any force, thought, fantasy or attitude which violates the harmony, unity or balance in the family of man and our environment.

Evil can be defined as any force, thought, fantasy or attitude which violates the harmony, unity and balance in the family of man and our environment. Is there any question that the images we nurture and process in our minds have a great potential for either healthy or unhealthy growth? For either good or evil?

Brain Activity of Special Senses

While humans have wondrous senses of seeing, hearing, smelling, tasting and feeling (by touch), in many areas we can't compare with the amazing senses of animals in the lower creative kingdom. It is awesome how acutely eagles see, bats hear, dogs smell, ants taste, and flies have a delicacy of touch. We have less need for these highly specialized capacities, because we rely more on the adeptness of our forebrain (see the Creative Mind Diagram, previously shown).

Many advances in modern medicine, such as cat scans, MRIs and x-rays, are designed to extend and expand the power of our five senses. However, many times we doctors rely too heavily on our technology, when we should go back to developing our five senses more in our clinical approach to patients. We should look, listen, touch and even smell more. Chapter two will address this more in detail.

EING #6: Purpose

Purpose is the sixth essential inner nutrient for growth. It can be defined as the faculty of mind that sets specific goals and plans which determine the direction of our destiny, giving meaning to life's aspirations.

Viktor Frankl, in my opinion, was the greatest psychiatrist of all time. He established "Logo Therapy"—therapy based on the meaning of words, which actually relates to the meaning of life. In his book, *Man's Search for Meaning,* Frankl says that striving to find a meaning in one's life is the primary motivational force in man, or "a will to meaning." This school of psychiatric thought makes the most sense compared to the other methods I studied in medical school and since.

Purpose: the faculty of mind that sets specific goals and plans which determine the direction of our destiny, giving meaning to life's aspirations.

Freudian psychology is useless, except for his discovery of the three structures in the mind: the ego, super ego and id. Transactional analysis is a modern version of Freud. Cognitive therapy by Beck and Burns has also influenced me greatly, but no one has made more sense to me than Frankl. Furthermore, his experience in a Nazi concentration camp is living proof that if we find a purpose in our life of suffering, we can endure anything.

The freedom to find and set the purpose and meaning for our life is essential for growth. Setting goals in harmony with that purpose each day is difficult, but is one of the most highly integrative forces in our personal growth. Dr. Frankl would probably agree that it is the pearl of great price we should seek to find.

As with the other nutrients, there are positive (healthy) or negative (unhealthy) purposes we can discover. "We should hold ourselves accountable...relate that purpose to our own personal lives," Viktor Frankl urged. Disraeli, a former British Prime Minister, once said in a similar way: "The secret of success is constancy of purpose." And Thomas Carlyle warned, "The man without purpose is like a ship without a rudder—a waif, a nothing, no man at all. Have a purpose in life, and having it, throw such strength of mind and muscle into your work as God has given you."

EING #7: Prioritize

The seventh EING involves the setting of priorities and values. Setting priorities requires the faculty of mind which sets our value systems and treasures of the soul for the highest good. Priorities and values are the real integrators in the brain, along with purpose.

Prioritizing: the faculty of mind which sets our value systems and treasures of the soul for the highest good.

How many of us have taken time to write down our priorities and values? What do we treasure? Where do we spend most of our time and money? Are these priorities and values positive or negative?

All of us have value systems that form the core of our attitudes and mid-brain integrative processes. What is a "value"? It can be defined as a thing, ideal, person, idea, purpose or relationship that we treasure, prize and deem important.

Authors Blessing and White have offered an extensive list of values to use as a tool in the manufacturing sector. Unfortunately, the medical profession as a whole hasn't come up with a comparable list of these items which are so essential to integrity and growth. Yet, some medical groups and a few individual physician's offices have at least prepared a mission statement that sets forth their values and purposes.

Values are not only neglected in most medical training, but they are often even frowned upon for fear of imposing one person's values on another. That, of course, should not be done. Each of us must respect—though not necessarily agree with—the diverse values of others. But that should not keep us from clearly stating and living our own convictions.

Value: a thing, ideal, person, idea, purpose or relationship that we treasure, prize and deem important.

The process of setting values occurred in my own life later than I would have liked. This book embodies a distillate of my own value systems, and I have written it for the consideration of others who are interested in personal growth. Looking back, I wish I would have engaged in this process as early as my teenage years. With some help, even teenagers are capable of setting their own priorities and values. Each of us can experience a new freedom, awareness and growth if we begin the process of clarifying and prioritizing our desires, values and purposes.

EING #8: Choose

Freedom of choice, the eighth essential inner nutrient of growth, is one of the most precious freedoms a human can enjoy. Choice can be defined as the faculty of free will which selects our options that are predetermined by our thoughts, desires, purposes and values.

Growth and creativity are stifled without this crucial EING. Our Creator gave us this gift that distinguishes us from all other creatures. Most animals act and react on instinct. In contrast, we humans have the freedom, if we are aware, to act on a higher level: We can exercise our free will. We can choose.

Choice: the faculty of free will which selects our options that are predetermined by our thoughts, desires, purposes and values.

We have a whole spectrum of options. We may choose the right or the wrong, good or evil, the lasting or the ephemeral. Our choices will ultimately be made by our attitudes which were predetermined by our thoughts, passions, priorities and purposes.

One of the favorite bits of wisdom I tried to pass on to my residents was this quote by Aldous Huxley, taken from *The Choice Is Always Ours*, an anthology on the religious life by Dorothy Berkley Phillips:

> The choice is always ours. Then, let me choose
> The longest art, the hard Promethean way
> Cherishingly to tend and feed and fan
> That inward fire, whose small precarious flame,
> Kindled or quenched, creates
> The noble or the ignoble men we are,
> The worlds we live in and the very fates,
> Our bright or muddy stars.

EING #9: Act

The ninth essential inner nutrient for growth is taking action in accord with our priorities. To act means to engage in a dynamic movement in reaction or response to stimuli and circumstances, predetermined largely by our attitudes and habits. It does little good to have purpose and priorities if we never act upon them. Yet many of us would have to acknowledge that we often fail to act upon our beliefs and values.

Many phrases have been devised to encourage people in this essential inner nutrient. Perhaps you have heard the Latin phrase *carpe diem*, which means "Seize the day!" Others say, "Just do it— now." Goethe inspires us with this poem:

> Are you in earnest? Seize this very minute.
> What you can do or dream you can, begin it.
> Boldness has genius, power, and magic in it.
> Only begin and then the mind grows heated.
> Begin, and then the work will be completed!

The freedom to act is essential for growth, as Oliver Wendell Holmes writes, "I find a great thing in this world is not so much where we stand as in what direction we are moving. To reach the port of heaven we must sail, sometimes with the wind, and sometimes against it, but we must sail and not drift nor lie at anchor."

Let's be sure to distinguish action from reaction. Most of our lives we are too busy reacting to stimuli and circumstances. We become proactive after we have cultivated the processes previously outlined. Acting, in my view, is equivalent to being proactive. The less we react to things, the more chance we have of successfully responding.

Action: to engage in a dynamic movement in reaction or response to stimuli and circumstances, predetermined largely by our attitudes and habits.

This is a learning process. First we become aware of our stimuli and situation, and then we evaluate our thoughts, feelings, desires, purposes, priorities and choices. With that foundation, we can act proactively rather than reactively. The key is awareness and the freedom to process what makes for the best response. This proactive approach is described in Stephen Covey's book, *Seven Habits of Highly Effective People.*

Members of the medical profession have been so busy reacting to all the changes, stresses, rules, regulations and laws that we fail to assess, process and respond with positive action—proactive leadership. In fact, we are so busy in our service to patients that we fail to unite our common purposes in one solid statement that could put things straight. Then we would hope that the legislators were inclined to listen proactively to the patient and their physicians.

One of my favorite authors, Wilferd Peterson, challenges us all to grow and be creative in taking appropriate action: "We must go all out. We must put pressure on ourselves to surpass ourselves. One turns on the fire through action. Action opens the mind to the inflow of ideas. Action stirs up the subconscious. Action primes the pump.

Action puts words on paper." Let us heed this helpful reminder.

EING #10: Persist

Action without persistence is like lighting a fire but then putting it out. Patience and persistence go hand in hand, and they constitute the tenth essential inner nutrient for growth. A strong vision of future success, coupled with perseverance, is crucial for actually attaining that success. Most worthwhile things come only after long, enduring effort.

Persistence can be defined as a continuous commitment to action, urged on by a strong belief that the highest good will come, regardless of adversity and circumstance. We all will face the frequent choice: Should I persist or should I quit?

Persistence: a continuous commitment to action, urged on by a strong belief that the highest good will come, regardless of adversity and circumstance.

Character formation is a long-term goal, involving many processes and circumstances which can easily overcome the weak and timid. Striving for excellence is a rough climb to the top. We should never try to measure our courage and endurance. The power to persist is always there if our thoughts, attitudes and habits are focused on our purposes and priorities.

This same quality of persistence is likewise needed in any long-term relationship, such as doctor and patient, pastor and parishioner, or husband and wife. Too many quit when things get rough, reacting instead of becoming more creatively active.

Building partnerships is an important theme of this book. Genuine partnerships take persistence. That is why patients and physicians should not either voluntarily or involuntarily quit a relationship without trying to fix it. Many managed care systems have violated this principle early on. Now some see the importance of staying with a trusted relationship if at all possible.

The attitude of persistence is also important in the healing of many chronic and so-called incurable diseases. Defeating deadly diseases requires a persistent effort, not something halfhearted. Saint Paul knew what persistence was all about, saying, "...but we also glory in tribulations, knowing that tribulation produces perseverance, and perseverance, character and character hope" (Romans 5:3-4).

A story has been told about two frogs that fell into a pail of cream. The sides were so slippery and steep that, despite all their efforts, they could not escape the pail. One frog decided it was hopeless. She gave up, sank to the bottom and drowned. The second frog refused to give up and kept churning away with all her strength. Suddenly she let out a satisfied croak, because there she was, sitting on a pat of butter, churned up through her own efforts. Persist!

EING #11: Response-able

The eleventh essential inner nutrient for growth is "response-ability." This is a different word than responsibility. Only the latter is found in the dictionary, which defines it as the attitude of a person who is accountable for his actions or choices and is willing to live by the consequences.

Response-ability, on the other hand, is the ability to respond, not react, to stimuli or circumstances. It is the habitude that springs from processing the previously mentioned EINGs, so we become pro-adaptive rather than maladaptive. To be pro-adaptive is similar to being proactive. It describes a positive manner of adjusting to circumstances, responding rather than reacting.

Response-ability: the ability to respond, not react, to stimuli or circumstances, so we become pro-adaptive rather than maladaptive.

Maladaptive habitudes usually come from negatively reacting to our circumstances. The consequence of these reactive behaviors is that we fail to grow. We may survive, but true maturity never comes. In order to become response-able, however, we must begin with a positive mental attitude, persisting and adapting positively to all of our circumstances.

We develop the capacity of response-ability by processing the other nutrients for growth. This is the ultimate goal before change and growth can occur. No growth comes from reacting. We may escape a crisis, but to prevent future crises we need to develop our *response*-ability instead of *react*-ability.

Pro-adaptive: a positive manner of adjusting to circumstances, responding rather than reacting.

We respond or react to various stimuli throughout life. No one escapes this challenging process—either to respond positively or react negatively to circumstances. The end virtue is responsibility; the process is response-ability. Throughout this process, we have the freedom to choose whether to discipline ourselves and grow or to remain immature by reacting negatively to our suffering, pain, conflict, stress or brokenness.

More than 30 years ago I read with zest William Glasser's book, *Reality Therapy*. His book changed the system of criminal punishment in California, and hopefully some other states followed the lead. His definition of responsibility is "the ability to fulfill one's needs and to do so in a way that does not deprive others of the ability to fulfill their needs."

Dr. Glasser's book presented a unique process of dealing with criminals and others who act irresponsibly. It works. Yet most criminals and delinquents are constantly reacting to the stimuli around them, never having learned this essential inner nutrient for growth: response-ability.

With 1.5 million individuals incarcerated in our society, shouldn't they be given the opportunity to learn response-ability and responsibility? They are literally a captive audience! Chuck Colson, imprisoned for two years because of his involvement in the Watergate scandal, is now pioneering prison ministries that present innovative models for transformed lives.

Most legislators, however, still struggle to get a vision of the changes needed in our very uncreative penal system. The high rates of recidivism are a testimony to the overall failure of our prisons to successfully bring reformation to people's lives. However, there are some positive exceptions, where incarcerated people do, in fact, discover the freedom to become response-able—even more so than many persons who are *not* behind bars. Becoming response-able is a learning and creative process achievable at any age.

EING #12: Change

Change, the twelfth essential inner nutrient, really isn't so difficult. We all have the freedom to change. However, change sometimes is made more difficult because we have to first handle the other processes and EINGs. Change is thus facilitated when we successfully process and combine the other inner nutrients for growth.

I define change as the faculty of mind necessary to renew or restructure our attitudes, transforming our person into a new identity and direction of growth. To grow is to change. To change positively, we must grow creatively.

Change: the faculty of mind necessary to renew or restructure our attitudes, transforming our person into a new identity and direction of growth; the powerful process of renewing, replacing, restructuring or transforming, which yields a new direction, identity and destiny.

Sometimes it is possible to change as did Scrooge on Christmas Eve—in a short, overnight vision of things past, present and future. Usually, however, change occurs slowly, methodically and imperceptibly, as in nature. If the limb of a tree is cut off, it heals slowly.

The Power of Books

Quite a few patients come into my office depressed, apathetic and filled with negative attitudes, looking for some quick cures and easy fixes to their problems. Often these individuals have just "run out of gas." They lack the energy to grow, change or just keep up with the pace of life.

Books provide one of the greatest powers to grow and stimulate the essential inner nutrients of growth. Our need to assimilate a variety of books is similar to the nutrients needed by our body. A well-balanced diet, containing all the necessary vitamins, minerals, fiber, phytoestrogens, lycopenes, etc., makes for health and growth. In a similar way, character formation requires a combination of various nutrients. To grow intellectually, socially and spiritually, we need the energy and power that books of a wide variety can supply.

We physicians have a hard time reading anything not related to medicine. It's impossible even to read the mass of medical literature coming our way. We select our reading materials carefully and try our best to grow in our medical knowledge.

William Osler, M.D., one of the greatest physicians of the 20th century, was well read in medicine, but also in books for spiritual growth. His essays are still timely and inspirational for many in the medical profession. Osler has been one of my role models. *The Life of Osler,* by Harvey Cushing, has been a prized possession, along with *Equanimitas* and various other writings by Osler himself. Few people understood the power of books to the degree he did, as shown by this quote from *Equanimitas*:

> To study the phenomena of disease without books is to sail an uncharted sea; to study books without patients is not to go to sea at all. Divide your attention equally between books and men. The strength of the student of books is to sit still for two or three hours at a stretch—eating the heart out of a subject with pencil and notebook in hand, determined to master the details and intricacies, focusing all your energies on its difficulties. Get accustomed to test all sorts of book problems and statements for yourself, and take as little as possible on trust. The Hunterian "Do not think but *try*" attitude of mind is the important one to cultivate.

In addition to scientific books, we need books that provide us with an understanding of the processes of growth in human character.

When does a busy physician get the time to read these books on subjects other than medicine? Well, many do find the time, and they and their patients are the richer and more empowered from that choice.

Creativity through books has power that is accessible to all. In *The Art of Living Day by Day,* Wilferd Peterson wrote:

> Books become a part of man, help to shape your character. The past and present live in books to guide you into the future. Someone wisely said, "It is what we read when we don't have to that determines what we shall be when we can't help it!" The spirit of man, the life of man, the discoveries of man and the adventures of man all will be found in books.

Outside of my family and my patients, books are one of the greatest sources of my personal growth. They stimulate me, call me to accountability, and challenge me to respond rather than react. Every conflict or difficult patient is a creative opportunity for me to grow. All we physicians need in order to have satisfying relationships with our patients is to relish their growth and invite them to help us grow. Sharing books (this being one of them) is a great way to grow together.

Work

Most of us physicians tend to be workaholics, and we need to take a good look and see what constitutes excellence in work. I believe all humans were meant to work—to produce something useful or beautiful. We had to work hard in medical school, and have kept working hard ever since. Although some have worked just to make money, others have focused on making sick people healthier. Helping to make people well again is a beautiful, useful thing.

It is quite revealing to ask ourselves the questions, *What are we working for?* and *Why are we in medicine, anyway?* Traditionally, physicians worked to serve their patients. However, managed care and the "for profit" systems of health delivery have often debased the service motive. The creativity of work in our profession has been badly damaged by rules, regulations, laws and policies which dehumanize both our patients and ourselves.

On the other hand, the expectations of many overworked physicians are changing for the better. Younger physicians want balance in work, play, family and other areas of their lives. Such a balance may be hard to achieve, yet is a worthwhile quest.

In my files I saved an essay by Wilferd Peterson, "Words to Live By—the Art of Work." I love this creative thesis on work:

> Work brings man to life, sets him in motion. Work is man in action doing things. Nothing happens until people go to work...Work creates the world we live in.
>
> The art of work consists of what you think about your work, how you feel about your work and what you do about your work. It is abolishing the concept of work as chains and slavery, and seeing it as freedom to create and build and help.
>
> It is striving to find work you can love, a job to which you can harness your heart. It is idealizing your work, turning a job into a mission, a task into a career.
>
> It is doing your present work so well that it will open doors to new opportunities. Tasks done at a high standard pave the way to bigger things.
>
> It is discovering the great healing power of work. If you are lonely...work! If you are worried or fearful...work! If you are discouraged or defeated...work! Work is the key to happiness.
>
> It is making your work you.
>
> It is putting the stamp of your unique personality on the work you do. It is pouring your spirit into your task. It is making your work a reflection of your faith, your integrity, your ideals.
>
> It is recognizing that work, not repose, is the destiny of man.
>
> It is going to your work as you go to worship, with a prayer of thankfulness and the aspiration to serve.

James W. Elliott said it all in nine words, "Work is life, and good work is good life."

Play

In a subsequent chapter is a section on play and work. While most of a physician's work day is anything but play, approaching even the most serious work with a somewhat playful touch contributes to the creative process. Working under stressful conditions in a relaxed manner will be far more productive than getting grim and tense about our work. This art of balancing time and maintaining an attitude of play while we work is a lifelong endeavor.

Aging

As much as I have loved the wisdom of William Osler, I don't share his views on aging, which he wrote in the early 1900s. His contemporaries chastised him for these statements, and I, too, would openly disagree with his view of the aging process. This is what Osler said:

> My second fixed idea is the uselessness of men above 60 years of age and the incalculable benefit it would be in commercial, political and in professional life if, as a matter of course, men stopped work at this age. In his *Bianthanatos,* Donne tells us that by the laws of certain wise states sexegenerii were precipitated from a bridge, and in Rome men of that age were not admitted to the suffrage and they were called d*epontani* because the way to the senate was per pontem, and they from age were not permitted to come thither.
>
> In that charming novel, *The Fixed Period,* Anthony Trollope discusses the practical advantage in modern life of a return to this ancient usage, and the plot hinges upon the admirable scheme of a college into which men retired for a year of contemplation before a peaceful departure by chloroform.
>
> And there is truth in that story, since it is only those who live with the young who maintain a fresh outlook on the new problems of the world. The teacher's life should have three periods: study until twenty-five, investigation until forty, profession until sixty, at which age I would have him retired at double allowance.

Now Osler may have in humor stretched his point, or he may have been serious about the bridge and chloroform. He did have a sense of humor, but I believe he was serious about the uselessness of those over 60 years of age.

In contrast with Osler's view, there are numerous examples of people who have extended their growth into their eighties and nineties. Hans Selye was vibrant and researching in his eighties. Arthur Rubenstein performed and recorded flawlessly in his early nineties. Albert Schweitzer, likewise, continued his work till his nineties. Norman Vincent Peale kept audiences inspired from pulpits and personal encounters till his death at age 95. Most of us personally know senior citizens who have accumulated and displayed great wisdom.

Viktor Frankl just died in 1999 at 86 years of age. Shortly before his death he said in an interview:

> I'll be 86 years old yesterday. I lectured here in California and soon I travel to Mexico to lecture. I have no objection to aging and becoming ever more old, as long as I may be able to claim that I am maturing. An old human being may to some extent lose his memory. He may lose the speed of his thinking and speaking, but all this may be compensated by the experience he has gained from the decades of his life.
>
> Personally, I am not disturbed by the thought of death or the transitoriness of life. It is my conviction that nothing is lost or destroyed. Everything is preserved and stored. Nobody can remove it from the past: what we have done, the work we have accomplished, what we have created, what we have experienced, whom we have loved, and even what we have suffered. Our past is a granary wherein the harvest of our lives has surely been deposited. In the book of Job we find, "You go in old age to your grave as harvest is brought in, in its time."

One of the tragedies of our times is the myth of retirement—a time to stop working and growing, living a life of ease and comfort. What I see more often in my patients who have "retired" is a sense of purposelessness, uselessness and boredom. Rather than experiencing a life of ease, they often are afflicted with frustrating stresses that come from their wrong mindset.

It seems obvious to me that the biological limits of man are increasing. Ages of 120 or more may occur as frequently in the years ahead as the centenarians today—who in the year 2000 numbered about 72,000 in America. Because of these stunning trends, we need to rethink how to keep creativity and productivity growing regardless of age. I am currently 75 years old, and I feel the best I have ever felt in my life. I am trying to keep physically, socially, intellectually and spiritually fit.

My life is full and joyous. The words of this book proceed out of the overflow of this abundant life, and I hope they will benefit many people.

In the words of Robert Browning:

> Grow old along with me
> The best is yet to be,
> The last for which the first was made
> My times are in His hands who saith,
> a whole I made,
> Youth shows but half.
> Trust God
> See all
> nor be afraid.

Accountability Questions

From time to time we need to ask ourselves some hard questions. This is essential for accountability. Those involved in doctor-patient relationships can profit from the following questions:

1. Do we value personal growth?
2. Do we have the freedom to grow?
3. What are the obstacles to our growth?
4. Are our relationships positive?
5. Where are we headed?
6. What is our mission?
7. Do we respond to each other or react?
8. Do we have a positive mental attitude
   - Most of the time
   - Some of the time
   - Occasionally
   - Rarely

9. Are we aware of our feelings and circumstances?

10. Are we enthusiastic in our work?

Instead of merely glancing at these questions, I encourage you to take the time necessary to fully ponder and digest them. Some of the answers may be hard to face, but they can be a key to unlocking new areas of growth.

A Final Challenge

Work, play, books and aging are integral parts of the growth processes. They are strongly affected by the essential inner nutrients of growth, and it is almost impossible to separate them from creativity.

The acrostic for essential inner nutrients of growth (EING) undergoes an interesting metamorphosis when the letter "B" is added: BEING. Our *being* and *becoming* are processes that we use every day if we are truly growing. Understanding the precise definitions of the essential nutrients of growth, and the order in which they occur, seems to me a logical solution to the question of how we change our attitudes and habits. Attitude is the all-important element in partnerships. The foundation of partnering is based on creativity and the processes of inner growth.

Let's aspire to facilitate each other's growth—helping each other understand where we are and what we want to become.

Chapter Two

Growing in

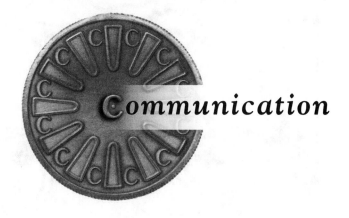

Communication

"If anyone has ears, let him hear" (Mark 4:9).

"Let every man be swift to hear, slow to speak" (James 1:19).

Again we must begin by looking at some key words that are vital for our growth:

▶ Rapport – connection   ▶ Look – *nomo fascies apraxia*
▶ Listen   ▶ Love
▶ Laugh   ▶ Lift

Nothing is more vital to our quality of life than communication. As George A. Miller has observed, "The most powerful stimulus for changing minds is not a chemical or a baseball bat. It is a word." If words are this important, we need to pay closer attention to how we use them.

The bridge is my choice for the symbol of communication. Perhaps the Internet would be more timely, since it has bridged the gaps in worldwide communications in a way that no static structure could ever do. Admittedly, the computer has dazzled us with its amazing speed in managing words and transmitting information from one place to another.

However, for thousands of years bridges have provided common pathways to connect people on two sides of a waterway. Until the era of the automobile, people crossed the bridge as a common meeting place and vehicle for exchange. A bridge that was broken down or destroyed would be sorely missed. They were a crucial part of the infrastructure, often taken for granted.

Much like the connection of a bridge, communication has been the common connection between persons, yet often broken down and a source of confusion. Both bridges and the communication of words and ideas may seem to be rather simple structures on the surface. However, it was long after graduation from medical school that I discovered, by studying my own inadequacy, just how complicated this business of communication really is.

It happened about 25 years into my family practice. As I was making hospital rounds one evening, at the nurses station I noticed a student nurse reading a book, *Looking Out / Looking In*, by Adler and Towne. I asked her what the book was about and became interested enough to glance through the Table of Contents. It was so compelling that I bought a copy, and I was so moved by its contents that I studied it like a bible.

Yes, I had a brief communications course in college: Communications 101. But it made very little impact. Not much was added about this in my medical training, though we were told that communication with patients is important. The problem was, no one really taught us *how*.

Adler and Towne started me on the journey to learning the processes of communication. I came to process my listening and speaking skills along with my scientific skills. After years of limited skills in communication, the processes began to become more clear. Some of us are too satisfied with our communication habits, unaware that we still have errors in our listening and speaking skills. Unwittingly, I still make errors in my connections.

Adler and Towne's definition of communication is a lot more technical than I prefer to use. Perhaps mine is too simple, but the rest of this chapter will give a glimpse of its complexity:

Definition: Communication is the powerful process of listening and speaking to another person, sharing our thoughts and feelings about something and listening as the other person speaks their thoughts and feelings as well.

Communication involves a connection of thoughts and feelings, through words and body language. This level of communication provides for richer and fuller meaning than is possible on the Internet. In a live dialog between persons, there is much more than the sharing of knowledge and facts. It is a live, two-way bridge.

Communication: the powerful process of listening and speaking to another person, sharing our thoughts and feelings about something and listening as the other person speaks their thoughts and feelings as well.

One of the most common criticisms of even the best physicians is, "He doesn't really listen to me." Often when speaking to patients we are accused of "talking in terms I can't understand." Or, "The doctor just doesn't explain to me what is happening."

There are breakdowns of the bridges of communication. We will be far more effective in our relationships with our patients and others if we commit ourselves to advance in our life journey by increasing our power of communication. In this book I am endeavoring to share many of the words which have become increasingly alive and meaningful to me over the past 25 years—a lot later in my career than I would like to admit. It should be our desire to grow in our ability to listen and speak with effectiveness and excellence.

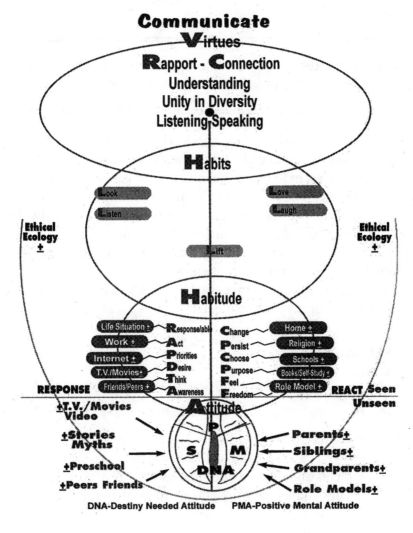

DNA-Destiny Needed Attitude   PMA-Positive Mental Attitude

Rapport

Establishing rapport is an important part of true communication. Rapport can be defined as getting connected to the whole person rather than superficially paying attention only to words. Rapport is the supreme virtue in communicating.

The word rapport is not often used in daily conversation. It is used more often in medical circles but not enough to my liking. It connects a physician in sympathetic and harmonious relationship to patients. This involves an interest in the whole person—his passions, feelings, perceptions, principles, beliefs and even his foibles and quirks.

Rapport: getting connected to the whole person rather than superficially paying attention only to words.

An increasing number of medical schools and residencies are becoming aware of the need for this emphasis. However, facts and technology still seem to dominate most doctor-patient relationships. And so it should. The science of diagnosing the cause of illness is our primary aim. Then we must treat the patient as well as the disease. We need the balance of rapport and science. When we combine true communication with a dedication to the science of medicine, a powerful process is created.

Over a period of years I have used the following memory device to increase my rapport with patients:

▶ Look
▶ Listen
▶ Love
▶ Laugh
▶ Lift

I will endeavor to break this down into practical steps, helping you see how you can establish and keep rapport.

To my patients and other lay persons I share my experience in the hope of making you aware of my desire to grow in this capacity. If you understand the process, you can hold me accountable to behaviors that demonstrate excellence in rapport. As I share these principles, I hope you will increasingly see how vital this matter of rapport is. As Ben Johnson once said, "Language much showeth a man; speak that I may see thee."

Look: Eye Contact

Our first connection to other persons is to glance and then look into their eyes. Eye contact is essential to begin and maintain rapport. Quite a few physicians are so busy feverishly writing notes for the medical record that much is lost in contact with the patient. If I do not see into a patient's eyes, I feel the encounter is dehumanized.

To look into someone's eyes is to look into his or her inner being, soul and emotions. So many feelings can be read in a person's eyes. In a similar manner, most patients are searching for the feelings and humanity of their physicians, getting behind our cold, scientific facades. Eye contact is one of the first bridges to rapport.

Look: *Noma Fascies Apraxia* (NFA)

Noma fascies apraxia is a very common disorder among physicians. This Latin phrase literally means "inability to put name and face together." Our second connection with our patients should be putting names and faces together, for there is no sweeter word to most people than their own name. Our name is our communicative identity.

I have to confess that I have struggled with this disorder for years. I have also come to understand why it is so much more common in physicians than salespeople, ministers or people in public relations. The fundamental reason is that physicians are more focused on understanding, diagnosing and treating diseases and illnesses than on memorizing the names and faces of their patients. Of course, patients come to us primarily as facilitators of their healing, not as a pal with whom to socialize. Nevertheless, healing occurs more readily in an environment of recognition and relationship.

Another thing that causes NFA by physicians is that we have written charts to prompt our lazy brains with the patient's name and other relevant information. This makes it easy to rationalize that there is simply no need to remember names and faces. Our receptionists do a much better job with name-face association than we physicians, and we are often content to leave it that way.

Noma fascies apraxia: a Latin phrase meaning "an inability to put name and face together."

But what if we are away from our office and charts, say at a ball game or church? We can easily be embarrassed by a failure to remember the face and name of a longtime patient. Knowing our weakness in this area, sometimes our wives can come to our aid by introducing themselves first. If you are a patient, please try to understand this common limitation among some physicians. Be patient with us as we endeavor to grow in this area.

LOOK: Uniqueness

We need to search for and define the uniqueness in each individual. Look for the characteristics that give them an identity—something to be valued as unique from anyone else on earth. Most people try to create an identity some way or other: tattoos, clothes, cars, hobbies, license plates, bumper stickers. Let's celebrate the identifying qualities of our character. People who do not have a healthy identity often end up either behind bars, on the streets, or in mental hospitals. Some patients have a very difficult time seeing their uniqueness.

LOOK: Common Ground

As we look for uniqueness, we also need to look for common ground. This includes similar interests, such as hobbies, values, purposes, principles and passions. In the sick room or medical office we communicate about the thing that has brought us together: stress, pain, brokenness, sorrow or sickness. However, the practice of medicine has been a joy and fulfillment for me and many healers when we also connect with the interests we share with patients beyond the sickness and disease. What a delight it is to share even briefly our common interests in family, hobbies or aspirations.

Patients can be proactive in this when time constraints allow—and physicians should endeavor to provide opportunities for such sharing.

Look: Awareness

As defined in chapter one, awareness means becoming cognizant of ourselves and the circumstances in the doctor-patient relationship. We need to be alert, alive and aware. For this we need to be rested, relaxed and truly in connection. We need to be relatively free from preoccupations, fears, anxieties and internal conflicts. This is a much sought after attitude of equanimity as we look into the eyes of another person.

Listen

My own thoughts about listening are expressed well by Earl Koile: "I feel like a terribly slow learner in acknowledging that only in recent years have I come to learn that listening is a primary way by which I can become a significant person in my own eyes and in the eyes of others, and I must continually relearn it." Listening is the most important skill and most prized gift we can give our patients. The greatest satisfaction in doctor-patient relationships comes from this capacity to connect and establish rapport.

Many patients go from doctor to doctor, minister to family, and then to friends, talk shows or bartenders, searching for someone who knows how to listen or is willing to take the time to listen. In the press of time and often because of a lack of skills, most of us fail at least some of the time to listen adequately. As we strive for excellence in listening, we need to model ourselves after those who are masters. These masters are successful listeners because they (1) observe non-verbal communications, (2) recognize the patient's agenda, (3) "say back" the patient's communications, (4) concentrate fully, and (5) empathize.

Let me briefly define these.

Listening: Non-Verbals

Have you ever considered how much is communicated by our facial expressions? A vast array of emotions can be portrayed, either consciously or subconsciously. In our scientific detachment, so necessary in the medical encounter, some of us doctors stone-face our patients and fear letting our feelings show. However, there is a time to let our patients see the emotions and humanity in our faces.

There are many different kinds of non-verbal communications. These silent messages and meanings are expressed by our body orientation (distancing), posture, gestures, facial expressions, eyes, voice and touching. Author David Augsburger states that "the emotional impact of words on others is 7% the choice of words, 38% the tone of voice, and 58% the body language, facial expression, posture and gestures." Other authorities estimate that 70% of all communication is non-verbal.

Physicians and patients can "read" each other to a considerable degree without talking. However, in the press of schedules we often ignore these non-verbals. Blessed are those who keep their awareness levels high and circumspect.

Sometimes our words are betrayed by our non-verbal language, and the unspoken message carries the greater impact. Ralph Waldo Emerson warned us years ago, "What you are speaks so loudly I cannot hear what you say." William Shutz says it this way: "Every thought, gesture, muscle tension, feeling, stomach gurgle, nose scratch, fart, hummed tune, slip of the tongue, illness...everything is significant to know and understand oneself...and the more one knows the more he is free to determine his own life."

Perhaps the biggest non-verbal to be aware of is attitude. Many attitudes are felt and observed in our communication. Excellent rapport demands a positive mental attitude (PMA); it can never be achieved or maintained when there are negative attitudes in either of the persons trying to communicate. We physicians should be held accountable to promote and model a PMA.

Listening: Agenda

Everyone who comes to a doctor has an agenda: a list of complaints, concerns or conditions. Most patients don't have these items written down, but they have an agenda nonetheless. Some proactive patients not only make a list, but even prioritize the items. I would like to see every patient get into that habit.

A hurried and harried physician can easily short-circuit the patient's agenda, often causing a mistaken prioritization of the patient's symptoms. Howard Beckman, M.D., found this in his research: "Most patients have between one and five things that they want to talk about...We found that in only half the visits do people get all of the symptoms out...doctors interrupt patients after 18 seconds on average...only 23% of patients were able to complete their opening statement."

Patients need to realize that time constraints are a real factor. Both patients and physicians must be aware of the agenda and negotiate how much can be done in the given time limits. Often more time must be found, either now or later, depending on the urgency.

Wise physicians will also realize that there is often a *hidden* agenda, which is typically more important than what the patient lists. Hesitations, vagueness and silence may be signals that something difficult to write down or talk about is trying to surface. I have to admit that I may have missed more of these through the years than I would like to know. I am trying to keep a finer sensitivity to these unlisted, suppressed desires and concerns. However, I also implore patients to courageously communicate their hidden agendas to the physicians they trust.

LISTENING: Say It Back

This skill should be a regular habit. One of the best listeners in my life is my wife. She has taught me so much, and yet I'm sure I won't ever reach her level of listening. Boy, does she read the nonverbals! Most of all, she has the practice of "saying back" what she picks up from my non-verbals.

Once again, the press of time often hinders us from clarifying what we thought we heard. It is surprising to physicians that patients generally hear only 20% of our instructions. That is why it is far more effective to write things down in communicating our needs, wants and instructions.

LISTENING: Concentrate

My office has been planned and constructed to reduce distractions and maximize concentration, enabling me to focus on the patient encounter. In spite of this, phone interruptions sometimes break my train of thought and cause me to lose my focus. Adler and Towne cite other reasons why we do not listen as we should:

- **Message overload.** It is impossible to listen all the time.
- **Preoccupation.** We can easily get wrapped up in personal concerns.
- **Rapid thought.** Our optimum rate to process information is 100-140 words per minute. Anything slower than this can cause the mind to wander.
- **Noise.** Physical distractions or discomforts that hinder our concentration.
- **Hearing problems.** This is much more common than you might think.
- **Faulty assumptions.** This comes from failing to check the other's viewpoint.
- **Talking temptation**. Talking sometimes has more apparent advantages than listening.
- **Lack of training.** We are not trained to be good listeners, so few of us do it well.

This list could go on and on, for many factors seem intent on hindering our concentration on patient needs. Most HMOs are not very subtle about their demands on physicians to see more patients. With a great emphasis on efficiency, the priority of excellence in communication is often lost in the shuffle.

Surprising as it may seem, time spent with patients does not always equate to excellence in communication. Some rare physicians can manage their words and listening skills so effectively that they actually spend less time than others. That takes concentration and experience, and is not possible for everyone.

So, what makes for excellence in communication? Consider the following formula:

Success = Excellence (not perfection) + Effectiveness and perhaps Efficiency

or

Success = E + E + E in communications

LISTENING: **Empathize**

Empathy will be defined and described in detail in a later chapter. However, here it is sufficient to say that every patient deserves the attitude of empathy in their health providers. The patient who is in pain needs us to listen with our feelings and not just our mind. We need to try to put ourselves in the patient's place—able to feel how their lives are being impacted.

Empathy: derived from Latin, em (in) and pathos (feelings), this is a deep inner feeling for another person, putting ourselves in their situation.

LOVE: **Be Friendly**

While we listen or speak, we need to communicate a warm and friendly attitude. Nothing positive can easily come out of a cold, hostile and unfriendly attitude. All too often, physicians project a demeanor of arrogance and authoritarianism toward their patients.

There was a time when physicians were in short supply, and attitudes did not seem to affect a physician's practice. However, in today's marketplace it is different. What will happen if I have a choice between two consultants with equal expertise, but one acts friendly toward me and my patients, while the other is distant, arrogant, surly and unfriendly? I will clearly choose the friendly one. It pays to be warm and friendly, but the financial rewards are only secondary. Patients should be treated as human beings—not "walking diseases" hired out to specialists.

There is also such a thing as being too friendly. Some physicians are so given to fraternizing that they are easily manipulated. We need to guard against losing that independence of thought and objectivity so necessary in medical discipline. That is why a physician who treats himself or his family often loses the impartial, unemotional, rational judgment that is necessary, especially in serious situations.

LOVE: **Touch**

How we touch, where we touch, when we touch, who we touch

is a powerful skill in communicating patient care. Some patients like to be touched, but some do not. Some physicians and caregivers tend to touch, while others are reluctant to touch. This is an important issue in the art of medicine. In many cases it will determine how well we connect with our patients.

A long chapter could be written on this subject. For now, however, it is enough to say that patients expect us not only to examine by touch, but to do it with finesse and gentleness. Too often our hurried exams are painful, and sometimes necessarily so. Our patients have a responsibility to keep us informed and sensitive to the level of pain they experience in our touch. Again, two-way communication is crucial.

Wise physicians will exercise great sensitivity as to where, how and how often they touch a patient. This is not something that always comes naturally, but rather is a skill that may take the better part of a lifetime to fully learn.

Love: Openness

For either the caregiver or the patient, freedom to express our thoughts and feelings is an essential part of creative communications. When the bridge of communication is open—no barricades, pot holes, prickly nails or barbs in the way—great things can happen. However, in some medical offices there is an atmosphere and attitude that only certain subjects will be heard. Freedom to communicate on any subject should be encouraged.

Is this freedom of dialog offered in our offices and patient relations? Or do our encounters rigidly stick to the scientific facts of diseases? Quite often a patient has exhausted all hopes of finding someone who will be open and listen to his very private and personal thoughts. We caregivers should not be shocked or dismayed at whatever a patient presents. We should invite openness and free dialog about any human hurt or suffering.

This openness has limits, of course. Time constraints in the schedule must be recognized by both doctor and patient. A general freedom to share should not be construed as a license for patients to expect unlimited time. While our desire is to promote freedom of dialog, we must maintain reasonable boundaries and balance.

Love: Acceptance

Almost any human suffering or circumstance can be endured and managed if we find another person who accepts us, believes in us, and finds us worthy in spite of our unique quirks and foibles. A person may be ugly or beautiful, penniless or wealthy, angry or friendly, but all need acceptance. That does not mean we accept bad behaviors, but we must always try to accept the inner person. Whether we accept or reject a person is quickly communicated in our attitudes. We may think that our judgments toward a person are successfully masked, but they seldom are.

Love: Suffering

We need to respond quickly and sensitively to those suffering with various kinds of pain. Establishing successful rapport depends upon our ability to perform this act of love and compassion. We all have experienced pain, and we shouldn't forget that feeling as we try to help others in pain. Even if we struggle to identify with the exact situation our patient is dealing with, compassion is the one thing we are expected to communicate.

Love: Thanking

Yes, we are grateful when our patients lavish thanks on us for our care. We like it and need that boost! However, we physicians often forget to thank *patients* for the privilege and honor of serving them. This attitude of gratitude will go a long way toward strengthening our rapport with patients.

Love: Serving

Are we serving our patients or ourselves? The attitude of whom we are serving is soon communicated by patients. They will respond to our treatment and advice much more readily if they sense that our motive is genuinely focused on serving them.

Laugh

When I say laugh, I mean humor. I realize that there are very few belly laughs in medicine. However, there is more humor than you might think. The tragic is often tied closely to humor. Nothing in the lower animal kingdom can be compared to humor. The hyena may laugh, the chimpanzee may smile, but only humans have true humor.

So, what is humor? I define it as a uniquely human capacity of mind which expresses or reacts to something funny with smiles or laughter. It is a kind of comedy that tickles the soul. As physicians, we can communicate our good humor and connect very positively with patients. I love to hear good humorous stories, especially if they come from real life. Many books could be filled with jokes about doctors and patients.

Instead of being serious all the time, we should tickle the child within us, maintaining our ability to laugh. We need to laugh with our patients, but not at them. At times we must laugh at ourselves— our souls battered by rules, regulations, lawyers and litigious patients.

Humor: a uniquely human capacity of mind which expresses or reacts to something funny with smiles or laughter.

We also need to keep our sense of humor when we see the ugly. Although ugly can be perceived as beautiful at times, that is only made possible through a good sense of humor. Expressing humor can provide an enormous power in communication and healing. The most articulate person on this subject was Norman Cousins, who wrote the excellent book, *The Anatomy of an Illness*.

LIFT: Arouse

We establish rapport in order to lift people out of their misery and helplessness. That is why they come to us. Patients depend upon the art of healing that a physician possesses. Often the patient's strength has been drained away, and the doctor is called upon to arouse the patient's spiritual and emotional reserves once again.

Certainly the powers of a physician are limited, but hopefully we can impart a power beyond pills, knives and physical therapy. Our expertise should include the power to lift up our patients by the arousal of some basic hopes in the partnership of healing and curing. Genuine hope is a great healer.

LIFT: the Power of Freedom

One of the important qualities to arouse in our patients is inner freedom, as already discussed. In order to inspire freedom for the patient, we must communicate that they have freedom to choose, act, persist and grow. We can suggest, encourage and nurture, but the patients themselves must exercise their freedom to choose and act.

LIFT: the Power of Imagination

Do we recognize and communicate to our patients the enormous powers of the imagination? We are often called upon to give a prognosis, but many times we are wrong. Sometimes our prognosis is unnecessarily gloomy, which only imparts discouragement to the patient. Instead, we need to ask the patient to imagine the best that is possible. Milton Erickson, M.D., has set down a law of the mind that says, "Whenever there is a conflict over the will and the imagination, imagination will always win out." Whatever we vividly imagine will inevitably come to pass.

LIFT: Arouse a Readiness

Do we as physicians communicate an understanding of our patients' readiness to be helped and healed, to grow and find a purpose for their lives? Many patients who come to us are not really ready for healing. That may seem strange, but many alcoholics, chemical dependents, food addicts, obese people and those with chronic pain are not ready to give up their dysfunctional lives.

Many diseases are actually self-inflicted, and people often hang on to their illnesses for reasons not entirely understood. For example, a food-addictive person who is obese may be using food as a crutch to overcome depression, loneliness or anxiety. Although it is better to soothe depression with food rather than alcohol, food addiction is a problem nevertheless. The challenge for physicians is to arouse in the patient a readiness to find a better answer to loneliness and depression. Is the patient ready? He must choose.

Now you may say this psychological stuff has no place in the office of a general practitioner. Leave it to the psychiatrists or the ministers! On the contrary, a great many family physicians and other primary care physicians are actively doing this kind of lifting. Primary care physicians are often in the most natural place to be aware of a patient's readiness to act. This is the key: waiting for when the patient is ready to deal with the issue. These times of decision often occur when no one else is around or available.

LIFT: Arouse Expectations

Interpersonal conflicts often arise when there are significantly differing expectations. We need to arouse and be aware of our patients' expectations. Unfortunately, caregivers are frequently unaware of these expectations, nor do the patients understand our expectations of them. We need to communicate these subtle, subliminal hopes and desires.

Clarifying expectations is not only an essential part of excellent communications, but also a great way to prevent conflict and dissatisfaction. That is why new patients should immediately receive information about a physician's expectations. A patient information brochure is helpful insurance in this regard.

LIFT: Arouse Hope

It takes so little time to lift a patient's spirit with hope. Yes, charlatans and quacks, nostrums and hucksters will always be with us, offering false hopes about unproved or even dangerous cures. The medical profession, in contrast, has been zealous to protect patients and the public against unproved remedies.

Hope: defined by Dr. Robert Schuller as "Holding On, Praying Expectantly."

The marketplace is wild with all sorts of claims to healing. We are besieged with "natural products," herbs, copper for arthritis, and an unending list of other alleged remedies. Many of these are unregulated, unproved and risky. While these products hold out hopes for dramatic cures, the scientific bent of mind is disciplined to question and wait for proof.

However, there are many things in medicine that can inspire hope—even without scientific proof. Scientific empiricism says that if a remedy works, we should use it even though we cannot explain it.

For example, take prayer. It is difficult to prove its effectiveness in healing, but countless millions of people have used prayer throughout the centuries as an important resource to bring healing and hope.

Hope is defined by Dr. Robert Schuller as "Holding On, Praying Expectantly." I cannot think of a better definition. Arousing hope through our communications is a powerful element of lifting.

LIFT: Arouse Enthusiasm

If a physician communicates indifference, apathy or a negative attitude, the patient will be let down. An enthusiastic, positive attitude in a physician has a great chance to lift a patient. If I am not enthusiastic about a medicine or treatment, I will not use it. However, if we communicate our faith and enthusiasm in a treatment alternative, a positive result will likely occur even if it is a placebo. Enthusiasm is caught by others. It's like spreading fire.

Physicians who are experiencing burnout or brownout will be less effective in their practices. Part of the struggle in medicine today is to maintain enthusiasm and a positive outlook in spite of the dehumanizing forces that confront us.

LIFT: Arouse Healing Powers

Physicians must be aware of the enormous powers that patients have in the healing processes. Many of these healing powers are intangible and immeasurable, yet very real nonetheless. As we grow in our awareness of where these powers come from, we must communicate the information to the patient.

It is arrogance for a physician to feel that he alone can heal or cure someone. Yes, surgery can cure many things. Radiation therapy and chemotherapy can also have wonderful results. But the most important powers come from the body's own healing faculties.

We physicians merely assist the body in its recovery from assault. We assist nature's healing processes, which are enormous and complex.

The twentieth century witnessed some marvelous progress in the healing of disease. We anticipate many wonders and miracles yet to come in this new century. However, the creative power which gave birth to the universe, our world, and all the wondrous creatures still holds all wisdom and power in His hands. Physicians and patients must partner with these creative forces of infinite wisdom.

Speaking

The wise old owl sat in the oak.
The more he saw the less he spoke.
The less he spoke the more he heard.
Why can't we be like that old bird?

The power of the spoken word was not taught in medical schools. In fact, only a few truly articulate physicians ever achieve excellent and effective speaking in their professional life. Their skills were likely honed on a high school or college debate team, certainly not in medical school. My brief sortie into the world of debate was a fiasco, and I did not persevere long enough to become as skillful as I might have. Consequently, I grew very little in my speaking "know how" and remained content with ordinary dialog. It is still a struggle for me to speak in public. However, I dream of being able to effectively empower, motivate and influence people through the principles of excellent speaking. This has become a lifelong quest— an art to be cultivated by commitment.

The words that proceed out of our mouths are a window to our thoughts and feelings. Often these thoughts and feelings are so intense that they erupt spontaneously. We are creatures often swayed by reactions and responses to various stimuli, either from our external environment or from our inner thoughts and feelings.

We need to go back to our paradigm of the essential inner nutrients of growth. The words that fill our speech are a by-product of the following areas:

▶ Thoughts   ▶ Feelings   ▶ Desires   ▶ Purposes
▶ Priorities   ▶ Choices   ▶ Actions

As we mature, our speech should become more response-able, instead of merely being reactive to the stimuli around us. Adolescents are typically volatile reactors, and their speech often reflects the inability to respond rather than react. The time-honored passage in Psalms describes our goal for excellent speech: "Let the words of my mouth and meditations of my heart be acceptable" (Psalm 19:14). Jesus likewise instructed His disciples:

> "A good man out of the good treasure of his heart brings forth good things [words]. An evil man out of the evil treasure brings forth evil things [words]"
>
> (Matthew 12:36).

If our words are uncontrolled—not formed in a response-able manner—our tongue can be as destructive as a carelessly tossed cigarette that destroys a great forest. For most of us, it takes a journey of many years to process words more response-ably. We all need to be aware of how reactively we speak in our communications.

More frequently than I would like, I continue to demonstrate "foot in mouth disease"—reacting instead of responding. I suppose that all of us will continue to struggle with this to some degree as long as we live. However, I am happy to report that my words truly are improving the older I get. Noted for his wisdom, King Solomon wrote, "A wise man's heart guides his mouth" (Proverbs 6:23). This is striving for excellence in speaking.

Checklist for Evaluating Our Communication

So, how can a patient evaluate the communication skills of a physician? In general, effective communication occurs when a physician:

❑ Listens to patients, whether or not there is agreement.
❑ Asks patients what they understand about their illness.
❑ Uses open-ended questions to give patients opportunities to explore their feelings.
❑ Refrains from conducting patient interviews in a tightly controlled manner, with rapid-fire questions or interruptions.
❑ Has an unhurried demeanor.

❏ Takes time for adequate explanations, drawing pictures when helpful.

❏ Makes eye contact while listening or speaking.

❏ States views modestly, not in an authoritative manner that discourages the patient's individual expression.

❏ Listens to psychological needs before ordering batteries of tests.

❏ Chooses words effectively when talking with patients.

❏ Explores patients' own perceptions, beliefs, hopes, fears and values.

❏ Allows patients to tell their stories in their own words.

Conclusions

Establishing rapport and getting connected with our patients requires a solid understanding of the inner processes of looking, listening, laughing, loving and lifting. The first four EINGs—awareness, freedom, thinking and feeling—are vitally important to the improvement of our communication skills. These require a determined quest to discover our patients' desires, purposes, values and choices. This is how excellent communication is attained.

Chapter Three

Growing in

Conflict Resolution

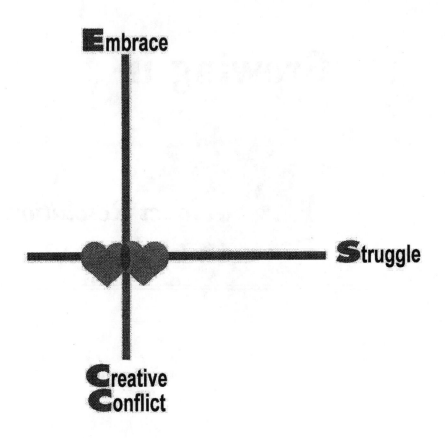

"Blessed are the peacemakers" (Matthew 5:9).

Peace is a prize virtue in families, communities and among the nations. The angels proclaimed at Christ's birth, "Peace on earth, good will among men" (Luke 2:14)—and this deep longing is the cry as each new millennium dawns. While there still are some per- verted souls bent on creating conflict, division and hatred, there is a vast tidal wave of humanity moving toward peace.

So how do we achieve this universal dream and desire? This chapter devises a simple paradigm—a picture of how to do this. The words may have a familiar ring, but I can assure you I did not encounter them in medical school or residency. Perhaps "peace" is something too abstract and soft to be handled by the many devotees of the physical sciences. Yet true medicine is more than an applica- tion of the physical sciences. It is a blend of physical, social and spiritual disciplines.

Here are some key words related to this:

▶ Conflict	▶ Interdependence
▶ Anger	▶ Win-Win
▶ Unity	▶ Peace
▶ Mediation	▶ Confronting
▶ Humility	▶ "Carefronting"
▶ Forgiveness	▶ Persistence

The three "Big Cs" in striving for excellence—creativity, com- munication and conflict resolution—have preeminence for me because of the influence of David and Vera Mace. This husband and wife team were marriage counselors for more than 50 years. People in crisis came to them with diverse problems and stresses, hoping to find solutions through these wise counselors. The Maces learned practical processes of how the families could communicate and resolve conflict. Often, however, the Mace team found that the problems got no better, partly because the counselees refused to talk about the things that mattered most. Many of the counselees also struggled to think creatively, build a positive attitude, and find new ways of living. However, this is the secret to satisfaction in rela- tionships, especially when there is conflict.

We shouldn't be surprised when we encounter conflict in our

relationships from time to time. Conflict should not be a baffling experience, but rather a natural phenomenon that we can strive to understand. Instead of being some strange and perplexing occurrence, we need to realize that conflict is actually inevitable—found in every profession, school, church, business, nation, friendship and family. In fact, wherever two people intimately share the same space, conflict will periodically arise.

It is unfortunate, however, that conflict is generally thought of only as a negative force. I want to propose that when we consider the process of conflict resolution, we find that it can be a powerful positive force in shaping our lives and character. Hard as that may be to believe, I want you to understand the following axiom: *Creative conflict is a crisis opportunity for change and growth.*

Conflict: the powerful process for change in a struggle/embrace relationship, arising from differing expectations, needs, wants, passions, powers, principles, priorities and purposes.

Conflict may be thought of as the dynamite that blasts away at our hardened, fixed ways—the things that hinder us from growing. It has the great potential to change our attitudes, biases, prejudices and rigid relationships. I do not remember a single lecture or seminar in my early scientific training that clearly addressed this wonderful phenomenon.

Natural Conflict

From Charles Darwin's studies of plants and animals comes one outstanding fact: To live is to struggle. Close to this fact is another: Males and females embrace and have union to perpetuate their kind. So there are these two phenomena, closely related but perpetually in tension: struggle and embrace. Much of my understanding of this paradigm springs from David Augsburger's book, *Caring Enough to Confront.*

In the history of the natural world there is continuous competition. This takes the form of tussles over territory and survival of the fittest, for individuals and for the species. The processes are mostly orderly, predictable and without abysmal violence. While one species may prey upon another in the food chain, there is no mass genocide in the same species except perhaps with the lemming. Only in the human species have conflicts and struggles for possessions, positions, power and superiority become heinous and massively destructive. Despite the nearly universal human longing for peace, it is apparent that humankind as a whole has little understanding of the processes of conciliation.

From my personal experience in the medical profession, there have always been too many turf wars, and they still exist today. It was true in Osler's time, a hundred years ago, when he said, "The wrangling of unseemly disputes which have too often disgraced our profession arise, in a great majority of cases on one hand, from this morbid sensitiveness to the confession of error, and on the other, from a lack of brotherly consideration and a convenient forgetfulness of our own failings."

So how can we define conflict? It is that powerful process for change in a struggle/embrace relationship, arising from differing expectations, needs, wants, passions, powers, principles, priorities and purposes. Armed with this definition, we can grow in our understanding, discovering how best to manage our conflicts.

Struggle and Embrace

These two forces or movements are opposite but complimentary emotional passions which spawn love-hate relationships. These emotions outwardly seem to be at cross purposes to each other. However, personal differences in our passions, expectations, needs and wants are bound to occur in any loving relationship. So the paradigm begins with our different perspectives in our struggle for unity and embrace.

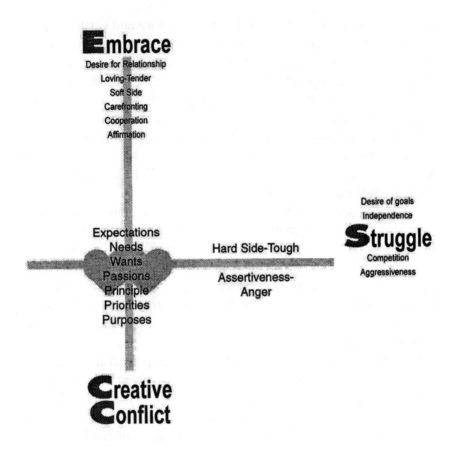

Embrace comes from a desire for relationship and is associated with soft forces pulling for unity or interdependence, affirming another person. Struggle, however, pulls us in another direction, toward independence and individual goals. Associated with this force is the tough side of relationships—adversity, anger, aggressiveness, competition and power moves.

You probably can readily see that some of the essential inner nutrients of growth in chapter one form the center of this paradigm. There will always be differences in how individuals grow in these nutrients, and often our conflicts stem from these differences. Conflict becomes maladaptive and negative when we *react* to our differences. In order to make conflict a positive creative process, we need to learn to *respond* and become response-able in our conflicts. This is how we can use the power of struggle and embrace to grow, change and adapt in a harmonious manner. It enables us to grow toward unity and interdependence, not disunity and extreme independence. We retain partnership, or at least a concern for relationship. We respond rather than react to our differences. Affirmation and assertiveness are two essential dynamics, each healthy emotions which help us avoid the hazards of anger, violence and broken relationships.

By plotting numerically our attitudes regarding relationships and goals, it is very easy to predict the outcome of conflicts.

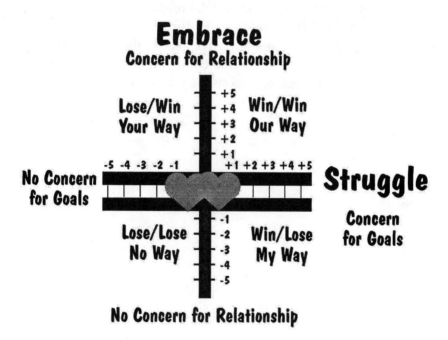

Our predetermined attitudes often cause us to fall into ruts in our methods of resolving relationship conflicts. What is needed is a plan to change our attitudes, and that is where I suggest we become response-able for a win-win outcome. Admittedly, this is not as simplistic as Shel Silverstein's jingle from his book *Where the Sidewalk Ends*:

I will not play at tug o'war,
I'd rather play at hug o'war.
Where everyone hugs
Instead of tugs,
Where everyone giggles
And rolls on the rug,
Where everyone kisses
And everyone grins,
And everyone cuddles,
And everyone wins.

Sometimes broken relationships are necessary. When conflict occurs, it may be appropriate to have an outcome of no way, your way or my way. However, in most relationship conflicts it is possible to process our differences to make for a win-win outcome: not my way or your way but *our* way. The rest of the chapter is about words not used often enough in the conflict arena. I will fill in the paradigm with a reasonable, responsible plan for conflict resolution.

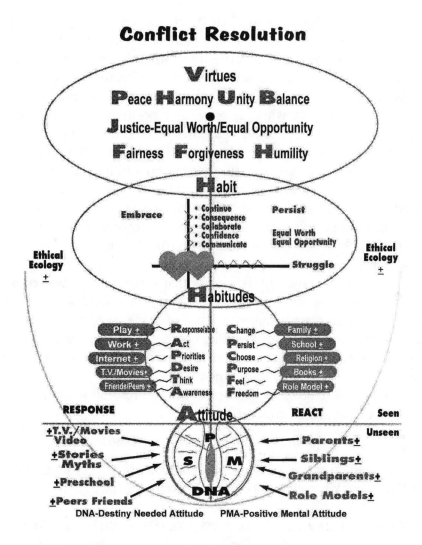

Conflict Resolution

Confrontation

Conflict is often thought of as a confrontation, a facing of two adversarial forces. This often is a negative win-lose process, with assertiveness high on both sides. Both sides are defensive and aggressive, with a high concern for one's own goals and rights. In contrast to this negative picture, David Augsburger has coined the beautiful word: "carefronting." He describes carefronting as "a new word for those who strive to keep relationships in a win-win mode of behavior by allowing all parties in conflict the freedom to assert their wants, values, goals and viewpoints." Carefronting does not imply capitulation to the views of others. Rather, it encourages us to care for relationship while asserting our positions, passions, perceptions, principles, priorities, purposes, needs and wants.

A high concern for relationship, when combined with a high concern for one's own goals, yields a great possibility for a win-win resolution of the conflict. Although carefronting should be a much-used word, few people are familiar with its power. It is a word that can change our attitudes and bring positive outcomes to our conflicts.Gaining a new perspective on conflict begins with a realization that it is possible to make every conflict an opportunity for growth. Conflict, after all, is a crisis that should not be wasted on negative thinking and reacting. From early childhood we have all learned how to react in anger in times of conflict. At a very young age we set our pattern for handling conflict, either fighting back or fleeing. What most of us failed to learn, however, was how to respond to our conflicts with win-win attitudes.

It is helpful to see how successful conflict resolution fits in with the inner nutrients of growth:

Conflict Resolution and the EINGs

We need to see how the Essential Inner Nutrients of Growth (EINGs) work together to help us resolve conflicts:

EINGs #1 and #2: AWARENESS AND FREEDOM – The first in restructuring our thinking for positive conflict management is to become aware of the freedom we have to respond rather than react according to our previous patterns. This also means becoming aware that there is a more adaptive way to handle conflict.

EING #3: THINK – We need to stop and think before reacting. To overcome the tendency to react with anger or fear takes a considerable amount of reading, thinking and soul-searching about how we are behaving. David Augsburger's book, *Caring Enough to Confront,* helped get me excited about discovering new ways of managing conflict. Though it is just a small book, it is packed with great ideas for restructuring our attitudes toward conflict.

Another book that awakened me to skills of conciliation was Likert and Likert's *New Ways of Managing Conflict.* The Likerts addressed conflict in the manufacturing sector, but their counsel is just as applicable to conflict in medicine or any other service industry. Not until the past 20 years did some of the large corporations become aware of the importance of conflict resolution skills. Despite these advances, many big businesses (including hospitals, clinics and physician groups) are still locked in the old reactionary ways.

Fortunately there is a wealth of new material now available to renew our thinking about handling conflicts. One of my favorites is *The Peacemaker,* a book by attorney Ken Sande in which he masterfully details the intricacies of successful conflict resolution.

EING #4: FEEL – Feelings of anger, fear, isolation, arrogance, jealousy, insecurity and many other negative emotions are typically involved in conflict situations. Unless these feelings are successfully dealt with, the conciliation process will be sabotaged. Anger, hostility and fear are the primary emotions that get in the way of conflict resolution.

Interpersonal conflicts rarely turn from negative to positive until we first become aware of our own feelings and inner conflict. Love-hate relationships usually stem from the struggle between two opposing emotions within ourselves. Introspection plays a crucial role in eliminating our negative feelings and replacing them with positive ones.

EING #5: DESIRE – An important ingredient in resolving conflict and pursuing conciliation is having a fervent desire for peace. Most of us do yearn for peace in relationships, but sometimes we fail to see that this must be a lifelong quest. New conflicts will arise as long as two people are intimately connected. Each conflict is a challenge for closer harmonious intimacy. The goal is to achieve and cultivate unity in spite of diversity.

EING #6: PURPOSE – Recognizing our purposes and goals is a vital part of resolving our conflicts. No one can fully do this for us. We must also try to ascertain the purposes and goals of the other person, putting ourselves "in their shoes" as the metaphor describes. It helps to write down the purposes and objectives of each party, so we can see which goals are presently at odds.

EING #7: PRIORITIZE – Our values and priorities often lie unwritten and unexpressed. In any conflict it is important to clarify our own values—the things that we believe are most important. Then it is important to seek the values of the other persons involved in the conflict. To respect the values and goals of others as much as our own, in spite of disagreement, is a huge step toward finding common ground. This is hard work, but conflict can be a great aid to personal growth, helping us discover our inner selves. There is little hope for lasting conflict resolution unless we are willing to probe what psychologist Virginia Satir calls our "wisdom box"— made up of our passions, perceptions, principles, priorities and purposes.

Other EINGs: Choosing to become response-able (EING #11) rather than react will be a natural consequence of processing the previous growth nutrients. This crucial choice (EING #8) allows us to act (EING #9) the best we can. To reset our attitudes, all we need to do is persist (EING #10), repeating our actions in a positive way (EING #9).

By understanding how the above processes relate to conflict resolution, we become responders rather than reactors, capable of change and adapting positively rather than negatively. We are then ready to consolidate our habits in the next step of maturation in conciliation.

Consider the following "Five Cs" that are essential habitudes for growth in the conciliatory process:

1. Communicate
2. Confide
3. Collaborate
4. Consequence
5. Continue

These can be illustrated by the following diagram:

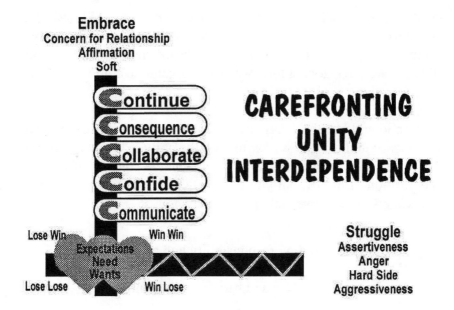

Embrace
Concern for Relationship
Affirmation
Soft

Continue
Consequence
Collaborate
Confide
Communicate

CAREFRONTING
UNITY
INTERDEPENDENCE

Lose Win   Win Win
Expectations
Need
Wants
Lose Lose   Win Lose

Struggle
Assertiveness
Anger
Hard Side
Aggressiveness

Let's look at these five habitudes in more detail.

1. Communicate

Instead of building walls in times of conflict, we must build bridges. We must employ all of the essential inner nutrients for growth and the processes of communication. In the absence of true dialog (a two-way bridge), there is little chance for resolution of the conflict.

Successful communication usually requires several distinct steps. First, we must *listen* to the other person, trying to hear their expectations, needs, wants, priorities or principles. This means more than superficial listening, for it involves delving into the meaning of their words and desiring to see their inner selves.

The second step is to say back what we thought we heard from the other person. This is important, for often they are not saying what we think we heard!

Third, we must try to empathize or see the other person's viewpoint and position. This does not mean surrendering our own view, but simply recognizing the deep-seated feelings and views of each other. We must acknowledge each person's right to hold and state his views—whether or not the views themselves are correct. As we learn to listen, say back what we've heard and empathize with another, we have gone a long way toward genuine communication.

2. Confide

A solid and healthy relationship can be built only by developing confidence and trust. If we begin with the attitude "I'm OK, you're OK," we are positioned to build respect. On the contrary, if we take the position "I'm OK, but you're not OK," we are likely to engage in a variety of negative actions:

A – Attack
B – Blame (avoiding responsibility and accountability)
C – Criticize
D – Defend ourselves and become argumentative

These four maladaptive reactions to conflict will inevitably prevent response-able growth. They will violate any trusting relationship. All too often, they are readily triggered early on in conflict, especially if we do not communicate clearly.

To have the attitude "I'm OK, you're OK" requires a healthy self-esteem, which many people do not have. This must be built by a separate process. If neither party in conflict has a good self-esteem, a real miracle will be needed to get a win-win outcome.

Often we become reactive in the face of conflict because the conflict exposes our weaknesses or shortcomings. As Benjamin Franklin once said, "Love your enemies, for they will tell you your faults."

Few people in history were as familiar with criticism as President Abraham Lincoln was. When asked his advice for handling criticism, Lincoln recommended a three-step process: 1. Consider the source, 2. Take the chip off your shoulder, and 3. Keep an open mind. Realizing that keeping an open mind was perhaps the most difficult thing to do, Lincoln explained, "As unreasonable as it seems, I always think to myself, 'It's just possible that this man knows what he is talking about.' On that assumption I see what I can learn from him."

3. Collaborate

Collaboration is defined by Webster's Dictionary as "working together." This is a significant word for us physicians, for we are by nature an independent lot. Bucking this tendency takes a serious commitment to work for unity. It means finding the common ground, seeing interdependence as the ultimate goal. There is almost always *something* which can be shared: a goal, value, need or want.

It takes a labor of love to clarify each other's expectations, needs, wants, priorities and purposes. Setting individual goals and plans requires time, trust, talk and sharing of feelings. It is essential to understand that unity does not mean conformity, but rather a collaboration designed to result in partnership. Respect for an individual's unique character traits must be prized and cultivated.

Collaboration: defined by Webster's Dictionary as "working together."

In the process of collaboration there may well be a healthy release of anger. In the midst of assertions and affirmations, confronting and care, collaboration can use the power of anger and channel its force into positive action. Like the power of steam in a steam engine, anger can transform conflict into a creative process.

In his book, *Feeling Good,* David Burns admonishes us to stop creating anger by our own cognitions (thoughts and feelings). "People don't make us angry," Burns says, "we make ourselves angry by our reactions—uncontrolled thoughts." William Blake, likewise, writes about the proper way to deal with anger in a relationship:

> I was angry with my friend.
> I told my wrath; my wrath did end.
> I was angry with my foe.
> I told it not, my wrath did grow.

Collaboration, communication and trust form a highly effective triad for handling conflict. If followed, these steps can keep us from reacting in conflict, helping us grow in response-ability.

4. Consequence

In any situation, we need to look ahead and consider the likely outcome of our actions. Positive processes yield positive consequences. Negative processes yield negative consequences. It isn't hard to figure out the desired outcomes most people desire when they have conflicts:

- Everybody wins something (win-win)
- Harmony
- Unity (interdependence with a degree of autonomy)
- Balance

What exactly is this peace that we long for in our relationships? Peace is *not* the absence of conflict, but rather may be defined as a successful outcome of the processes of conflict resolution. Like endless waves breaking against the seashore, this pattern of conciliation – conflict – conciliation – conflict is an inevitable reality of life.

> **Peace:** not the absence of conflict, but rather a successful outcome of the processes of conflict resolution.

Fairness and justice must be desired goals in our conflicts, but they are often very difficult to achieve. The reason fairness and justice tend to be so elusive is often because we see them only from our own self-centered perspective rather than objectively. This self-centered focus on "getting my rights" (what I think I'm entitled to) often takes center stage in trying to resolve our conflicts. Objectivity gets pushed aside.

In extreme cases, these matters are relegated to the legal profession, yet physicians and caretakers are also often drawn into conflicts with patients and their families. The vocabulary of legalese is foreign to most of us, but we must do our best to understand the legal processes which manage a great many conflicts in our society.

The medical profession today is greatly affected by the processes of the legal profession and legislation. The sword of Damocles hangs over every physician's head: the fear of malpractice suits and other litigation. Personally, this is one of my greatest fears, haunting me at every patient encounter. Despite the fact that I have never suffered through a malpractice suit in my 48 years of practice, I have no guarantees that I will not one day become a victim.

Legal experts have concluded that more than 90% of the medical malpractice claims are frivolous and founded only on a patient's imaginary "right to compensation," even if there was no negligence by the doctor. Regardless of a physician's quality of care, poor medical outcomes often invite grief, anger, blame and criticism. The end result of this conflict is often an adversarial confrontation in a court of law.

Most physicians love the practice of medicine but are dismayed and discouraged by this current adversarial climate. This leaves us feeling victimized by a legal system where it is all too easy for people to file lawsuits just because they are dissatisfied with the outcome of their surgery or treatment. Some lawsuits are, no doubt, justified, but many are filed irresponsibly. The rules should be changed to entertain such lawsuits only when there is some kind of reasonable basis for the claim of malpractice.

Dr. Otis Bowen, a former governor of Indiana, managed to correct this unjust process by requiring a medical panel to review the claim before it went to court. This model reform gives physicians in Indiana a great deal more protection from these frivolous malpractice claims. Of course, some patients and lawyers still are blinded by a reckless pursuit of their perceived "rights," but this procedural safeguard at least weeds out many of the unwarranted claims.

I realize that our legal system in America may be the best in the world regarding a person's freedom and rights. However, too often we miss a lesson we could glean from other countries: With freedom there is a need for response-ability. As I understand it, in most European countries there is a severe penalty paid by those making false and frivolous claims. This has not been so in America. As much as I would like to see penalties placed on those who make irresponsible claims, I do not see that revolution occurring anytime soon. There seems to be too much money at stake.

Now a word about lawyers. Lest I be censured for seeming to attack lawyers, I am not. Perhaps some lawyers will actually support me as I describe my perceptions of the legal processes in our country. The fact of the matter, it seems to me, is this: Lawyers are enmeshed in negative processes, and negative processes get negative results. The processes are essentially confrontational and adversarial, designed to produce a win-lose outcome. Typically, neither side attempts to create a better relationship between those in conflict. Relationships are, in fact, usually worsened by the confrontational legal arguments, especially in divorce proceedings.

Mediation is a legal proceeding that is rarely used. I have often wondered why the mediation process is not utilized more frequently. It is difficult to find a lawyer who has been trained in the mediation process or even offers it in marriage and business disputes. Where it has been used effectively, each party in conflict wins something and also has greater possibility of preserving working relationships. Mediation seems to me to be the answer.

Mediation

Mediation may be defined as the process of resolving conflict with the aid of a neutral third party, with the goal of preserving the best possible working relationship and outcome among the participants. As mentioned previously, a good example of successful mediation is Indiana's process of handling malpractice claims before they become adversarial in court. If a patient has a claim against a doctor, for whatever reason, that case is first submitted to a panel of physicians who will review the case. A lawyer and a layman also serve on this panel.

Mediation: the process of resolving conflict with the aid of a neutral third party, with the goal of preserving the best possible working relationship and outcome among the participants.

Under Indiana's system, a physician charged with malpractice has the choice of his case being settled out of court or of going to the review panel. The panel of mediators reviews all the records and pertinent facts. If the case if found frivolous, without merit, it is dismissed with no further action. If the complainant is found to have substantial grounds for bringing the suit, the case may then be taken to court.

A review panel is in many ways a mediator, keeping the courts from being overburdened with frivolous claims. Indiana's model of mediation has a biblical basis:

> "If your brother sins against you, go and tell him his fault, between you and him alone. If he hears you, you have gained a brother. If he does not hear you, take with you two or three others so that by the mouth of two or three witnesses every word may be established. If he refuses then to listen, go and tell it to the church. If he still refuses to listen, then let him be as a heathen or tax collector" (Matthew 18:15-17).

Notice: Jesus encourages the use of third parties when there is a conflict. There must be a desire to preserve a working relationship, a desire to heal the hurts and work for fairness and justice. At the last step, if all else fails, take it to court. But we need to realize that if we battle it out in court, adversary to adversary, no one will win except, perhaps, the lawyers. This is a negative outcome, with little chance for forgiveness and no opportunity for growth.

Why is it in America that this amazingly positive process of mediation is little known or used? Why hasn't it been popularized as one of the greatest processes in conflict resolution? For example, in labor-management disputes it is usually employed just as a last resort. And why aren't more states following the lead of Dr. Bowen's model legislation in Indiana? The public needs to be concerned about finding the answers to these questions.

Attitude Adjustments

There are three more attitudes which need to be considered in achieving successful outcomes in conflict:

▶ Arrogance
▶ Humility
▶ Forgiveness

Arrogance: an attitude of self-satisfaction, self-superiority and self-sufficiency.

Arrogance may be defined as the attitude of self-satisfaction, self-superiority and self-sufficiency. It is a temptation for any professional who has high goals and intellectual powers. However, our patients do not see this as a positive attribute. Arrogance is something we often don't see in ourselves, and we are therefore often surprised when this attitude triggers negative feelings in our patients. In some cases the hostile feelings are so severe that the patients may be tempted to pursue a lawsuit if their treatment doesn't go satisfactorily.

We physicians need to be aware of the arrogance we inadvertently project. This haughty attitude will be changed only as we realize that true partners have equal standing in the doctor-patient relationship. Of course, physicians have superior knowledge on some matters, but never enough. We are dependent on others and need to continue seeking consultants who can supplement our database. In partnering we are not above our patients, even though they hopefully will respect our leadership and ability to coach them in the healing processes.

So, how do we know if we are projecting an arrogant attitude? If we are satisfied with our past knowledge base and see no need to seek new knowledge or skills, we are arrogant. If we believe our own powers are sufficient, not recognizing the powers in our patients and the innate, wonderful healing processes crafted by our Creator, we are arrogant.

Heaven knows, there is a great need for reversing this common attitude in our profession. We could prevent many conflicts and vastly improve our relationships. How can this change occur? By embracing humility—the very opposite of arrogance.

Humility

Humility can be defined as the virtue achieved by recognizing our own limitations and our need for assistance from others and from our Creator. While arrogance conveys an attitude of superiority to others, humility is never self-satisfied or self-sufficient. It recognizes that interdependence makes us much stronger than independence.

Humility: the virtue achieved by recognizing our own limitations and our need for assistance from others and from our Creator.

Oliver Cromwell once challenged his colleagues, "Gentlemen, I beseech you by the bowels of Christ to remember for just one moment that you may be wrong." That is a good reminder: We may be wrong! Wise physicians will recognize that, despite their great learning, there is always a chance that they are wrong in their diagnosis or treatment. We are not omniscient. Galileo thus encourages us "to pronounce that wise, ingenious and modest statement, 'I don't know.'"

"*Our* way" is better than "*my* way." Humility has equal regard for the passions, perceptions, principles and values of others. It is capable of saying, "I was wrong." Such an attitude makes room for forgiveness. It is willing to admit mistakes. In the process of considering the consequences in conflict, the word forgiveness hardly finds a place. And yet, forgiveness is probably the most potent healing process of all.

Dr. David Hilfiker, in his book *Healing the Wound,* aptly addresses the issue of mistakes and forgiveness. He points out that the process of mediation allows for forgiveness, restitution of relationship, and real justice. In contrast, the usual legal processes scarcely allow for true repentance, apology and forgiveness.

All healthy relationships are built and sustained on trust. Doctor-patient relationships are no different. Without humility and the possibility of forgiveness, the healing profession is greatly weakened.

Our present litigious society has fostered an atmosphere of suspicion and sometimes even hostility between doctors and patients. This toxic environment is not conducive to trust or healing.

As already mentioned, Likert and Likert's book, *New Ways of Managing Conflict,* pioneered new concepts of conflict resolution in the industrial sector of our society. The corporations which implemented their ideas have been rewarded with a considerable reduction in intramural conflicts. However, many corporations still haven't caught on to the great benefit of understanding the processes of conflict prevention and resolution. The medical profession, likewise, is slow to awaken to the creative powers in resolving conflict. There still is too much fighting among physicians and patients. Arrogance is still modeled in many medical centers, rather than exemplifying the disciplines of conciliation and humility.

Persistence

Persistence is not only one of the essential inner nutrients of growth, but is also one of the essential habitudes in conflict resolution. Too many marriages and business partnerships give up prematurely, without realizing that with a greater understanding and a dogged determination, conflict can be resolved. In any conflict, it takes both sides to care and confront, to work at relationship, to own anger and assert our needs while we respect and embrace each other.

Persistence: a continuous commitment to action, urged on by a strong belief that the highest good will come, regardless of adversity and circumstance.

Persistence means "hanging in there." It is tough but tender. Because there is an unending cycle of conflict and conciliation in any relationship, only persistence will bring the sweet joy of harmony, unity and balance in spite of diversity and nonconformity. Peace is achieved by persistently processing our differences in a win-win creative manner.

In his book, *The Greatest Salesman in the World, Part 2,* Og

Mandino writes:

> There is no better school than adversity.
> Every defeat, every loss, every heart break
> Contains its own seed, its own lesson
> On how to improve my performance...next time
> Learn from past mistakes.

Do you seek the seeds of triumph in every adversity? We should take Mandino's wisdom to heart. In every conflict or difficulty, let's not waste a single opportunity to grow.

Questions for Partners in Conflict

1. Do we care enough about relationship to "carefront" and assert?

2. Do we demonstrate both the tough and the tender of our feelings and thoughts?

3. Do we communicate by...
   > ...listening?
   > ...saying back what you have heard?
   > ...empathizing?
   > ...seeking to understand?

4. Do our actions help to build respect, trust and self-esteem?

5. Do we invite...
   > ...openness?
   > ...honesty?
   > ...I'm OK, your OK?

6. Are we responding to each other, not reacting by...
   > ...attacking?
   > ...blaming?
   > ...criticizing?

...becoming defensive?

7. Are we working to...
    ...collaborate?
    ...unify?
    ...find common ground?

8. Do we clarify...
    ...expectations?
    ...needs?
    ...wants?
    ...priorities?
    ...goals?

9. When significant differences threaten, do we seek a mediator rather than a lawsuit?

10. Do we practice...
    ...humility?
    ...forgiveness?
    ...avoiding an arrogant attitude?

11. When a relationship is in crisis, do we...
    ...stay to the end?
    ...persist until the conflict is resolved?

12. Do we have a positive attitude toward the creative potential in conflict?

Chapter Four

Growing in

Confidence

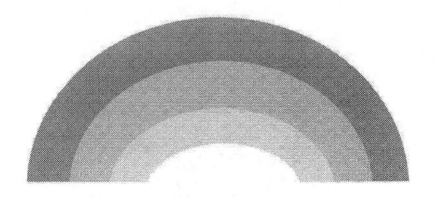

*"In quietness and confidence shall be
your strength"* (Isaiah 30:15).

A rainbow is a soft, spectacular symbol of promise and hope, as the sun's powerful rays reflect through dark clouds. In some ways, character is like a rainbow, a "many splendored thing." They are both seen only rarely, and even then they can only be seen from a special vantage point. Beautiful character, as the rainbow, is awesome to behold. Beauty may be defined as a perception of something that stirs the soul to smile, admire and desire.

A rainbow is made up of countless droplets of water, tiny spheres which are each capable of reflecting the sun's rays so that they reach our eyes at exactly 42 degrees from the sunlight. The back surfaces of the droplets act as tiny mirrors, creating a prism that refracts the sunlight into differing wave lengths. The result is unparalleled beauty, as the seemingly "ordinary" sunlight bursts into a band of vivid colors.

Beauty: a perception of something that stirs the soul to smile, admire and desire.

Can you stretch your imagination to see a similarity in the beauty we see in human character that is full of confidence? Some unseen, immeasurable, creative powers enter our brain and are then processed and reflected through our eyes, our face and our actions. The reflection displays our inner thoughts, perceptions, attitudes and imagination, making them outwardly visible to other people.

Our attitudes are merely a reflection of the truth, perception, thought and inspiration that enters our brain through the words we hear or read, and the images we take in through our eyes, ears and other senses. Though they might not be able to literally "read our mind," people around us do get a perception of what we are taking into our brain. They can also often catch a glimpse of the processes we use to handle the sensory input we are receiving.

When our attitudes are positive and confident, they provide a beautiful, multifaceted rainbow of refracted light. Negative attitudes, on the other hand, produce dark clouds that often eclipse the light not only from us, but also from those around us. Our attitudes are shaped primarily by the powerful force of our belief systems, whether positive or negative. When our beliefs are grounded in positive faith, an inner light is produced that will be reflected outwardly to others.

Many of the concepts presented in this chapter are rather foreign to traditional training in the art and science of healing. My purpose is to share my struggle to blend matters of faith, hope, trust, respect, truth and beliefs into the everyday practice of medicine. Again, we will be looking at some key words found in the growth paradigm, as they relate to growing in confidence:

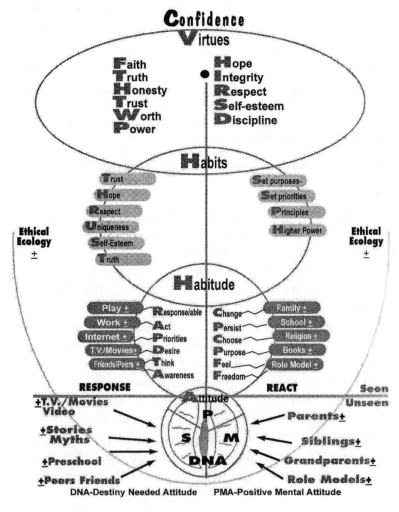

As I look back on my medical training, I am baffled that spiritual matters (unseen and immeasurable) were totally ignored and neglected. It was arrogantly assumed that the science of medicine was the only answer to human diseases and problems. However, we are now seeing in medical literature a new desire to openly acknowledge the enormous powers of a patient's faith, belief systems, attitudes and even prayer. Recently there has been a vast amount of documentation about the influence of a patient's attitudes on his recovery. Matters of faith, though they may not seem very "scientific," are often key ingredients in spawning the kinds of attitudes that facilitate healing.

Nevertheless, many doctors avoid such subjects. This is a sad truth, but it usually stems from our insecurity in dealing with spiritual realities. We feel more in our venue when we discuss factual and scientific medical issues, but we are often uncomfortable venturing into the faith arena.

In the interest of providing maximum help and healing to our patients, it is time to share more openly regarding the impact of faith, beliefs, thoughts and feelings. These qualities, along with other EINGs such as desires, purposes, priorities, values and choices, have a dramatic effect on human well-being. For too long, the medical profession has ignored spiritual growth as a key to unlocking human potential. In fact, faith may well be the greatest process of personal growth.

Confidence

Confidence is an important quality to define. To me, it is the powerful process of believing in our Creator, ourselves and others, which inspires trust, respect, hope, courage and dignity as we see our worth as a person. Confidence embodies an entire cluster of words relating to matters of faith and beliefs:

▶ Faith   ▶ Hope
▶ Truth   ▶ Wisdom
▶ Trus   ▶ Self-worth
▶ Spiritual disciplines ▶ Creator

Defining confidence is a lot like defining a rainbow or describing

97

character. Like droplets of water in a rainbow, growing in confidence involves a myriad of beliefs and thoughts. Thousands of books have been written on this subject of growing in faith and confidence. Yet, this spiritual growth is often neglected by those who value only their intellectual and social growth.

Most of my patients, and other people throughout the world, believe in some kind of supreme being or supreme intelligence— the architect and creative force that shaped our universe and created the infinite processes and forms of life. They acknowledge that there is an awesome power that surrounds us and dwells within us in varying degrees. Many call this power God or Allah. Others refer to a Father in heaven. But call this mysterious, unseen, creative force what you will, it is here, there and everywhere.

Confidence: the powerful process of believing in our Creator, ourselves and others, which inspires trust, respect, hope, courage and dignity as we see our worth as a person.

During my medical school days I was lifted to a new respect, admiration and wonder at the complexity, orderliness and dependability of the processes in the human body. The structure of the cells, genes, organs and interactions was marvelous to study. However, while many of the processes and structures were clearly definable, there remained a considerable degree of mystery. The more I learned, the more I became aware of how many questions about the body and mind were still left to be explained and understood. Particularly fascinating were the enormous mysteries locked up within our most amazing organ—the brain. Arnold Beckman has said, "God is the sum total of the vast unknown."

I share Albert Einstein's profound statement, "The fairest thing we can experience is the mysterious, the cradle of true science and true art. He who knows it not, can no longer wonder, can no longer feel amazement, is as good as dead, a snuffed out candle." As I look at the macrocosm, the microcosm, and this visible world of wonders around us, I cannot help but affirm a powerful conclusion: There is a God, a creative force with power so incomprehensible that I scarcely comprehend it.

If this conclusion is so inescapable, why doesn't the medical profession openly admit and espouse this belief in our everyday practices? Many physicians are beginning to do so. However, there is also great value in the scientific discipline of detachment from emotion, seeking information that can be proven, tested and verified. This we must continually do. Perhaps Michael Faraday had it right when he said, "The truth of science has ever had the task of evolving herself from the dull uniform mist of ignorance and also repressing and dissolving the phantom of the imaginations."

Many people have commented on the nature of our pursuit of truth. Ham and Salter, authors of *Physician in the Making*, once told their medical students, "It is easy to slip into false belief...The scientist must not only have a passion for facts, but also a mind clear of prejudice." Thomas Huxley adds, "Sit down before fact like a child, and be prepared to give up every preoccupational notion. Follow humbly wherever and whatever abyss nature leads, or you will learn nothing."

For years I tried to adhere to the strict discipline of science—the hard stuff. As the years passed, however, my faith experiences and interaction with patients caused me to increasingly marry the two disciplines, scientific and spiritual. I have concluded that spiritual and scientific disciplines are not foes but compatible. In fact, it may well be that both components are indispensable in treating patients as whole human beings—not just as composites of their organs and diseases.

Faith is belief in action. As a physician I have become convinced of the need to break the bondage of pure science—slavery to the factual and observable—in order to partner the best in science with the best in spiritual forces. Yet this is not easy to do for those of us who have for years worshipped the "God of Science."

Dr. Bernie Siegel, author of *Love, Peace, Healing,* has been a star for us to follow. As a surgeon he broke the barriers of "technological correctness." Others have followed in his steps. Norman Cousins, for example, found similar ground in his book, *Head First: the Biology of Hope.* However, pioneers such as Siegel and Cousins have had only minimal acceptance among the many physicians still shackled by the limits of pure science.

Norman Cousins' book convincingly demonstrated that:

> ...our belief systems are the activators of the healing systems. Our beliefs represent the unique element in human beings that makes it possible for our minds to affect our bodies. How we respond intellectually, emotionally and spiritually has a great deal to do with the way our bodies will function. Our confidence, or lack of it, has an enormous influence in our recovery from serious illness. Our beliefs can actually influence our body chemistry, converting hope, robust expectations, and the will to live into positive factors in our battles against illness. While our belief systems are no substitute for competent medical attention in serious illness or vice versa, both are essential.

Cousins goes further, "The belief system is not just a state of mind. It is a prime physiologic reality. It is the master switch that gets the most out of whatever is possible." His studies are reinforced by numerous scientists who call this medical frontier psychoneuroimmunology. His book describes the abundant evidence for the impact of faith, beliefs and positive mental attitudes on healing.

According to Cousins:

> The physician must supply not just the scientific competence but the spiritual nourishment his patients need...The most potent medicine available to the physician is the confidence placed in him by the patient. The next most potent medicine is the physician's ability to harvest the natural drive of the human body and mind to overcome its maladies...Patients tend to move in the direction of their hopes and fears. If they have strong confidence in themselves and their physicians, they tend to have a better outcome than if they are morose and defeatists.

Attitudes are built on beliefs. Positive beliefs produce positive attitudes. Negative beliefs produce negative attitudes. And, as Cousins suggests, these beliefs and attitudes have an inevitable impact on our healing processes.

Pioneers such as Siegel and Cousins have made a bold departure from many physicians' dependence on science alone. They have helped to create a strong groundswell of interest among patients and physicians who desire a clearer understanding of "how to" blend the scientific and spiritual disciplines. It is challenging to acquire knowledge of either one of these disciplines, let alone both. Few physicians have successfully combined the two. Most who have done so are outside the circles of academic medicine, where the prevailing cultural forces tend to inhibit new ideas or a thrust into spiritual disciplines.

Dr. Patch Adams, popularized by Robin Williams' movie a few years ago, is another pioneer that we should emulate. In his efforts to humanize medicine, Adams demonstrably moved entrenched traditions and pointed his patients and colleagues to the unity of science and soul. Willing to engage in unconventional methods, Adams found that his patients responded in remarkable ways. We, too, need to be willing to "color outside the lines" at times in order to reach maximum effectiveness. Another good role model for young physicians to follow is Dr. Ben Carson, author of *The Big Picture.* Carson is as articulate in his faith as he is in the highest disciplines of science and technology.

Let's begin to look at some key words never fully expressed or taught in medical schools. These will greatly facilitate the partnering and healing of patients who have a faith perspective. Although this book is designed to whet your spiritual appetite, you will have to work out the "how to" by much more reading and other information than is contained here. Out of thousands of books and spiritual experiences that I've encountered, I am only able to share a small portion in these pages.

Truth

No confidence is developed without a commitment to the unflinching pursuit of truth. This is the foundation of trust, hope, respect, honesty and integrity. Truth can be defined as an absolutely dependable belief, word, fact, idea, perception, principle, value or way that stands the test of time and trial.

Truth is the basis of our search, whether in science or in spiritual understanding. It provides the necessary infrastructure for solid growth in other virtues: fidelity, honesty, integrity, respect, hope, courage and dignity. Bit by bit, finding truth will build character. The greater our desire for truth, the greater our confidence.

Truth: an absolutely dependable belief, word, fact, idea, perception, principle, value or way that stands the test of time and trial.

Wisdom

Wisdom is the treasury of truth which is accumulated by using the power of discernment to refine our knowledge and experience. The sages, philosophers and spiritual leaders throughout the centuries have offered us their treasury of truth. It is for each of us to process these gems of truth and wisdom to help us grow in our passion for additional insights. This is not a momentary experience but a lifelong journey.

Wisdom: the treasury of truth which is accumulated by using the power of discernment to refine our knowledge and experience.

I particularly admire the many young people who have set their hearts on acquiring a treasury of truth early in life. However, many of us have acquired a great deal of our wisdom late in life. Perhaps that shouldn't be too surprising, since spiritual experience and wisdom is not necessarily acquired in high school, college or even medical school.

True wisdom is only received by those who have a passion for it. Solomon, reputed to be the wisest man of his day, writes of the high priority we should place on gaining wisdom: "Wisdom is supreme; therefore get wisdom. Though it cost all you have, get understanding" (Proverbs 4:7)..."Buy the truth and do not sell it; get wisdom, discipline and understanding" (Proverbs 23:23). The poor souls who are lazy or timid in their pursuit of the truth will never find it. As a result, they will forfeit their confidence for living.

Trust

On every coin and bill printed in U.S. mints are inscribed the words "In God We Trust." How did that happen? What does it mean? Do people really believe it?

The original founding fathers of America had a basic belief that a trusting relationship with our Creator and other people must be the foundation for a positive, unified society and monetary system. Our economy could not exist without a high degree of trust in our government and in the integrity of our currency. While no human organization or device is totally reliable, our Creator (God) is the paragon of perfection and dependability.

In a free society, trust is the foundation of positive relationships. It is the glue that binds us together. Likewise, if there is no trust in a doctor-patient relationship, healing is virtually hopeless. Effective caring and curing are only possible where there is an atmosphere of trust. Physicians who sense that this fundamental quality of trust is absent will do well to terminate the relationship and suggest another physician. And if a patient can't trust the physician, he should share his feelings and initiate a change. Trust can sometimes be restored after it is broken, but this is only possible where there is open dialog.

Although not a foolproof list, there are several behaviors that generally indicate a physician who can be trusted. Such a physician...

...calls back when he says he will.

...can be depended upon to do as he says he will.

...gives a high priority to honesty, particularly in his financial affairs.

...has a professional demeanor that inspires trust.

...levels with you when things aren't going right.

...is willing to admit mistakes.

...acts decisively.

...has high ethical standards.

...has a high degree of scientific knowledge and technical skills.

...exhibits a continuing search for new knowledge.

...makes eye contact.

...treats you with friendliness and respect.

...is willing to disclose his humanity.

...keeps confidential all private matters.

The list could go on, with items beyond his license and his specialty credentials. Such credentials in themselves are of little value. The fact that we have "M.D." behind our name is a sign that we passed the basic medical competency test, but that does not necessarily mean we are trustworthy. A Board Certification, likewise, is an indication that we have a base of knowledge, but that will not, of itself, inspire trust. Trusting relationships are ordinarily something that must grow and develop.

In their book, *The Leadership Challenge,* Kouzes and Posner offer this assessment of the process of building trust: "Trust is a risk game. The leader must ante up first." In this way, we physicians must demonstrate attitudes and actions which inspire trust. Solomon advises us that our ultimate trust must be in our Creator: "Trust in the Lord with all your heart and lean not on your own understanding. In all your ways acknowledge Him and He shall direct your ways" (Proverbs 3:5-6).

Respect

I learned quite a lesson on respect when my youngest daughter, Holly, was only six years old. One evening I came home from the office about supper time. Things were chaotic for my wife, who usually has good control of things. The dog was barking at the front door, the phone was ringing, someone had spilled ink on the floor, and a couple of the kids were arguing with each other. I was trying to restore order and asked the kids to help. I was getting no place.

In my frustration to get cooperation, I struck my fist noisily on the table and raised my voice. "What's the matter? Don't I get any respect around here?" There was silence until Holly said with six-year, saucy, snappy eyes, "You get all the respect you need at the office!"

That cracked us all up—and order eventually was restored. Holly had put respect into the proper perspective. It isn't automatic, but has to be won and deserved. Incidentally, I have normally enjoyed a great measure of respect at home, perhaps more than I can explain.

Respect is defined by Webster as a sense of worth or excellence toward another person. Often an M.D. degree does inherently command a considerable degree of respect in America. However, the most important kind of respect is that which is engendered not by our academic degrees or other achievements, but by who we are.

Respect: defined by Webster as a sense of worth or excellence toward another person.

Here again is the distinction between expertise and excellence. Popularity often goes to those with expertise. Respect and deep admiration usually go to those who have endured hardships and overcome enormous obstacles. This takes character. A good example of this difference was illustrated several years ago when Michael Jordan and Dennis Rodman were both players on the Chicago Bulls. It was undoubtedly an achievement just to play on an NBA team, but there was quite a difference in the level of respect accorded to these two players. While Rodman was known mostly for his trouble-making and his flamboyant hairstyles, Jordan was known for his sportsmanship, expertise and moral leadership.

Hope

Hope is one of the most therapeutic gifts that a patient can receive. As Erik Erickson has said, "Hope is the earliest and most indispensable virtue inherent in the state of being alive. If life is sustained, hope must remain, even when confidence is wounded or trust impaired." And, as William Shakespeare wrote, "The miserable have no other medicine but only hope."

Hopes and expectations are just a whisker apart from each other. Both hopes and expectations tell us of our deepest desires for positive outcomes—for cure, for healing, and for life with joy. The

Reverend Robert Schuller provides one of the best definitions I have seen for hope: "Hope is holding on, praying expectantly." Note the acronym in Schuller's definition: Holding – On – Praying – Expectantly.

Hope must be coupled with the will to hold on and persist, even in the face of adversity. Just a bare thread of optimism is often enough to rekindle our spirits and set the stage for healing and growth. It is a form of courage and determination that life will be better in the future than it is now.

Hope: defined by Dr. Robert Schuller as "Holding On, Praying Expectantly."

Years ago I learned a powerful lesson from Milton Erickson, M.D. With regard to hope and expectation, he gave this fundamental law of the mind: "When the subconscious mind dwells upon an idea, it tends to realize itself." All we have to do is put an image deeply into our mind and keep revisiting that image. As someone once said, "Whatever we vividly imagine, ardently desire, sincerely believe, and enthusiastically act upon will inevitably come to pass." This is something I have come to believe passionately.

The key to hope is persistence, as indicated by the "Great Physician" in His Sermon on the Mount:

"Seek and you will find.
Ask and you will receive.
Knock and the door will be opened to you" (Matthew 7:7).

Hope is not a stagnant or abstract force, but rather something filled with great power to bring change. The promise of hope is shown in Jesus' words, "If you have faith as a grain of mustard seed, nothing will be impossible to you" (Matthew 17:20). If we have the seed of hope, we will continue to grow despite any adversity or circumstance that would come against us.

This powerful lesson from Jesus, the Master of confidence,

encourages us to continually hope and pray for growth and healing. However, that doesn't mean that every disease will be cured in this life. While numerous miracles of healing are occurring everyday, sometimes we must persist in hope even when we see no improvement in our condition. Yet, in Bernie Siegel's view, all disease can be managed with joy and optimism, as we learn to make the best of our circumstances.

Whatever our patients expect to happen in their treatment and their encounter with us can be as powerful as any medication prescribed. Time after time, placebos and sugar pills have demonstrated the incredible power of expectations. In fact, many "cures" can be attributed to the placebo effect. It is not my policy to ever prescribe a placebo. A medicine or drug has to give me confidence that it will be of benefit or I won't use it. However, in double-blind pharmaceutical tests, the placebo effect is amazing. The placebo will often give just as good a result as a legitimate drug.

Thoughts and feelings, whether positive or negative, potently affect medical outcomes in a patient. The thoughts and feelings of the physician, likewise, will greatly affect the outcome. If the physician is hope-filled, confident and positive in his attitudes, the patient is much more likely to respond well to his plans for treatment. Whether the physician realizes it or not, his enthusiasm, or lack of it, is readily felt by his patient.

Norman Cousins affirms, "It is a perversion of rationalism to argue that words like 'hope' or 'faith' or 'grace' are without physiologic significance. The benevolent emotions are necessary because they are regenerative. The will to live produces a responsive chemistry." Samuel Johnson, likewise, states the remarkable power of hope: "The human mind does not move from pleasure to pleasure but from hope to hope."

Self-Worth

More than 100 years ago, Dr. William Osler told a group of fledging physicians, "If you don't believe in yourself, how can you expect other people to do so? If you have no abiding faith in the profession, you cannot be happy in it." It is surprising how many people of high achievement, M.D.s included, have a poor self-image and a low sense of worth.

Many intelligent and talented people get their sense of worth by what they do—not who they are. Often a person's cockiness, arrogance or authoritarian approach is actually a cover up of their lack of confidence and self-esteem. David Augsburger warns us that "within each human person there is a deep need to be heard or be a real person, a person of importance, who merits attention and recognition."

Much has been said about self-esteem, but I like Dr. Augsburger's concept of personal value and worth as a God-given right. It is not just something we conjure up by our own willpower, but something that is imparted to us by an understanding that we are a valuable creation of God.

Dr. John Rosemond has warned that in their desire to develop self-esteem in their children, parents have too often coddled them and made them more egocentric, more self-centered. True self-worth is not a matter of egocentrism, but rather stems from gratitude to God for our uniqueness as an individual.

David Augsburger reminds us that a person's worth and value must not be based upon outward success. Instead, it is something that is intrinsic to who we are, an inherent quality to be claimed and celebrated. According to Augsburger:

> We must disconnect self-esteem from success, self-respect from failure, self-worth from performance, self-regard from competition, self-confidence from appearance. My worth is not increased by winning, your worth is not increased by being right. Nothing can increase it or reduce it....It is a personal value of infinite worth to be prized by all. No amount of money, fame or power can build genuine feelings of self-worth.

Unfortunately, there are all too many professionals who still haven't learned this lesson. In my case, I discovered these words by Augsburger long after my graduation from medical school. A physician who is still trying to prove himself, not yet secure in his self-worth, will be continually striving for achievement and recognition. When we are operating from this insecure, unhealthy motivation, it becomes much more difficult to be an effective instrument of healing for others.

For every person on earth, our fingerprints, DNA, immune systems, reactions to circumstances, needs, wants, feelings, perceptions, dreams, values and goals are unique. Each person is a distinct individual, with special value. All of us in the medical profession need to hear this. Many bureaucrats and businessmen try to reduce the practice of medicine to nothing more than a mass-production assembly line. All medical caregivers must take responsibility to affirm the unique value of each patient.

Today the economic pressures are pushing healthcare providers to be more efficient and use more standard treatments. Individualized care has been replaced by managed care. Decisions once made by physicians and patients are now effectively controlled by insurance companies and HMOs. The result of these trends is that we are losing the battle for the individual.

Cervantes said, "It is difficult to make it our business to know ourselves, which is the most difficult lesson to learn." Shakespeare linked it differently: "Know thyself, to thine ownself be true, and it shall follow as day the night. Thou canst not be false to any man."

Many physicians know disease and technology far better than they know themselves. Writing this book has helped me to clarify my self-understanding, but I regret that this understanding came later in life than it should have. In their book, *Looking Out / Looking In,* Adler and Towne write, "Concept of self is perhaps our most fundamental possession. Knowing who we are is essential, for without a self-concept it would be impossible to relate to the world."

Purpose

Likewise, the self-esteem of our children would be far better off if we helped them find a purpose and meaning for their life. Instead of being self-absorbed, they need to learn how to serve mankind and be a part of the solution to the world's problems. By over-indulging our children in an effort to make them happy, we are likely to make them self-centered. That is just one reason why good kids in our affluent homes sometimes go wrong. Instead of helping to solve the world's problems, they themselves become part of those problems.

Having a sense of purpose for our life is a powerful force in establishing confidence for living. Quite often, teenagers flounder with indirection until they find the one high purpose for their lives, into which they can channel their undivided efforts. Solomon warned long ago that those who have no vision for their lives will perish in aimlessness and apathy (Proverbs 29:18).

As I look back over my life, I see that one of the greatest sources of my self-worth came from P.J. Gustat, my high school music teacher. He was like the teacher in *Mr. Holland's Opus,* imparting vision and encouragement to countless teens. Every teenager needs a Mr. Gustat. He inspired a fresh sense of purpose for my life, which greatly boosted my self-esteem.

After my teen years, by far the most important people in my life have been my wife of 50 years and my children. My family has helped me to grow in confidence by one of the best "how to" skills ever devised: self-disclosure. This skill of self-disclosure is not always easy or comfortable for physicians. We were taught early in our careers to keep aloof, objective and private with our patients.

There clearly is some merit in refusing to disclose ourselves to just anyone. However, there is also a great benefit in learning to discretely disclose ourselves to our patients—and *fully* disclose ourselves to our families. In the safety of our families we are free to grow, without pretense, masks or charades. A great deal of confidence is generated when we can share our inner selves in true intimacy, as I have with my wife. I am grateful for all the times when her unconditional love has provided me with renewed confidence and courage.

Sidney Jamard suggests, "When a man does not acknowledge himself—who, what, and how—he is out of touch with reality. He will sicken and die. No man can come to know himself except by disclosing himself to another person." Growth is facilitated as we engage in healthy disclosure and sharing. Our self-image is strengthened, and our destiny is released to exciting new potential.

Power

Our power for living comes from the design of our "personal power package," as shown by the rocket ship in the following diagram:

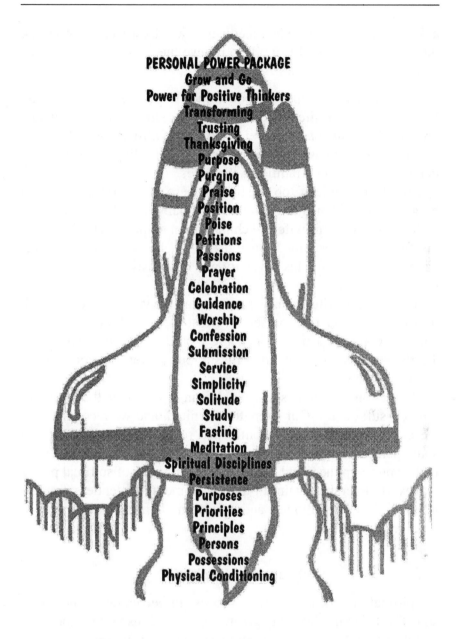

PERSONAL POWER PACKAGE
Grow and Go
Power for Positive Thinkers
Transforming
Trusting
Thanksgiving
Purpose
Purging
Praise
Position
Poise
Petitions
Passions
Prayer
Celebration
Guidance
Worship
Confession
Submission
Service
Simplicity
Solitude
Study
Fasting
Meditation
Spiritual Disciplines
Persistence
Purposes
Priorities
Principles
Persons
Possessions
Physical Conditioning

Many patients I see in the office have simply run out of gas. They have allowed their "personal power package" to be depleted, and the rocket is in danger of crashing to the ground. The "tiger in the tank" is gone, and they've lost their confidence for living. They've given up—browned-out or burned-out. Sometimes I feel like I'm running a filling station rather than a medical office. However, all too often the only "gas" desired is a pill to relieve the symptoms. This is an incomplete remedy at best.

Yes, various medicines are potent aids to people who are reeling from the storms of life: adversity, sickness, stress, sorrow, pain and brokenness. Some people seem to have been afflicted with far more that their share of woes. Nevertheless, true healing must often go deeper than pills and traditional therapies.

Take the example of Job, the biblical hero of suffering. Where did he get the confidence to overcome his many trials? How could he endure the loss of his wife and children, not to mention his boils and his financial devastation? On top of that, he was taunted by his friends, who told him his adversity was obviously due to God's displeasure with him.

Job's example illustrates our need to tap the vast reservoir of faith in a power higher than ourselves. Most of us will, at one time or another, come to a point when life's burdens are overwhelming. That's where faith comes in, a mysterious power that comes from outside ourselves.

During times of great stress or suffering, we realize the futility of our self-sufficiency. Our strength is limited, and we recognize that we can't do it ourselves. Confidence returns only when we find some person or force that is able to give us hope again. After we realize our emptiness and weakness, this infusion of spiritual power makes life tolerable again. In the meantime, the relentless press of adversity has helped to test and refine our character, teaching us to be overcomers.

Sources of Inspiration

Spiritual growth is a lifelong process in becoming a whole person. The Bible has been my greatest source of inspiration for spiritual direction. It has been my compass and guide, presenting matchless virtues and wisdom in a written record of man's struggle for relationship with our Creator. The Bible remains the longest best-selling book in history. It is the stimulus for healing and growth for millions of people, the road map for recovery from every adverse circumstance. Hidden in its pages are the character qualities our Creator wants to breathe into the soul of every man and woman, making us the beautiful persons we were meant to be.

Hidden secrets from the treasury of wisdom in the Holy Word were the source of power for the spiritual giants in history, those who strove mightily for spiritual excellence. Those who pursue the truths of the Bible find themselves on a sunlit journey, where each grain of wisdom is like a droplet of water in the rainbow.

Seeking the truth of Scripture must be more than a mere intellectual exercise, for it requires a commitment to the "how to" of spiritual growth. Biblical virtues are the culmination of character traits of excellence cultivated by the processes of striving for growth in our thoughts, attitudes, actions and habits of excellence. While the Bible provides the general guideposts, laws, principles, values and goals, each person must discover how to apply these through understanding the processes of growth.

One contemporary writer who has inspired me more than any other is Wilferd Peterson. His book, *The Art of Living*, is packed full of insights and actions to restructure and renew our attitudes. It gives many practical suggestions on "how to" grow and change.

The many books of Norman Vincent Peale have been another great source of encouragement. These include classics such as *The Power of Positive Thinking* and *A Treasury of Courage and Confidence*. Robert Schuller, minister of the Crystal Cathedral in California and the "Hour of Power" television program, has provided similar inspiration through his speaking and his books.

Another writer, Og Mandino, has written many books which focus on techniques for developing confidence. *The University of Success* contains the insights of 52 different writers who are seekers of wisdom. They share powerful skills for growing personally and spiritually.

Spiritual Disciplines

Richard Foster's book, *Celebration of Discipline—Pathway to Spiritual Growth*, has also been a particular source of inspiration for me. Foster shares 12 great dimensions of spiritual growth, which I hope will one day be recognized in medical schools. His spiritual disciplines are very relevant to the practice of medicine, and they could unleash powerful forces in the healing and growth processes of our patients.

Let me give you a brief synopsis of the disciplines Foster presents:

1. Meditation. This powerful spiritual discipline enables us to center, concentrate, contemplate and connect our creative imagination with our Creator, through a relaxed mind and body.

2. Prayer. This is the powerful discipline which seeks to communicate with God, the creative power outside ourselves, in order to receive help in changing our responses and attitudes through processing our...

> ...passions and emotions
> ...petitions
> ...relationships
> ...praise
> ..purging (removing negative emotions)
> ...purposes
> ...thanksgiving
> ...trust
> ..transformation.

The greatest power in prayer is its ability to change our attitudes and relationships through the above elements. Although prayer wasn't taught in the curriculum of my medical school, the use of prayer in medicine is finally beginning to be studied scientifically and accepted in some healing situations. Prayer is one of the most effective ways to renew, restructure and transform our attitudes, and it seems clear to me that a positive healing attitude is a great asset in medical and surgical situations. As physicians we need to ask ourselves how we can help nurture a positive attitude in our patients amid troubling circumstances.

3. Fasting. This powerful discipline seeks renewed spiritual sustenance and growth by a prayerful, voluntary deprivation of food.

4. Study. Through books, nature and new ideas we are enabled to restructure, renew and transform our minds by the processes of concentration, comprehension, curiosity, reflection and repetition.

5. Solitude. This is the discipline which seeks aloneness to inspire quietness and listening to the wonderful creative forces in nature and in our souls, to overcome loneliness, isolation and conformity.

6. Simplicity. This discipline sets us free from the seduction of material things and the quest for material success. Instead of greed, hoarding and conformity, we are liberated to seek God's kingdom above all else. We learn to give and share, and are freed from slavery to anything but living, serving and growing.

7. Service. This discipline teaches us to become servants, responding with individual consideration to the needs of others.

8. Submission. One of the most misunderstood spiritual disciplines, submission creates freedom, unity and harmony in our relationships as we yield our way to God's way. This does not lead to conformity or a loss of identity, but simply a replacing of arrogance with humility.

9. Confession. This powerful discipline involves the purging and purifying of our souls. It facilitates healing and brings the forgiveness of our sins. Through confession we are brought into fellowship with sufferers, sinners, saints and support systems.

10. Worship. Through acts of prayer, praise and thanksgiving, this discipline enables us to experience the presence of God, His Son and the Holy Spirit.

11. Guidance. This discipline involves seeking instruction through group experience, the company of those committed to unity and interdependence.

12. Celebration. This is the powerful spiritual discipline of joy, By lifting us to laughter, smiles, simplicity, song, dance and tears, this joy brings freedom from negative emotions such as anxiety, anger, fear and self-centeredness.

Perseverance

Confidence and perseverance are qualities that go hand in hand. Even a person who is normally confident can have that confidence undermined if he becomes slack in the spiritual disciplines. The rocket ship that once was so well energized by its personal power package, gradually runs out of the resources necessary to continue its ascent.

Sometimes its power is sapped by something as basic as a lack of physical fitness. This is one of the most basic disciplines needed for a healthy and productive life. Maintaining our bodies at peak efficiency cannot be a seasonal fad but must be a lifelong quest. A body that is physically fit may face disease and disability, but the desired goal is to always make the most of our physical endowments. Few of us were meant to be Olympic athletes, but even the elderly need to continue the processes of vigorous exercise, balanced nutrition, adequate sleep, and personal cleanliness.

In his various books, Dr. Kenneth Cooper has illustrated the "how to" achieve this important virtue of fitness. He has inspired millions of Americans to consider the basic processes of caring for our marvelous human machines. If people prized their bodies like they do their new cars, our bodies would have much less sickness and much more energy.

In additional to the disciplines necessary to fill our spiritual tanks and maintain the fitness of our bodies, we each need to maintain our "emotional tank." This requires determining the activities and relationships that provide "energy in" instead of "energy out." In particular, the people we connect with as our support systems—such as family, friends and mentors—should be vital sources of strength and well-being.

In the final analysis, we will find inner resources of confidence to the degree that our character has been shaped by the basic godly virtues of faith, hope and love. Filled with these virtues, our "rocket" will never lack the power it needs to soar to amazing heights. Take a moment and consider your own "power package" from the items listed on the rocket paradigm above.

Chapter Five

Growing in

Compassion

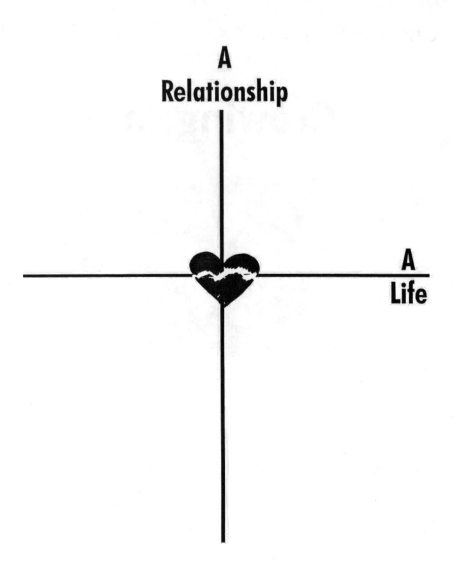

A
Relationship

A
Life

"And now abide faith, hope, love, these three; but the greatest of these is love" (1 Corinthians 13:13).

"Blessed are those who mourn, for they shall be comforted" (Matthew 5:4).

Shocking as it may seem, the word "compassion" is not found in even the most recent medical dictionaries. That doesn't reflect a lack of interest among those in the medical profession, but the omission of this crucial word in medicine should cause us concern. It also makes it all the more important that we come up with a clear definition of compassion. Only then can we take it out of the realm of the abstract and harness it as a workable, activating force in the healing process.

Before examining the concept of compassion, let's consider some key words that are related:

▶ Suffering   ▶ Touch
▶ Acceptance   ▶ Sensitivity
▶ Recognition   ▶ Healing
▶ Mercy   ▶ Empathy

The word "compassion" is made up of two Latin words, *com* (with) and *pati* (to suffer). When these two words are combined, the meaning becomes clear: Compassion means a willingness to "suffer with" another person. However, I would like you to consider a more dynamic definition, that provides more depth of meaning: Compassion is that powerful process of suffering with another person to help in the healing of sickness, sorrow, stress, pain or brokenness, enabling the person to grow again.

Compassion: the powerful process of suffering with another person to help in the healing of sickness, sorrow, stress, pain or brokenness, enabling the person to grow again.

People become patients (sufferers) when negative circumstances happen, causing them to become vulnerable, wounded or hurt in some way. Depending on the severity of the circumstances, those who are wounded and hurt may have their growth suspended. They reach out and call for help so they can be healed and grow again.

Severely wounded people can be compared with having a flat tire on our car. We are incapacitated from further progress down the road until the tire is fixed. If we are mechanically inept, unable to repair the tire ourselves, we must cry out for help so we can get going again. We look to someone who has the power, skill and desire to help, someone with the compassion to respond to our hurting circumstance.

Sensitivity

Without sensitivity, compassion will always fall short of its intended result. Sensitivity can be defined as the degree or measure of our emotional response to human pain or hurt. Norman Cousins contends that sensitivity is not a stagnant quality, but something we can learn and cultivate. Stating that our capacity to respond emotionally is a learned skill, Cousins says, "A casual or apathetic response to human hurt or pain is a sure sign of educational failure."

Sensitivity: the degree or measure of our emotional response to human pain or hurt.

Cousins is simply describing what many patients feel when we respond in our cool, detached scientific mode. Yes, this detached approach to human suffering is all right when handling the mechanistic correction of an acute appendicitis or broken leg. The skill and know-how of curing diseases is what modern medicine does so superbly. However, in other situations there is a great need to be sensitive to the emotions and heart-wrenching suffering the patient is experiencing.

If we review the 12 essential inner nutrients for growth, we will see that our capacity for developing higher degrees of sensitivity is enhanced by:
1. growing in awareness of the suffering around us
2. gaining freedom to respond instead of react
3. thinking about the "five sisters of mercy," which I will describe below
4. getting in touch with our feelings and the feelings of our patients who are suffering
5. sharing our desires, with creative imagination about

how to help the situation
6. finding meaning and purpose in suffering
7. setting priorities and valuing people over things
8. choosing the appropriate level of sensitivity
9. act—begin to get involved
10. persistently follow through with empathy and compassion
11. become response-able
12. seek a change in attitudes

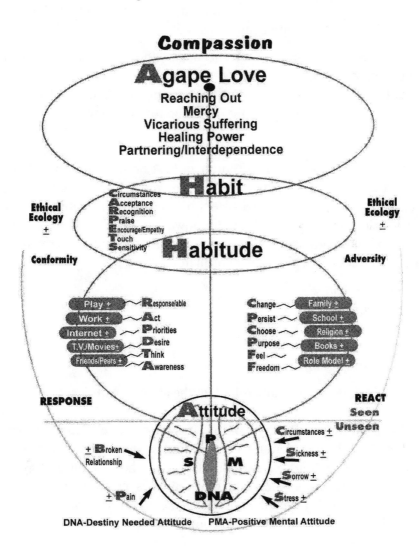

Just as the EINGs can help us grow in our compassion, there are also factors that can quench it. Edmund Pellegrino, M.D., notes that in our medical care systems sensitivity and compassion can be eroded or extinguished by such things as:

- technology
- depersonalizing institutions
- replacing care by individuals with a team
- medical education focusing on "man the object"
- rigidity in medical education that does little to help the student develop his own humanity

Pellegrino's warning must be heeded by those who desire to grow in compassion. Because of the negative factors he cites, growing in sensitivity is much like a fish trying to swim upstream. Only the resolute will succeed in defeating these enemies of compassion.

Mercy

Perhaps our level of sensitivity can best be measured by what I call "the five sisters of mercy." Before we are ready to pursue the sensitivity required by these sisters of mercy, our relationships are only casual and superficial—at the lowest level of sensitivity. This is where all relationships must begin, but after a while we hopefully will progress to the five sisters of mercy:

1. sympathy
2. concern
3. caring
4. empathy
5. compassion

Let's take a more detailed look at these vital qualities.

Sister of mercy #1 – Sympathy: It is appropriate to vary our sensitivity level in consideration of our circumstances and relationships. Sympathy is feeling (*pathos*) with (*sym*) another person. It may be an expression of condolence or recognition, such as sending a card upon occasions of death, birth or sickness. These remembrances, though quite minimal, are much appreciated by the recipients.

Sympathy: Feeling (pathos) with (sym) another person.

Sister of mercy #2 – Concern: This quality may be defined as an attitude of marked interest in serving the patient more than self, characterized by the giving of greater consideration to the needs of another person in community. Webster's definition is only slightly different: "an attitude of marked interest or regard in relationship through a personal tie; getting involved."

This character trait shows a deeper involvement than sympathy. The attitude of becoming a servant is handled in a later chapter, for it is a distinct process that is different from the other sisters of mercy. The kernel of growth in this sister of mercy is clearly seeing human need and then responding to that need.

Concern: an attitude of marked interest in serving the patient more than self, characterized by the giving of greater consideration to the needs of another person in community; the powerful process of becoming a servant, responding with individual consideration to the needs of others.

Sister of mercy #3 – Caring: It is often rather arbitrary to determine where this quality belongs on the sensitivity scale. While it is a much-used word, the dictionaries don't define it very clearly. Although it is an attitude that is readily visible, it is often difficult to explain.

Let me take a stab at defining this attitude with the dignity it deserves: Caring is an attitude which is positive, warm, friendly and responsive to those who suffer, marked by a reaching out of our hand and heart to help. Caring is often a composite of sympathy, empathy and concern. There is probably no more serious indictment heard regarding many physicians and nurses today, especially those in HMOs, than "they just don't seem to care." Patients can readily spot the attitude of caring, or the lack of it.

Caring: an attitude which is positive, warm, friendly and responsive to those who suffer, marked by a reaching out of our hand and heart to help.

In 1920 Dr. Frances Peabody revealed his attitude toward patients when he wrote, "The secret of the care of the patient is caring for the patient." This classic article is a "must read" for every caregiver. Peabody says, "The treatment and cure of diseases may be impersonal, but the care of a patient must be personal."

Sister of mercy #4 – Empathy: Empathy is another word derived from Latin: *em* (in) *pathos* (feelings). It is a deep inner feeling for another person. True empathy—putting ourselves in the same situation as another person—is a very draining experience. It means not only feeling the suffering of another, but also trying to respond to their needs.

Empathy: derived from Latin, em (in) and pathos (feelings), this is a deep inner feeling for another person, putting ourselves in their situation.

It often takes a great deal of effort for a caregiver to imagine what the person's suffering is like. Even so, empathy is an attitude all of us can develop, even when we haven't suffered exactly the same pain or circumstance. Robert Hogan, M.D., describes empathy as "a willingness or tendency to put one's self in another's place and to modify one's behavior as a result...It is clearly an important aspect of moral growth."

Sister of mercy #5 – Compassion: The greatest sister of mercy is compassion. People with this highly valued character trait have something very special: a sense that they have actually *experienced* and *identified with* the suffering of the other person. In a very real way, the compassionate caregiver has "been there" and can therefore empathize more deeply.

A physician or nurse who has never experienced deep hurt, sorrow or tragedy is handicapped in such situations. The greater our suffering and brokenness, the greater will be our capacity for compassion. However, this axiom only is valid *after* we have successfully gone through the pain process. Only then, once we have experienced healing and begun to grow again, can we be of much help to others who are hurting. A healer must be healed before his compassion is truly responsive or response-able.

The capacity "to suffer with" is the greatest character trait or attitude a healer can possess. The more we have suffered and been healed, the more compassionate we can be. Perhaps this is the meaning of Jesus' beatitude, "Blessed are those who mourn, for they shall be comforted" (Matthew 5:4). We might add, "...and have great capacity to comfort others" (see 2 Corinthians 1:4).

Compassion: the powerful process of suffering with another person to help in the healing of sickness, sorrow, stress, pain or brokenness, enabling the person to grow again.

A few illustrations may bring this a little closer home. Alcoholics Anonymous has amazed the world by helping alcoholics more successfully than most physicians, psychiatrists, ministers, psychologists or social workers—unless, however, these professionals themselves have been alcoholics. Only an alcoholic knows what it is like to hit bottom after years of denial and self-inflicted suffering. A.A.'s twelve-step program for recovering alcoholics makes full use of "the company of the truly compassionate"—other alcoholics.

My son and one son-in-law are highly skilled obstetricians and surgeons, and they've delivered hundreds of babies. Although they are empathetic and caring, they have obviously never fully "been there"—really suffering the pangs of childbirth themselves. They gladly offer the gift of empathy, but true compassion eludes them in such cases.

However, two female obstetricians have joined their medical group. I believe that those women, having had their own experiences with childbirth, have a greater capacity for compassion to those in labor. This is particularly true if the female doctors truly grew and found meaning in their suffering. For example, woman physicians who delivered their babies easily—with just a few grunts, as some women do—would not really feel the pain as deeply as those whose labors were long and arduous.

My wife and I were a bit surprised when daughters Jenny and Sandy decided to go through medical school. Yet we certainly applauded their achievements, along with two daughters who have become nurses and another who teaches school. The women who now comprise over half of the medical school population and well over half of the teaching profession enrich these professions with their special gifts of compassion. They generally bring more compassion and tenderness, qualities often more associated with the "gentler sex." Such women have already changed the complexion of healthcare in our country. The nursing profession, meanwhile, has for a long time taught, lived and breathed the soft stuff of medicine. While their examples point us to compassionate healthcare, we physicians have often trailed behind, still trying to balance mercy and science.

Each physician and caregiver has experienced his own unique set of difficulties and diseases. I cannot be fully compassionate to alcoholics, heart patients, diabetics and those with a host of other common diseases I haven't experienced. I can, however, grow, develop and employ the other four sisters of mercy in my practice.

Pain is a common denominator for all of humankind. We have all experienced broken relationships, stress and pain of various kinds. These uncomfortable circumstances have prepared us to understand and respond with compassion when we encounter similar conditions in other people. Even if our difficult circumstances were not identical to theirs, the healing we received after deep hurts can often radiate to others.

Jesus' story of the "Good Samaritan" (Luke 10:25-37) does not specify the exact depth of mercy that was given to the victim of robbers. This could have been an act of compassion, empathy, caring or concern. It really doesn't matter which sensitivity level was demonstrated, for the Good Samaritan obviously displayed a deep sensitivity to a human being in suffering circumstances. He cared, and he reached out to help.

Dr. Frances Peabody comments, "The good physician knows his patients through and through, and his knowledge is bought dearly. Time, sympathy and understanding he lavishly dispenses, but the reward is to be found in that personal bond which forms the greatest satisfaction in medicine."

Sometimes physicians have a great capacity for empathy toward their patients but fail to have compassion for their own frailties and suffering. Often God is the only one who knows the suffering secretly endured by physicians. Yet, if patients have truly good partnerships with their physicians, there may well be a great opportunity for the five sisters of mercy to work through the patients to meet the physicians' needs. Compassion and empathy need not be a one-way street.

In my early medical training I saw a few stellar examples of mercy modeled. However, I have learned far more about mercy from my wife, children, office nurse and nurses in hospitals. Medical schools can't afford to continue neglecting this important quality for every physician. It is time we teach the "how to" of compassion and mercy.

Several other key words have high power and priority in the process of learning compassion:

▶ Acceptance   ▶ Recognition
▶ Praise   ▶ Touch

Let's take a closer look at these crucial words.

Acceptance

Acceptance can be defined as an attitude which looks to the intrinsic worth of a person and values the potential of the inner person, regardless of status, intelligence, external dress, or obnoxious behaviors. Edmund Pellegrino, M.D., reminds us "to accept the patient for what he is and not what we think he should be. Accept the strivings of all persons—the ignorant and the intelligent, the successful, the failure, the poor, the wise, the weak, the strong, and even the evil."

> **Acceptance:** an attitude which looks to the intrinsic worth of a person and values the potential of the inner person, regardless of status, intelligence, external dress, or obnoxious behaviors.

This doesn't mean we have to agree with people's behaviors. We can extend acceptance to people and yet, at the same time, "carefront" their obnoxious behaviors. This kind of "tough love" is what we all need, but it is incredibly rare. It is much easier to either wink at obnoxious behavior, or else to launch into a judgmental tirade that accomplishes nothing. Genuine acceptance does not preclude the need to also carefront people from time to time.

Many of our conflicts stem from a rather common scenario. Friction occurs when the inner characteristics of another person— their passions, perceptions, principles, purposes and priorities—are at odds with our own. Change and growth will only occur when we learn to accept people who are different from us.

Sometimes we need to learn acceptance of an unpleasant situation or circumstance. Elisabeth Kubler-Ross points out that acceptance is one of the last stages of the grief process. Our grief over a death or loss will ordinarily continue until we are finally able to embrace and accept the situation as it is. Regardless of the severity of the circumstances, we will always have a ray of hope if just one person is nearby to stand with us in our sufferings.

Erma Bombeck wisely says, "A child needs your love the most when he deserves it the least." That is probably the best definition of the spiritual concept of "grace." As physicians we need to understand the four ways people may deal with an unfortunate circumstance, illness, pain, brokenness or even death. In general, we will get either...

1. **Mad** – striking back in anger, attacking, blaming, criticizing, putting up defenses, isolating or withdrawing.
2. **Sad** – feeling depressed, guilty, condemned or self-destructive.
3. **Insightful** - learning to see other possibilities, as we

listen, study, pray and meditate.

4. **Glad** – embracing acceptance of the situation so we can get on with our lives and start growing again.

As a final thought about acceptance, consider this observation by Norman Cousins: "Human beings have been able to comprehend everything else in the world except their own uniqueness."

Recognition

Although recognition is closely related to acceptance, it has more to do with social acclaim or the individual's right to given attention and focus. This gift of recognition is an extremely powerful motivator. Ric Masten says it this way:

> Put me in your human eyes, come taste the bitter tears I cry.
> Touch me with your human hand, hear me with your ear.
> But notice me! Damn you, notice me.
> I am here!

Patients must be separated from the crowd and not allowed to be lost in the shadows. Many people in our modern, fast-paced society find themselves feeling much like the Invisible Man, not recognized or cared for by anyone. Physicians have an opportunity to substantially reverse this trend in the lives of their patients. Instead of feeling invisible, insignificant or worthless, when a patient is with us he should be made to feel as if he is the most important person in the world. As William James reminds us, "The deepest principle in human nature is the craving to be appreciated."

Some physicians do quite well in showing recognition to their patients—but they fall short in another area. It is possible to give so much time and recognition to our patients that we fail to honor those closest to us: our spouses and children. Some of us actually find it easier to offer compassionate recognition to patients, co-workers or friends than to family. As we pour out our lives to serve our patients, we need to beware taking for granted those who are closest to us, our loved ones.

Praise

In their book, *The One Minute Manager*, Dr. Spencer Johnson and Ken Blanchard demonstrate the incredible impact of conveying praise and encouragement to those around us: "To help people reach their full potential, catch them doing something right." This is one of the most neglected opportunities to reinforce the processes of healing and growth. We need to be quick to recognize the efforts of our patients and family members when they are doing things right, instead of finding reasons to nag them for their shortcomings.

As pointed out in *The One Minute Manager,* it often takes only a few seconds to offer a compliment to someone. We physicians thus can't claim to be too busy for this important practice, because in mere moments we can encourage a patient on the specific ways he is assisting his healing processes and growth. It helps, as Johnson and Blanchard suggest, to "look the person in the eye, shake hands, or give a thumbs-up sign or an appropriate hug for any small achievements."

Physicians are often given praise and thanks for the care given to patients. We feel the need for that encouragement as an impetus for our perseverance and growth. So let's not forget to keep compassionate praise going both ways.

Touch

With all of the gadgets, instruments, procedures, needle-poking and steel probes associated with modern medicine, a patient can go a whole day without a touch from a human hand. The human touch wields a great power to convey sensitivity and compassion. Yet quite often I hear the great disappointment of patients who remark after their visit to a doctor, "He didn't even touch me."

A gentle touch is almost indispensable to the healing process, and patients seem to instinctively recognize this. They understand that much can be found by the physician's examining hand, and they have grown to expect that kind of personal involvement in their care. Many diagnoses and conditions are still found through a doctor's sensitive diagnostic palpation rather than through high-tech medical paraphernalia.

Physicians also must be careful about *how* they engage in touch.

Gentleness is expected by patients, and a brusque, hurried, forceful touch will often aggravate their pain. Sometimes our diagnostic procedures or treatment will predictably and unavoidably result in a certain degree of pain. In such cases, we need to let our patients know in advance that pain may be involved. They have a right to know what to expect. This is part of being compassionate—suffering with them. It helps, of course, if we have undergone the same procedure, enabling us to share from our personal experience.

Touching is not without its hazards, unfortunately. The legal climate in America has created a coolness and even coldness that often stifles the healing processes involving compassion. Because of paranoia regarding "inappropriate touching," there is a dark cloud of fear and suspicion hovering over doctor-patient relationships. We want to reach out in compassion, but we certainly don't want to be charged with harassment or exploitation. Our hospitals have too often been transformed from warm-fuzzy institutions of healing to cold-prickly prisons. Fearful of even the most appropriate hugs and touching, we forfeit many opportunities for showing genuine affection, sympathy and praise because of fear of legal redress.

It is true that improprieties in touching sometimes occur in the medical profession, as they do in other professions. Teachers of young students and physicians with vulnerable patients must be very discrete in their behavior so as not to violate a trusting relationship. Wisdom dictates that, wherever possible, we have a witness in the room when performing any procedure that could be misconstrued.

The future of healthcare in our country will be adversely affected if the present climate of paranoia is allowed to continue. Can legislators devise laws, rules and regulations that protect patients from improper touching but also preserve the freedom of caregivers to express genuine affection? Are today's physicians and teachers supposed to be wooden and emotionless characters, devoid of the nurturing touches that so powerfully molded and motivated our childhood? Aren't appropriate touches important throughout someone's life?

Unfortunately, there is no way to successfully legislate attitudes. Try as they may, I doubt if anyone can write effective rules to clearly differentiate between appropriate and inappropriate touching. Although there are legitimate concerns by caregivers, let me encourage you with this: Touching done with true compassion and empathy is rarely misconstrued.

Healing

During my years as a physician I have come up with the following definition of healing: The process of managing and mobilizing all the powers possible in our reaction or response to circumstances, sickness, sorrow, stress, pain or brokenness, mostly by changing our attitudes so we can grow again. My understanding of healing has been greatly enriched by two marvelous books: *Love, Peace and Healing* by Bernie Siegal and *Head First: the Biology of Hope* by Norman Cousins. These two texts have inspired me with possibilities for change in our healing systems in America. I can't improve on their comprehensive and creative principles and postulates.

Healing: the process of managing and mobilizing all the powers possible in our reaction or response to circumstances, sickness, sorrow, stress, pain or brokenness, mostly by changing our attitudes so we can grow again.

However, in this brief section I want to share a paradigm of healing which has been very workable and useful in my practice. It is a perspective that has grown in me while preparing this book the past 15 years. The paradigm springs from my realization that, despite the amazing medical progress of the past century, the vast majority of human suffering still cannot be cured—it can only be managed. This is true of the major diseases that afflict our patients today:

- Arthritis
- Hypertension
- Alcoholism
- Diabetes
- Allergies
- Asthma

The list could go on and on. Our remedies for such diseases are incomplete, not total cures. Our remedies are incomplete because we have an incomplete understanding of the true causes of these diseases. Often the cause is genetic in nature. No doubt we are at the dawning of an age where many genetic and immunologic disorders will be cured.

Medical practitioners are becoming increasingly aware of the priority of *preventing* diseases, instead of just treating them after they occur. Perhaps this should be our first priority, but it usually isn't. Most of the treatment given in our offices and hospitals is in the nature of crisis care, not prevention. Hopefully our priorities will shift as we see that the paradigm of healing is also a paradigm for prevention.

One of the problems with crisis care is that it focuses mainly on treating the symptoms. Do you see how shortsighted it is to be satisfied with treating symptoms, rather than searching for ways to prevent or cure? Such an approach is worthy only of quacks and nostrums. However, the doctors are certainly not the only ones to blame for this faulty approach. Patients often fail to pursue even the most basic preventative health measures, coming to their physician only to remedy a situation that has reached crisis stage. Like a car owner who never changes the oil, too many patients neglect their health until their bodies have a breakdown.

I have found that there are three main approaches to healthcare:

1. **Prevention** – Many illnesses are easily preventable, and we need to do all we can to keep these from occurring.
2. **Curing** – Some diseases can be totally eradicated with proper treatment.
3. **Healing** – Many diseases are not curable, and in such cases we are limited to doing the best we can to manage them.

If we are going to understand how compassion and the sisters of mercy are useful in healing, we need to consider an appropriate model of healing. The key is a change of attitude—since many of the disorders, hurts and circumstances will not change. One of the greatest testimonies to this fact is found in Reinhold Niebuhr's powerful "Serenity Prayer":

God grant me
the Serenity to accept the things I cannot change,
the Courage to change the things I can,
and the Wisdom to know the difference.

Applying Niebuhr's prayer to our discussion of healing, success in healing involves three steps:

1. Acceptance of our circumstances
2. Seeking help
3. Changes in our attitudes, so that we respond by becoming proactive to change

A wise healer and physician will guide the patient to a realization of these elements. He will be a positive guide as the patient tries to discern where the power comes from to achieve the changes. As there are three steps in healing, there are also three sources of power:

1. Power within the grasp of the sufferer
2. Power within the support system, including the physicians, family, friends, etc.
3. Supernatural power, which is beyond the physician, the patient or the support system

I often diagram this for my patients, showing them the respective roles of the Superpower (God), the doctor and the patient. This has helped many patients gain a new understanding of the essential three-way partnership in the healing process:

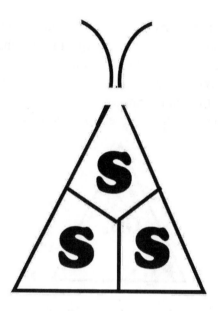

Balanced Partnership

This above paradigm is more than a nice, innocuous theory. It shows the balanced partnership between three distinct powers: the sufferer, the support and the superpower. The sufferer, of course, in the patient. The support includes physicians, family, friends and counselors. The superpowers are non-human spiritual entities, such as God, the Creator, or other objects of devotion.

This paradigm should lead to a discussion of specific things a patient or physician can do or change. Healing is facilitated by this process of interdependent partnering. It requires collaborating, dividing response-abilities, and clarifying expectations of who is to do what. For example, although only physicians have the power to prescribe medicine, only the patient has the power and responsibility to have the prescription filled and take it as directed.

It is not effective partnering if I merely tell a patient to lose weight, stop smoking or exercise. Although these might be good advice, and I might suggest them in some cases, I realize that such matters are ultimately their choice, not mine. Physicians need to be careful not to infringe on the proper role of the patient in making decisions for his own health and welfare.

Many conflicts between doctors and patients can be prevented by simply taking time to clarify roles, expectations and goals. This is not too difficult, and it will provide wonderful benefits in the healing partnership. When we empower patients to understand their proper role, fantastic results can occur.

Some patients look at the partnership like this:

Big Doctor / Little Patient

This isn't a good setup, for the doctor has most of the power and the patient very little. Self-help has often been scoffed at, because most patients don't realize *how* to do more for themselves. That is why there are thousands of self-help books.

Focus on the Family, located in Colorado Springs, is a tremendous resource for those who are suffering in some way beyond the usual scope of the family physician. They provide books, pamphlets, video cassettes galore, giving people the "how to" needed to assume their response-abilities in the healing partnership. Reading, listening and searching for resources such as these will strengthen a patient and build personal power back into the partnership.

A few patients—fortunately not many—want absolute control over the healing partnership. This usually dooms the process to self-destruction.

Big Patient / Little Doctor

After there has been a clarification of the respective roles of the physician and the patient, I often suggest that neither of us has all the powers necessary for optimum healing. I am frank to admit that there is a greater power than either doctor or patient, and I ask the patient about his beliefs. About 90% point to the space at the top of the diagram, indicating their belief in God.

Most of my patients believe in a higher power—vague as that terminology may be. They sense the existence of a power outside of themselves. I am not ashamed to say that the Creator of the universe, who established structure, movement and all the processes in the body, has incomprehensible wisdom.

Our work as physicians and patients is to let the natural healing processes go to work. All too often, we meddle in matters outside our proper sphere. Our environment is a blatant example of how man has messed up the creation of God. We all need to seek out the master plan and design which the Creator has set before us.

Honest physicians and patients will acknowledge that, despite their best efforts, their power is limited. Spiritual powers, on the other hand, add a special healing dimension to the doctor-patient partnership. If we utilize these available spiritual resources, we will materialize the greatest potential for healing.

I always feel sorry for the person who has great suffering and no faith, either in himself, his physician or our Creator. In fact, that is the only truly hopeless condition. Fortunately, I don't see this very often.

The maximum healing comes from a growing, dynamic faith in

ourselves, our physician and God—our Superpower. A wise physician will go beyond all his scientific and technologic "know how." After the patient has been empowered to do everything and change everything he can, the physician should take the next step, helping the patient leave the rest up to the chief of all medicine, our Creator.

Here is a prayer I often pray with my patients:

Prayer for Healing

O God, our Creator and Heavenly Father,
We are not alone. You are always available.
Your power and love surround us.
Help us to feel Your presence now.

Help us to keep from reacting negatively to our suffering
And circumstances in our own feeble human ways.
Help us to respond positively to the powers
You have provided within us and outside of ourselves,
To better manage these difficulties.

Show us how to overcome and manage
Evil thoughts, emotions and attitudes.
With your powers, changes and healing
All things are possible.
Lift us to freedom, forgiveness, joy, peace and love.

Give us a positive faith, a positive hope,
A deep compassion through which great
And wonderful things can happen
In our lives and through us.

With Your Spirit recreate us,
Renew us, transform us.
Change our attitudes to reflect
Your glory, power, love
And our confidence in healing and growing.

All this we ask and believe
In the name of Jesus of Nazareth,
The Great Physician,

Your Son, our Savior.
Amen.

Physicians need to recognize that millions of suffering people have found hope and healing through faith-based ministries. Whether in churches or on TV and radio programs, spiritual leaders have transformed countless lives. The medical profession could enhance its powers by partnering with the great spiritual leaders of our times. Two ministers and authors who have especially impacted my perspectives on healing are Norman Vincent Peale and Robert Schuller. They stand out as some of the most powerful proponents of faith in healing. We physicians would be wise to blend their systems of healing with our own.

Let's not laugh at self-help books, for they can be very valuable. However, it is the height of arrogance to assume that we are so self-sufficient and self-satisfied that we need no power greater than ourselves. By excluding the Creator from the healing process, some physicians and patients trust only in themselves, and consequently "have a fool as their doctor."

One of the hottest medical controversies in recent years has to do with a fundamental difference in approach between those who rely on traditional, scientific remedies and those who advocate alternative medicine. Of course, we also live in a day when some purported remedies are neither scientific nor truly alternative—they are simply deceptive, intentionally designed to rip off gullible consumers. In the face of these different options, all claiming to work best, laymen are understandably confused. How can the average person discern what remedies and treatments are actually good, trustworthy and empirically sound?

Scientific medicine has as its highest priority to find the cause of disease and achieve a cure by eliminating the cause. Despite all the success we have had following this approach, the causes of many diseases remain obscure and mystifying. However, medical researchers don't give up easily. Regardless of setbacks and disappointments, they will keep on striving to find new causes and remedies.

Some diseases admittedly have causes that are multifaceted or obscure. In some situations, there is no immediate cure on the horizon. In these cases the priority is to find ways and methods of *man-*

aging diseases, even though we cannot cure them. While such things as surgery, radiation, chemotherapy and antibiotics have achieved many miracles, at times even these wonderful advances reach their limits of effectiveness.

Renewal

Healing is the transforming and renewing of our minds and spirits. We desperately need this kind of genuine healing, something beyond pill power or surgery. What we need many times is psycho-surgery, the excision of negative thought and attitudes. Where in modern medicine do we find this power for inner surgery? Most physicians share the same faith I do, but often we are so set in our scientific disciplines that we fear breaking with the traditions we've been taught.

Compassion is not antiscientific. It is compatible with the greatest of scientific know-how. But we need to learn how to go beyond our scientific skills and be more compassionate in our healing arts.

Viktor Frankl, the psychiatrist who survived the horror of Auschwitz, gives us a profound insight into suffering when he says, "To live is to suffer. To survive is to find meaning in the suffering." Frankl then cites three ways we can find meaning and fulfillment in spite of our suffering:

1. Doing a good deed or creating a work
2. Experiencing something loving or loving someone
3. Bearing witness of the human capacity to turn any tragic situation into personal triumph, if the situation or tragedy cannot be removed or changed.

Robert Schuller, likewise, provides us with this terse, powerful thought to remember when we confront suffering: "Turn your scars into stars." And Dostoyevski prayed this prayer: "There is only one thing I dread; not to be worthy of my sufferings."

Great character is born out of great suffering. St. Paul understood this when he wrote the Corinthians:

I most gladly boast of my infirmities so that the power of Christ may rest on me. That is why I take pleasure in my weaknesses, in hardship, in injuries, in persecutions, and in difficulties. For when I am weak, then I am strong (2

Corinthians 12:10).

How did Paul survive horrible circumstances? With a positive attitude! He saw that even the worst situations could have a redemptive purpose, helping him to grow.

We do not need to cave in to the adverse circumstances we face. We were created with the powers to manage and overcome even the most overwhelming negative forces in our lives.

Power for Partnering With Compassion

1. Is the office or hospital atmosphere warm and friendly?

2. Is acceptance of each person felt?

3. Is empathy present?

4. Are there obstacles in compassion?

    ...technology
    ...lack of communications
    ...lack of recognition
    ...lack of praise

5. Is sympathy freely expressed?

6. Are basic needs sensitively sought?

7. Is there compassionate reaching out to those who are suffering?

8. Is there a quick response to pain?

9. Are support systems in place?

10. Is there balance in knowledge, combining technology with compassion and empathy?

11. Are "Superpowers" considered in the healing process?

12. How high on the sensitivity scale are we?

13. Is there an effort to help find the meaning of suffering?

Chapter Six

Growing in

Carefulness

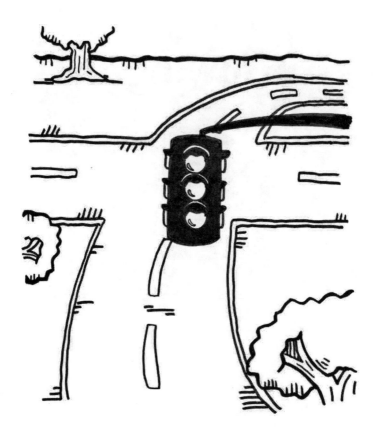

"Life is a daring adventure or nothing at all."

—Helen Keller

The practice of medicine is a risky business. When I embarked on my practice in 1952, I had little or no awareness of all the risks a physician assumes daily. Gradually, years after my graduation from medical school, the enormity of risk management became frightfully apparent.

For more than 20 years I practiced the best I knew. Then, in 1975, Dr. Otis Bowen asked me to become a member of the Medical Licensing Board of Indiana. At the time, I knew little of the functions of this professional panel of physicians, osteopaths and chiropractors. I simply knew that its purpose is to make the practice of medicine safer for the public.

That eight-year commitment changed my life in many ways. I found that the MLB (Medical Licensing Board) members had to acquire skills as legislators, judges and educators while we continued our own practice of medicine. This book would never have been written had I not accepted Dr. Bowen's challenge to participate in public service. It was a privilege to serve on the board, helping physicians become more aware of how to be careful in their practices.

One thing became very clear after eight long years of experience on the MLB: Carefulness is a process, a virtue that can be learned. Becoming aware of risk is an attitude, and it cannot be legislated. It must be learned and taught from the beginning of medical school and throughout our careers.

Carefulness can be defined as the powerful process of becoming aware of risk, its potential and its pitfalls, by becoming thorough, vigilant and wary. This chapter on carefulness is all about managing risk, and there are several key words that are related:

▶ Risk management	▶ Trial and error
▶ Competence	▶ Assessment
▶ Attention to detail	▶ Thoroughness
▶ Concentration	▶ Holistic

Risk can never be totally avoided. Think of all the risks we take every day when we jump into our cars. As soon as we turn the key in the ignition and start down the road, we subject ourselves to the possibility of horrendous accidents. Why do we take such risks? Aren't we frightened to put our vulnerable human bodies in two tons of steel, driving down a narrow asphalt strip and whizzing past deadly vehicles that we miss only by seconds and inches? Yet we take that risk many times each day.

Carefulness: the powerful process of becoming aware of risk, its potential and its pitfalls, by becoming thorough, vigilant and wary.

Sometimes we are oblivious to the risks, acting surprised when collisions occur between these hurling masses of steel, plastic and glass. But we can't dwell morbidly on these risks, for then we would never venture out on the highway at all. There are lessons that physicians can learn about this analogy.

Most accidents on the highway, as in the practice of medicine, are preventable. Wilferd Peterson makes this important point in his book, *The Art of Living Day by Day*:

> Your automobile does not possess a brain or a heart.
> Whether it is an instrument of death or destruction, or a
>   vehicle of safe and sane transportation, depends on you.
> You must think for it, guide it and command it.
>
> Your auto cannot judge and decide, only you can.
> Your auto cannot be courteous, only you can.
> Your auto cannot control its speed, only you can.
> Your auto cannot determine whether or not you are fit to
>   drive, only you can.
> Your auto cannot be patient with people, on foot or
>   driving, only you can.
> Your auto cannot cooperate for the common good.
> Your auto cannot observe the rules of the road.
> Your auto cannot practice the golden rule.
>
> Your mental attitude is the key to safe driving. You can
>   demand calmness, poise and emotional control of your-

self when you take the wheel. You can say a prayer each day for the guidance and safety of yourself and all other drivers. You can expect the best from other drivers while you keep alert for the unexpected. Driving with hands and feet, eyes and ears is not enough. Also drive with your head and heart.

The same principles apply to the practice of medicine. There are enormous chances for error and human disaster, made possible by either the patient or the physician. Most of this risk is unavoidable for the physician. Medicine is both art and science, and neither is exact. The risk is compounded by the fact that every patient is unique. His character and chemistries are to be discovered in the practice of medicine—that's why it's called the *practice* of medicine.

The word "practice" comes from the Greek word *practikas,* which means practical work. Patients often get the idea that we are experimenting on them when we "try" certain remedies. Indeed, there is no way to predict for certain how an individual will respond to a given medicine or treatment. Patients must simply understand this fact. Despite medical advances, this fact will never change. That is one reason why follow-up visits are so crucial.

In his book, *Healing the Wounds,* Dr. David Hilfiker has revealed the complexity of managing mistakes, either for physicians or patients:

> The environment in which physicians are trained does not encourage them to talk about their mistakes, or their emotional responses to them. Indeed, errors are rarely admitted or discussed once a physician is in private practice... Although mistakes are not usually sins, they engender similar feelings of guilt...The only real answer for guilt is spiritual confession, restitution and absolution. Yet within the structure of modern medicine there is simply no place for this spiritual healing. We need to find healthy ways to deal with the emotional responses to those errors. Our profession is difficult enough without having to wear the yoke of perfection.

Mistakes happen in all professions and walks of life. For example, mistakes are made in the manufacturing sector, and wise management has come to accept this fact. Management often encourages the process of trying new things, even if they fail, in order to solve problems. The very basis of entrepreneurial activities is taking risk. The resulting dictum in business is this: "If you haven't failed enough, you haven't tried enough."

In medicine, however, there are many unsolved problems, and yet physicians are usually wary of trying new solutions. Although prudence and caution is understandable, physicians must be allowed the freedom to keep trying new things. That is the basis for scientific empiricism: If we aren't getting results, we must try something different. Patients need to understand that. Many decisions in medical practice are matters of balancing probabilities and uncertainties.

A physician committed to carefulness is committed to excellence, not perfection. Again, we can best view this important quality in light of the essential inner nutrients for growth:

1. Awareness: We must become aware of the risks. This is not an option but an imperative if we are to survive, thrive and strive for excellence. Of course, even at the end of life's journey, we will be unaware of some hidden risks and traps. However, through the wisdom of experience and the processes of discernment, we can grow in our awareness. Many medical liability companies now offer risk assessment programs to physicians who want to reduce their risks in practice. Unfortunately, though, most of these companies are not yet equipped to address a key component of risk avoidance: the physician's attitudes. And physicians are not, by and large, interested in analyzing their interpersonal relationships with patients anyway. Too often, physicians only wake up to the importance of their attitudes after they are forced to defend a malpractice claim.

2. Freedom: It is wrong to think that patients will gain safety from overly restrictive laws, rules and regulations. The best solution is an inner freedom from negative attitudes. This is the only remedy that can truly enhance the safety of patients, while bringing joy back into the practice of medicine.

3. Thinking: Physicians will reap great benefits from thinking, studying and taking Continuing Medical Education courses regarding the risks we face. Most of us are vaguely aware of the importance of how we treat our patients, but we often don't take the time to improve our interpersonal skills as much as we study the scientific journals.

4. Feeling: Our feelings are too often suppressed and kept in the dark because of our intellectual pursuits. We get in trouble when we don't recognize our emotions such as anger, frustration, anxiety, apathy, arrogance and fear. An awareness of negative emotions is the first step to finding a positive way to manage conflicts with our patients or colleagues.

5. Desire: One of our primary desires should be to provide a safe place for our patients to find healing and curing. If we use our creative, imaginative powers, safety precautions can be achieved. It is not by rules or regulations, but by attitudes that will help us become response-able and not habitually react to our circumstances.

6. Purpose: A higher safety profile will only be achieved as we set specific goals and purposes to change our processes and practices. We must have a clear mission to become aware of pitfalls and traps inherent in the practice of medicine. Each of us needs to devise a plan for personal growth in risk awareness.

7. Prioritize – We will never achieve excellence in our attitudes, skills and knowledge unless we make it a priority. Our practices must treasure effectiveness over efficiency. This will require attention to detail, thoroughness and vigilance. Relationships must be valued and partnerships continually cultivated.

8. Choose: After setting our purpose, priorities and values, we must make a deliberate choice to pursue them without distraction or deviation. This choice means committing ourselves to a well-defined plan of action.

9. Act: We act on behalf of patients when we have clear plans, priorities and values and have chosen to faithfully adhere to them.

10. Persist: Both physicians and patients must follow through on their commitments—persisting to pursue excellence no matter what obstacles they face. We cannot merely abandon patients. If a relationship must be terminated, this should be done with sensitivity, perceiving the best possible outcome. This means valuing qualities such as trust, respect and empathy.

11. Response-able: After all of the above microprocesses are methodically explored and discovered, we become response-able. Now we can change our attitudes, which is a key to achieving the carefulness we need.

12. Change: Growth only occurs when we are willing to review and restructure our attitudes. These attitudes eventually become habitudes which make the practice of medicine safer.

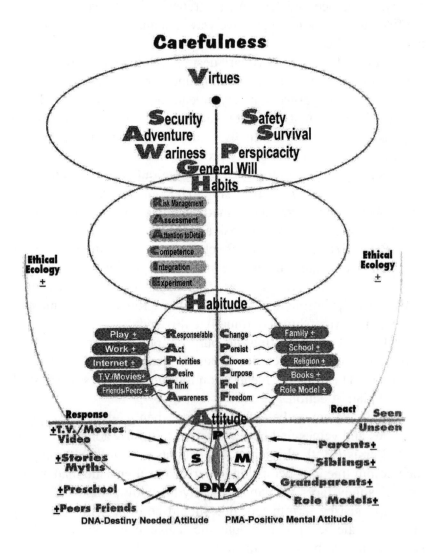

Many physicians have their pilot's license and fly airplanes. Flying has always been a great interest of mine, although my air time is rare now. Flying involves a complexity and challenge that I wish everyone could experience. Yet, while an airplane pilot endures arduous training and continuous education, it is far less complicated than the practice of medicine.

Piloting people in their healthcare journey will always be more complex than flying a jumbo jet. Near perfection is expected of pilots, and perhaps that is possible, since an airplane is far more predictable than people. However, weather is another matter, and predicting people is almost like predicting the weather. Even if you think you have someone figured out, they are often about as changeable as the weather.

Difficult as it may be, excellence should be the standard in both flying and medicine. Carefulness must be learned and practiced, and this requires an increasing awareness of the pitfalls and potentials. Airline pilots must be awake, alert, attentive to detail, and aware of all the possible hazards. They need to develop attitudes similar to Wilferd Peterson's safe driver analogy. Even though they follow detailed checklists and guidelines, there will be errors at times. However, as either pilots or physicians, our hope is that human error will be minimized as we continually strive for excellence.

There is no way the Medical Licensing Boards can scrutinize the performance of physicians in the workplace. A physician's performance has to be so bad that he breaks a clear law, rule or regulation before anything is done. Rather than pointing to a standard of excellence, MLBs merely deal with gross incompetence, fraud, chemical dependency and senility. The licensing boards do not monitor physicians' attitudes of carefulness nor their growth in the 12 processes described in this book. Nor would I want legislators or certifying bodies to adjudicate attitudes and character traits. That is out of their domain. However, we desperately need a public partnering with physicians to bring a new level of accountability to the medical profession.

So why will the certifying bodies and specialty boards always fall short in their ability to evaluate physicians? Because they measure only cognitive skills—ability that is based on knowledge and technology. This is the main substance of medical school training, but it is quite a different thing than true competence.

Competence

How do we define competence in medicine? During my term with the Medical Licensing Board, I was appointed to a position on the Flex Committee. This committee, assigned the task of devising a national standard certifying exam for physicians, was composed of members of Medical Licensing Boards from 48 states. This was the Federation of the Licensing Exam Committee—FLEX for short.

Competence: a balance of knowledge, skills and attitudes.

We selected test questions and devised the examinations which every physician needed to take, certifying that his knowledge was competent to be licensed in his state. This test is the *sine qua non* by which a physician is licensed. Even after passing medical school or specialty boards, he must have passed the Flex test.

For eight years our committee worked diligently to strengthen this exam. However, when we tried to define the word "competence," most examiners recognized that knowledge base is not equivalent to competence. In fact, the concept of competence still holds many mysteries ill-defined.

The paradigm below illustrates the nature of competence, with attitudes in the middle of skills and knowledge:

The S-A-K Diagram shows that competence is not just a single quality, but rather a balance of:

1. **Knowledge:** a growing, dynamic knowledge base
2. **Skills:** in both technology and human relationships, and
3. **Attitudes:** an awareness of attitudes that make for growth and partnership.

In medical school, competency meant merely passing the exams and making the necessary grades. Some of the best physicians today were not at the top of their class in medical school, but came from the middle or bottom. In fact, some who were in the top percentiles in medical school were abject failures in the real world of medical practice. How could this be? Not because of incompetent knowledge, but incompetent attitudes, character traits and people skills.

My experience in academia verified that some students with marginal knowledge were given specialty certification simply because they passed the test. A number who lacked the character traits defined in this book were passed on to the public as competent physicians. I observed that schools don't know what to do with students that are competent in areas of medical knowledge but incompetent in their attitudes and behavioral skills. Such traits just don't matter very much in our educative processes. We don't spend much time in our schools teaching creativity, communications, conflict resolution, confidence, compassion, carefulness and the other vital skills of an excellent doctor.

Sadly, many physicians actually had more competence in their attitudes and character *before* they were admitted to medical school. Instead of nurturing healthy attitudes and character, the pressurized medical culture can have a negative effect. Robin Williams' *Patch Adams* movie clearly illustrates the dehumanizing educational experience most of us had in our school days.

Of course, the medical schools and residency training centers in America are the best in the world. As knowledge factories, they are superb. Their success in producing top-rate physicians is a credit to the many dedicated teachers who inspired us by their model of excellence in lifestyle and character. Were it not for these men and women who went beyond medical facts to impart true illumination, I am afraid my education would have been a dismal failure. Yet a lot more change is needed in the culture of our training centers, and they would do well to follow some of the precepts of Patch Adams. Growth in attitudes and character is too important to be left to chance and personal initiative.

Dr. James Davis, president of the American Medical Association in 1958, addressed this issue:

> I urge you members of licensing boards to insure people who pass the test for licensing will also be able to pass the more difficult test of human values, emotional strengths and selflessness which requires us to pass throughout our entire careers...Is competence (scientific knowledge) enough? No! Competence must be coupled with genuine caring, compassion and concern for our patients and the whole of humanity. As you assess the students' knowledge...look further...examine also their character, their motivation, their dedication to find out what kind of a person one truly is...Put more emphasis on service and caring, because we can see that the dynamics of a successful doctor-patient relationship is more than intuitive. It takes proper training to learn to relate positively to patients in crisis. We cannot nourish our patients unless we are spiritually healthy ourselves.

Dr. Davis is describing the qualities needed for care-fulness. His short, insightful message has been lost and should be rediscovered and reiterated.

There is enormous competition for what must be taught in our medical schools and specialties. With the base of medical knowledge expanding at an ever-increasing rate, choices obviously must be made as to which subjects to cover. The public's spiraling fascination with alternative medicine is a symptom of our medical schools' failure to teach enough about such things as nutrition, environmental medicine, food allergies, hypnosis and acupuncture. It also points out the simple fact that competency is not some destination marked by a diploma or certification; it is, rather, a lifelong struggle to continue learning and growing.

Technological skills are revered and taught superbly in medical schools. Specialties that use high-tech are consequently very attractive to students, and that's usually where the money is, too. Behavioral skills, on the other hand, are usually relegated to the behavioral scientist. Somewhere in the curriculum there needs to be a balance between the technological and the behavior.

Competent Habitudes

Since attitudes and character issues are rarely addressed in our present-day educational processes, how will these important characteristics be taught? The answer, at least for now, is to develop the physician-patient partnership so successfully that we become accountable to each other. A physician open to personal growth should welcome the patient's perception of our attitudes and behaviors. Even as our wives and children have helped us grow, so can our patients.

Some medical practitioners might object to my emphasis on attitudes, saying that such qualities are invisible and therefore irrelevant. However, this is a tragic mistake. Attitudes *are* visible, clearly reflecting our values, goals and purposes. Nothing will change the direction of our lives or our medical practices more than an adjustment of our attitudes.

For either physicians or patients, attitudes play a major role in our relationships. Our competency in human relations will be challenged all of our lives. Physicians need to champion the process of learning excellence in this area. Relational excellence doesn't have to be a nebulous concept, but should have parameters that we can assess.

Assessment

We physicians should be on the forefront of providing leadership in the process of assessment. Plato once said, "An unexamined life is one not worth living." As Norman Cousins points out, "Great medical teachers have always impressed upon their students the need to make careful assessments of everything that may interact in the course of the disease."

We must assess three distinct attributes:

- Facts
- Feelings
- Attitudes.

Factual assessment simply involves the physician's competence in grasping the necessary knowledge base. This kind of assessment is done today in many different medical specialties, as in the American Academy of Family Practice. This is not a one-time assessment, but something that must be periodically updated. Since 1973 I have been re-certified every seventh year as a family practitioner. Each time this board-certified status has been updated, I have been required to sit for a seven-hour exam. Many specialties have a similar requirement.

Feelings may be the most uncomfortable area for many physicians to assess. Some doctors model Sergeant Joe Friday's famous attitude, "Just the facts, ma'am." Yet, such an approach ignores the very important role that feelings play. They inevitably influence every other area of our lives: thoughts, behavior, relationships, etc. We need to be willing and able to assess whether the patient, or we ourselves, are angry, sad, apathetic or offended.

Attitudes must also be assessed, including the attitudes of both patients and doctors. John Gardner stresses physician-patient accountability in this way, "I would lay it down on a basic principle of any human organization: that the individuals who hold the reins of power in any enterprise cannot trust themselves to be adequately critical. The only protection is to create an atmosphere in which people can speak up." In this regard, many medical offices have wisely prepared patient-satisfaction questionnaires which allow patients to express their feelings about our services. If openly embraced by both patients and physicians, such attitudinal questionnaires could conceivably be great educational tools.

Of the various kinds of assessment that are needed, none are more vital than self-assessment. Ben Franklin was a master at this, but his method of self-assessment is not very well known today. He gained considerable wisdom and maturity by making it a lifelong practice to focus each week on one virtue that he wanted to improve. His process of self-improvement involved assessing his performance each day and then picking a new virtue each week.

For more than 15 years now, it has been my practice to do the same thing with each of the 12 processes in this book. This approach has given me a great confidence that my own self-assessment and growth in these personal dimensions will give me increasing effectiveness, personal power, and successful relationships. My own experience has validated Edmund Pellegrino's observation:

> The task in later life is only little helped by post-graduate courses, tapes, films, television, and all the highly vaunted media of mass communication and education. These will always be ancillary to the unglamorous hard work of self-study, critical and meditative appraisal of one's experience, and imitation of the best role models.

Although our patients may not be in a position to judge our intellectual or technologic competence, they can tell us how they feel about the way we behave toward them. Receiving this kind of feedback is crucial for our continued growth.

Pellegrino suggests the following ways that professional groups can assure the competence of their members:

- Relicensure and recertification
- Setting standards of performance
- Providing opportunities for remediation
- Maintaining contact with colleagues and submitting to peer surveillance.

As important as these matters are, I would be opposed to legislation requiring them. Specialty boards should provide the incentives, but legislation would likely prove impossible to enforce. In fact, many laws already on the books are unenforceable. I am reminded of one law I saw not long ago: A farmer can be fined for having Canadian thistle on his farm! That's just one of many ludicrous examples of the misguided legislation being enacted each year. Such laws are often devised with the best of intentions, as an attempt to champion causes that stem from some failure in past leadership. However, in practice, the proposed legislative remedy can make the situation even worse.

The present methods of hospital credentialling, likewise, need to be reassessed. For a great many years, hospitals in our state have been reviewed periodically by the State Board of Health and the Joint Commission on Accreditation of Healthcare Organizations. The JCAHO has more than 6500 items on its checklist for hospital review. Hospitals pay big money for this accolade from JCAHO. Yet, although many hospital administrators go through the necessary hoops, few physicians and administrators are enthusiastic about the effectiveness of this credentialling. As far as I can see, it is like most other certification processes—dealing primarily with minimum standards and organizational procedures.

While these may be important details that must not be ignored, excellence cannot be separated from the hospital's character, values and espoused mission. In the final analysis, the attitudes of physicians, nurses and support personnel are what make for excellence. Since the JCAHO assessment ignores these key indicators, it may be asked whether the 6500 markers are merely whitewash—covering up the issues that really matter.

The JCAHO will not die, but perhaps it is time for it to have a new vision. I know of several hospitals which have had JCAHO's top rating and full accreditation, yet there's no way I would consider them excellent in the process of carefulness.

The National Data Bank

In the latter 1970s, the Federation of the State Medical Licensing Boards created an organization called the Physicians Disciplinary Data Bank. By 1981 most of the licensing boards of the individual states channeled information on disciplinary actions and malpractice claims into this one place. The purpose of this data bank is to keep track of physicians under disciplinary action in one state who want to move to other states with no record of the actions. This information has been kept confidential and used primarily by state licensing boards.

In 1988 the federal government created its own national data bank for the same reasons. The degree of access to these banks differs. However, an important feature of both banks is confidentiality, designed to protect physicians from undeserved negative publicity. Yet there have been efforts to open up these banks to the public. The

U.S. government data bank is more lax as to confidentiality, and some consumer advocates urge that it be opened up entirely to the public.

Although accountability is a very valuable asset to our profession, there is also something frightening about providing the public with a list of names without knowing the circumstances of the charges against them. The danger is that this could easily spawn witch hunts. It also doesn't take into account the possibility of rehabilitation: What if a physician was disciplined many years ago for alcohol or drug abuse, but is now a model citizen? Or what about the excellent surgeons who have faced poor outcomes and malpractice suits due to no fault of their own? Many of the nation's top physicians have had claims against them in spite of their heroic work in some extremely difficult circumstances.

It is often possible for patients to see and feel a physician's attitudes and behavior, but even the most discerning patient is hardly able to judge the competence of his physician's technical skills. Only medical peers can do that. The data banks, therefore, include not only the incompetent or evil doctors, but also many good or excellent physicians who have done nothing wrong. In the face of pressures to divulge all information to the public, I implore legislators to leave well enough alone!

Concentration

In order to provide competent healthcare to our patients, it is crucial that we be thorough and give attention to detail. This is often easier said than done. Physicians like myself who have ADD tendencies may face a lifelong struggle to:

1. Concentrate - keep focused
2. Give attention to details
3. Be thorough.

All of these behaviors are vitally important to the virtue of carefulness. K. Hildebrand points out, "A sense of purpose simplifies life and therefore concentrates our abilities, and concentration adds powers." Sir Isaac Newton adds, "If I have made any improvement in the sciences, it is owing more to patient attention than anything else besides." Concentration is a matter of consecration, a veneration of the objects of our study—the patients.

As Sir Beckeley Moynihan, M.D., enjoined us years ago, "A patient can offer no higher tribute than to entrust you with his life and health...and with the happiness of his family. To be worthy of this trust we must submit for a lifetime to the constant discipline of unwearied effort in the search of knowledge and attention to detail in every operation that we perform."

There are many specific areas in our everyday practices that require particular attention to detail, thoroughness and concentration. Most practices have devised a well-organized list of warnings and pitfalls about routine office procedures. Although details are beyond the scope of this book, it suffices to say that every practitioner needs a detailed plan and policy regarding the following items:

1. Delegation. For example, it needs to be clear who handles the various office duties, such as answering the phone.

2. Record-keeping. Excellence in this area involves such things as accuracy, legibility, timeliness, documentation and confidentiality.

3. Information management. This includes reports, letters, charts and other important documents.

4. Consultations. Procedures must be clear as to when and how patients are referred to other doctors.

5. Practice coverage. When the primary physician is on vacation or otherwise unavailable, another doctor must assume interim care.

6. Scheduling. Medical offices need basic understandings regarding how scheduling will be done, and what time periods are available for appointments.

7. Terminating relationships. Every office needs clear policies for the procedures to be followed when the office's relationship with a certain patient is being terminated.

8. Billing and collections. It is important that this area be handled with excellence, for it can cause either a positive or a negative effect on patient relations.

9. Employees evaluation and management. Each employee's

work should be periodically reviewed and assessed so that growth can be encouraged.

When I first began practice many years ago, I was unaware of the many details that would be involved. Not only that, but the complexity has increased exponentially as the years have gone by. I've discovered that there's a lot more to being a doctor than just hanging up the shingle: M.D.

Holistic Medicine

The field of medicine now includes at least 28 specialties and a number of subspecialties. The upside is that patients have a lot of options when they choose a physician. Doctors specializing in areas of narrowed interest will normally offer higher degrees of expertise in their chosen field.

There is also a down side to the trend toward specialization. Patients are often shuffled from one specialty to another, making it hard for any one physician to get the whole picture. This medical model is not only restrictive, but it is also a lot more expensive. Many more tests and procedures are ordered, because each doctor has an intense interest in his own specialty.

Even if some specialists are involved, there is a great value in having one physician who can get an integrated picture of the patient's medical condition. Some physicians have done an outstanding job in taking this holistic approach, seeing an overview of the patient's physical, emotional, social and spiritual self. These holistic doctors see patients not as a bundle of disparate systems but as united, integrated, whole persons. Some specialties are particularly suited for this holistic perspective: family practice, pediatrics, internal medicine and obstetrics.

Holistic medicine can be defined as that discipline which seizes the unity of a person—his physical, intellectual, social and spiritual well-being—and his potential for growth. I do not consider this alternative medicine or quackery. Quite the contrary, I see it as the ideal healthcare delivery system. However, the process of achieving that ideal is still muted in our present system. Fragmented as our system is, there needs to be a unifying, integrated plan. Hopefully, that will not be planned and led by the government alone. But where is the leadership to come from?

Many family practitioners and other primary care specialists have concluded that we need to improve the processes of communication and referral. They are seeing the need for one physician to integrate the plan of treatments, diagnoses and ongoing care. Someone needs to understand the person as a whole and then convey that perspective to the team. That is a part of carefulness.

Holistic medicine: the discipline which seizes the unity of a person—his physical, intellectual, social and spiritual well-being—and his potential for growth

---

The widespread patient acceptance of alternative medicine is due largely to the fact that much of our mainstream medicine has lost sight of the interrelated nature of the systems in a human body. While we may rightfully be somewhat skeptical of unproved remedies, we also need to humbly admit that we don't have all the answers for many of the diseases we face. Instead of a knee-jerk reaction that automatically rejects alternative remedies, we need to keep an open mind, while seeking scientific proof and validation.

Guarding of the Guild

Medical specialties typically try to keep the standards of their practice high by certification. However, this noble intent is often corrupted by another, less admirable motivation: guarding of the guild . By guarding the guild, I mean protecting their economic interests. This is usually done covertly, under the guise of protecting the public from substandard care.

The implication is that a physician who doesn't have a board certification in a specialty or procedure is clearly not competent. Yet that is not necessarily so. Throughout the years, many family practitioners have done excellent surgery, especially in remote places where there was no guarding of the guild. In urban areas there is often a great deal of conflict over surgical and obstetrical privileges. Many times the real issue is not competency at all, but merely professional jealousy and the desire to protect a virtual monopoly.

This kind of ugly competition in the medical profession is an unfortunate fact of life, both past and present. Nevertheless, a coming excess of physicians in the marketplace will give our profession a great opportunity to come up with creative solutions. This can still engender healthy competition, which will cause us all to sharpen our skills and increase our effectiveness.

Certification may have benefits, but it does not assure high standards. A significant number of physicians who are fully certified in their specialty do not display high standards. These marginal physicians are rarely challenged, disciplined or confronted by their peers. Certification thus offers a security blanket for protecting members of the guild.

Achieving high standards requires something more than certification, legislation or the present processes of peer review. I would like to see a process in medicine much like the airlines use—a performance check. Every pilot, private or commercial, is required to have not only a physical but also a flight performance check. For private pilots this is every two years.

The remaining issue is this: Who will check on the checkers? Some assessors tend to be very lenient, accepting low standards. Others insist on high standards, perhaps higher than necessary. One thing for sure, our profession needs to reconsider the processes of carefulness and accountability. Our present procedures do not assure the public of the excellence which it deserves.

Carefulness Questions for Partners

1. Does the office have an atmosphere that welcomes your comments?
2. Is there a patient-satisfaction questionnaire?
3. Are the physical examinations thorough?
4. Is there a proper attention to details?
5. Does the physician clarify the risks and complications involved in the discussed procedures?
6. Is the schedule managed in such a way that appointments are available when needed?
7. Is the physician's certification valid and current?

8. Has the physician continued to take medical education courses?
9. Does the office do what it can to minimize distractions?
10. Is the physician's attention focused on his patients?
11. Has the office worked to eliminate interruptions?
12. Is the office clean and orderly?

Chapter Seven

Growing in

*"Whoever desires to be great among you, let
him be your servant"* (Matthew 20:26).

The character trait of concern was previously mentioned in chapter five as one of the Sisters of Mercy. The word concern has lost some of its dynamic, emotional, passionate power, perhaps due to the blasé definition found in Webster's dictionary: "Concern is a marked interest or regard for relationship through personal tie, to implicate or involve; a matter of consideration."

The English word "concern" comes from the Latin word *concerere*, which means to be related to, to mingle with, to mix. The World Book Dictionary defines concern as "having to do with, to have an interest for, to be the business affair of."

Concern: an attitude of marked interest in serving the patient more than self, characterized by the giving of greater consideration to the needs of another person in community; the powerful process of becoming a servant, responding with individual consideration to the needs of others.

Perhaps a better definition of concern would be the powerful process of becoming a servant, responding with individual consideration to the needs of others. As you can see from my definition, I believe that becoming a servant is the very essence of what concern is all about. I use the words concern and service interchangeably to represent the same ideal character trait. In addition to the need for a heart of service, concern involves the following key words:

- ► Satisfaction
- ► Altruism
- ► Productivity
- ► Competition
- ► Humility
- ► Expectations
- ► Creative capitalism
- ► Profit
- ► Entrepreneur
- ► Involvement

Service brings the dynamic back into the definition of concern. I hold on to the word concern, to bring it alive and also because it begins with C to fill out my paradigm of commitment.

One of the reasons I like to use the word "service" is because it has become a by-word in both the manufacturing and service industries in America. It has climbed nearly to the top in corporate mission statements and values. The IBM Company, for example, says that its business focuses on three things:

1. Concern for customer
2. Respect for customer
3. Commitment to service with excellence

If service is so valued in the world of business, shouldn't it be even more important to us in the practice of medicine? Yet, do we as physicians have a clear idea of what it means to serve our patients? Is it a character trait that we are committed to emulate? If so, how do we grow in this key dimension of concern?The answer, as we have seen in other chapters, is that we grow in this character-building process by first clarifying the essential inner nutrients of growth associated with concern and service.

One of the virtues associated with concern is altruism. It may be defined as a concern for meeting the needs of others, taking pleasure in enabling people to satisfy their needs. This does not imply the neglect of our own needs, but rather seeks to equalize the opportunity for all persons to share in the common good.

Altruism: a concern for meeting the needs of others, taking pleasure in enabling people to satisfy their needs.

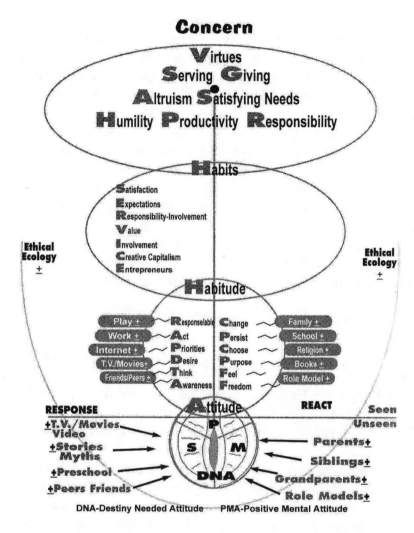

Concern

Virtues
Serving **G**iving
Altruism **S**atisfying Needs
Humility **P**roductivity **R**esponsibility

Habits

Satisfaction
Expectations
Responsibility-Involvement
Value
Involvement
Creative Capitalism
Entrepreneurs

Ethical Ecology ±

Ethical Ecology ±

Habitude

Play +
Work +
Internet +
T.V./Movies+
Friends/Peers +

Response/able **C**hange
Act **P**ersist
Priorities **C**hoose
Desire **P**urpose
Think **F**eel
Awareness **F**reedom

Family +
School +
Religion +
Books +
Role Model +

Attitude

RESPONSE **REACT** Seen

+T.V./Movies
Video
+Stories
Myths
+Preschool
+Peers Friends

Unseen

P
S M
DNA

Parents+
Siblings+
Grandparents+
Role Models+

DNA-Destiny Needed Attitude — PMA-Positive Mental Attitude

We can gain an understanding of how to develop a servant attitude by again reviewing the EINGs:

1. Awareness – It is crucial that physicians have an awareness of human need in our society. The family of man throughout the world is hurting with unbelievable poverty, starvation, malnutrition and disease. Our strife-torn world is desperately in need of people who can impart peace and assist in conflict resolution. All societies need a boost in education to rid the populace of the specter of ignorance. Our families are breaking apart at an alarming rate, and the need for positive role-modeling is urgent. Confusion over sexual behavior is widespread, producing a worldwide epidemic of uncontrollable sexually transmitted diseases. And we need a cultural revolution that will bring positive, wholesome entertainment on TV, movies and other media.

Physicians cannot afford to stick their heads in the sand and ignore these conditions. If we are to bring healing, we must have our eyes wide open to the needs. We should strive to be aware. The seemingly endless list of human hurts, circumstances, sorrows, suffering, stress and brokenness must be confronted with positive hope and action.

2. Freedom – It is not enough to be aware of needs—we must be free to respond to them. To be able to respond we must first free ourselves from negative attitudes and emotions such as apathy, anxiety and anger.

3. Think and 4. Feel – We should use our freedom to think and feel more deeply about unmet human needs.

5. Desire – As we think and feel, we begin to get a vision of what would be desirable in this world.

6. Purpose – Desire is incomplete until we begin to devise a purpose and plan. This requires setting personal goals as to how we will meet human needs, setting our own plan for making the world a better place.

7. Prioritize – As we consider our purpose, we will have to examine our priorities and values. Where should we commit our resources, time and money? How can we best serve those in need?

8. Choose – In today's busy world we are bombarded with competing pulls on our time and resources. Our choices of values and priorities will have either a positive or negative impact on our ability to relieve human needs.

9. Act – Our positive choices must be acted upon. This requires a decision to become involved in positive movements and support systems. Those who are isolated in their feelings and self-serving pursuits will be ineffective in helping others.

10. Persevere – A life of service is not for the faint of heart. Since there will always be suffering and human need, a lifelong journey of service will require persistent involvement in concern for others.

11. Response-able – The needs and suffering in the world are so vast, we cannot merely react. We must become response-able to these needs.

12. Change – As we become response-able instead of reacting, we develop the habitude of serving by first changing our inner environment. Only as our attitudes change can we hope to change the world around us. Specifically, our attitudes need to be changed from apathy, disinterest, non-involvement, and negative or angry reactions. Instead, we need attitudes that are positive, empathetic and proactive in responding to human need.

Sir William Osler, our great founding father of modern medicine, challenged his medical students with this admonition:

> ...that we practitioners of medicine are here not to get all we can out of life for ourselves, but to try to make the lives of others happier. This is the oft repeated admonition of Christ: "He that findeth his life shall lose it, and he that loseth his life for my sake shall find it!" If the children of this generation would lay hold of this, there would be less misery and discontent in the world. It is not possible for anyone to have better opportunities to live this lesson than you will enjoy. The practice of medicine is a work, not a trade; a calling, not a business. A calling in which your heart will be exercised equally with your head.

I wonder how many medical students have heard those words in their medical training? It was only in my reading of Cushing's *Life of Osler* and *Equanimitas* that I savored his powerful message.

Other great leaders also have shared their value of service:

Leo Tolstoy: "The sole meaning of life is to serve humanity."

Albert Einstein: "It's high time the idea of success be replaced with the idea of service. Try not to be a man of success, but rather try to become a man of value."

Albert Schweitzer: "I don't know what your destiny will

be. But this I do know, that only those of you who will be really happy are those who have sought and found how to serve."

Dale Carnegie: "The rare individual who unselfishly tries to serve others has an enormous advantage. He has little competition."

Brian Connelly: "Along the way of our service to others and community, we learn there is an enormous sense of satisfaction, purpose and worth."

Involvement

Let's not forget that concern for the needs of others is one of the Sisters of Mercy, as discussed in chapter five. To become involved with the needs of others is to respond to community needs.

A tragic story that occurred in New York City years ago points to the matter of involvement in community needs. Austin Street is a quiet, respectable neighborhood, the better part of the Kew Gardens. Late one night in the spring of 1964, a young woman named Catherine Genovice was stabbed on the street in three separate attacks by a lurking assailant. Twice the attacker was frightened away, so that 30 minutes lapsed between the first and third attacks. After the third attack, Catherine Genovice was dead.

The thing that makes this story so incredible is that 38 different people watched—but did nothing. During that half hour, not one person even lifted the phone to call the police. Later, police questioning these 38 onlookers discovered that they weren't even ashamed or embarrassed. They shrugged off the questions and replied that they just didn't want to get involved.

An appropriate response to human needs, especially those nearby in our own community, is our civic duty and privilege. Because the needs are sometimes overwhelming, it will take considerable thought in prioritizing our responses. This is especially difficult in light of all the fundraising organizations that are constantly soliciting our contributions. Some of these causes are deserving of great support, while others squander far more money than they are investing in the community.

Needs

Whenever we consider our community or the surrounding world, one thing is clear: The needs abound. Many service organizations and religious groups are actively responding to human needs: Kiwanis, Lions Club, Optimists, churches, synagogues, United Way, Red Cross and National Cancer Society, just to mention a few. Throughout the years, America has demonstrated to the world a commendable sensitivity and generosity. Now we ought to keep this same spirit alive back home in America.

A closer look at physicians in America will find the vast majority searching to find a way to preserve that spirit which seeks to help people in need. The value systems and dynamics of economic trends have tested the most dedicated physicians to be people of service and value.

"Managed care" has caused healthcare systems to set a high priority on efficiency and profits. In such an atmosphere, the focus on human need is frequently lost. The patient very easily becomes a commodity and the physician a mere provider. Even the language of our present-day medical climate has become very impersonal— often driven by the processes of economics.

Creative Capitalism

In spite of my deep desire to concentrate on relieving the suffering of my patients, I have found myself thrust into the business world. It is a reality that I cannot escape: To be successful and stay in practice, I must regularly balance the business, art and science of medicine. Our services in medicine must have...

...value
...recompense
...profit
...productivity
...competition.

Many physicians are trying to find a way to serve their patients with excellence, while still making a living. In today's climate, this requires what I call "creative capitalism." The essence of creative capitalism in medicine is in retaining the freedom to serve the needs

of patients with:
1. Maximal effectiveness
2. Quality productivity / excellence
3. Reasonable profits, in an atmosphere of
4. Friendly competition.

As mergers have created larger and larger healthcare systems, there has been a tendency for all of these basic elements to be eroded. Although physicians have for years been among the highest paid professionals, many physicians now are struggling to make the kind of living that was once expected. Some are even getting out of medicine, either out of frustration or because of the greater incentives they find elsewhere.

In 1984 Dr. Charles Davidson offered some great wisdom in the New England Journal of Medicine:

> We must be reasonable in our own demands for recompense. Doctors deserve a good living, but not an extravagant one. Greed and medical care are not compatible. We must take the major responsibility ourselves for cost containment, not to leave it to the government or the corporations or we lose our independence. We must be cognizant of costs, not overusing technology. We must ask, "Is this procedure, test, operation necessary?" Control consists of our determination to see that the care we provide: 1.) is the best to be had, 2.) costs only as much as is necessary, and 3.) is available to all...If we lose control of the way we practice our profession, both we and the public will suffer. Much of the choice is ours.

Since Davidson's warning in 1984, physicians *have* lost much of their leadership and control in the matter of how best to serve the public. We have been too divided, too independent, and too busy caring for patients to stop the steam-rolling effect of government processes and "managed care."

As we see the failures of government regulations and managed-care systems across the country, we must ask, "Could we have stopped all the ill-advised experiments of legislators and insurance companies?" Probably not. Rather, the need is for informed patients in partnership with physicians to speak to the crucial values of service in the new, managed-care context. As healthcare continues to evolve, physicians must find new ways of serving and meeting patient needs. These changes must take on a new look—providing innovative, win-win solutions for patients, physicians, hospitals and other participants in the healthcare system.

Hard as it may often be, medical care providers must again see their profession through the paradigm of serving. Personal and professional growth will come as we respond to human need in positive, creative ways. The first changes must come in our attitudes, giving us new hope that progress truly can be made in utilizing our physical, human and financial resources better. One of the most fruitful changes that can be made will be a new emphasis on preventive medicine.

Humility

The character trait of humility is closely tied to the process of becoming a servant. For example, humility and concern are displayed when a busy doctor takes time to partner with his patients in teaching them the best preventive medicine.

Our patients have seen enough of the opposite trait: arrogance. Perhaps arrogance is too strong a word to describe the negativity often found among medical practitioners. After all, most of this behavior is exhibited without any awareness of the attitude we are projecting. A more apt description of this arrogant attitude might be "hubris," a gentler term.

Humility: the virtue achieved by recognizing our own limitations and our need for assistance from others and from our Creator.

Understanding the difference between hubris and humility can help us grow in the great process of serving our patients. Changing from hubris to humility may be one of the most difficult tasks we face. However, while the medical profession has offered plenty of examples of hubris, we certainly don't have a monopoly on this negative character trait. Hubris seems to occur most often in people who have high goals and standards.

Where hubris is present, a variety of negative qualities and behaviors will typically accompany it:

1. Authoritarian relationships
2. Status-seeking
3. A desire to be served
4. A self-sufficient, independent attitude
5. A self-satisfied resistance to change
6. An attitude of superiority, regarding self as greater than others
7. Seeing and seeking only our own way
8. Facades rather than honesty and transparency
9. Difficulty forgiving those who fail.

An attitude of humility, on the other hand, has very different results:

1. Creates partnerships, empowering others in non-manipulative ways
2. Seeks equal rather than superior status
3. Seeks to serve rather than to be served
4. Seeks interdependence, acknowledging the need for partners
5. Seeks to make things better rather than remain satisfied with the status quo
6. Seeks the help of others
7. Seeks "our way" instead of "my way"
8. Removes facades and fosters an atmosphere of openness
9. Facilitates forgiveness, acknowledging that we all fail from time to time.

Pastor and author Charles Swindoll has defined humility in a way that destroys the common misconception that it entails meekness, passivity, self-abasement and a lack of healthy self-esteem. His description is very powerful and positive:

It is a non-defensive spirit when confronted...

...an authentic desire to help others
...absolute honesty
...no ulterior motives, no hidden meaning
...no hypocrisy, duplicity or political games
...no manipulation of others
...it is real, genuine, transparent humanity with an open
    admission of our weaknesses
...having needs and admitting them.

When we study the characteristics of true leadership in a later chapter, we will find that they are closely aligned with those of humility. The greatest leaders are those who *serve* their constituents, those "under" them. They exemplify humility rather than hubris.

The paradigm below illustrates how a physician's office is often perceived:

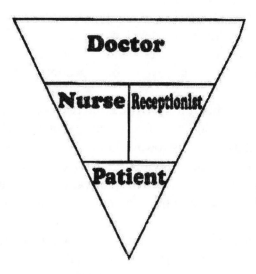

According to this paradigm, the physician has the greatest powers, while the patient has the least. This is a good example of hubris. Fortunately, I think a better paradigm is possible:

In this paradigm, the patient is the center and the physician is the leader of the other caregivers, all devoted to serving the patient. That is humility, quite a contrast to the typical attitude of hubris.

Viktor Frankl challenges us with a moving maxim: "The more one forgets himself by giving himself to a cause to serve or another person to love, the more human he is and the more he actualizes himself." We weren't taught this in our early training. Some physicians never learned it; some never will. Yet, traits of true humility can be learned at any time we desire. All we need to know is the "how to," and then we can develop our accountability systems with our partners.

It's really not difficult to recognize the two behaviors, hubris and humility. However, our present-day educational systems seem to naturally gravitate students toward hubris. Many fledgling medical students went into medicine with high ideals of desiring to help and serve patients. That was a powerful motivation for enduring the hassles, hard work and deprivations encountered during the early years of training.

Many idealistic young students experience a disillusioning culture change when they begin making rounds with attending physicians and professors in years three and four of medical school. The students begin to take on the negative values and attitudes of some teachers, senior staff, researchers and nurses who have become cynical, disgruntled or self-serving. A culture of negativity has a way of yielding negative processes that warp our medical education.

It doesn't take long for students to see where the big money is, as well as an easier life. Often this unintended "education" occurs when students overhear the conversations among faculty and staff. These conversations are often a reflection of the way we physicians react to the pressures of managed care, economics, litigation and the toxic climate created by governmental rules and regulations. In such an environment, students are often more affected by physicians' frustrations than by our positive excitement about serving our patients.

In large hospitals and medical centers the ideal of service with true humility is quite often forgotten or poorly translated. We struggle with how to provide quality care to our patients and yet survive in today's marketplace. We need more than simplistic answers to this dilemma. We must take care that we are truly responding to human needs, rather than merely reacting to crises created in a culture of negative processes. However, if we keep the service and concern motive high, create powerful partnerships, and emphasize preventive medicine, there is hope.

Partner Satisfaction

How are we doing so far in serving our patients with excellence? Have we taken time to ask our patients for feedback? Many hospitals are now aware of how important patient-satisfaction questionnaires are for determining the quality of their services and public relations. Surprisingly, we in the service industries are often far behind the manufacturing sectors in getting public feedback and satisfaction ratings. A small minority of physician's offices are finally beginning to test the public waters of criticism. We might not always like what we hear, but we need the input of our patients, nevertheless.

We shouldn't waste a single opportunity presented to us by criticisms or complaints. At such times we have a chance to demonstrate true humility. Hubris will get us no place. Humility means attempting to define our patients' expectations in order to meet or exceed them. Instead of displaying arrogance or independence, we become partners striving together for excellence.

Despite our best efforts, we will have unpleasant encounters with patients from time to time. Often the situation can be remedied by simply offering the patient a questionnaire that solicits his or her honest feedback. The first step in arriving at a solution is to determine what happened—sincerely trying to discover what could have been done better. We must never forget that most conflicts are the result of differences in expectations, needs, wants, passions, principles, priorities and purposes.

If patients and physicians understand the importance of achieving satisfaction and excellence, some wonders will occur. However, satisfaction is not a coincidence, it is a process. The process begins when physicians truly desire to become servants, meeting the needs of their patients. But patients have an important role to play in this as well: They must clearly communicate their needs to the physicians. When these simple procedures are followed, satisfaction will usually be achieved.

Of course, there will always be patients and physicians who have some unrealistic expectations. For example, physicians may encounter patients who want narcotics or antibiotics when they are not indicated. In such cases, there is a difficult area of understanding that needs to be worked through. Not only should physicians have an attitude of serving their patients with humility, the patients, likewise, must have a proper attitude, not fawning or obsequious toward the physician.

Below is a patient-satisfaction questionnaire that can be used by patients to enhance the services of their physician striving for excellence. Such a vehicle for communication and feedback helps to facilitate our partnering to its fullest expression.

Partner Satisfaction Scale

We want to serve you with excellence. We invite you to help us do that by filling out this short questionnaire. Feel free to make frank comments on the line following each question. Your views are important to us.

How do you rate us?

	Excellent	Good	Fair	Poor
1. Welcomed you in a courteous and friendly manner?	4	3	2	1
2. Phone calls answered in a prompt and friendly manner?	4	3	2	1
3. Ease of obtaining or rescheduling appointments?	4	3	2	1
4. Staff informed you when doctor's schedule was delayed?	4	3	2	1
5. Doctor really listens to all of your problems and complaints?	4	3	2	1
6. Did you understand after explanation and instructions?	4	3	2	1
7. Do you like the way we handle your criticisms and our differences?	4	3	2	1
8. Staff and doctor show genuine caring and compassion?	4	3	2	1
9. Do we inspire your trust and confidence?	4	3	2	1
10. Do we allow freedom for you in choosing your options?	4	3	2	1
11. Are we attentive to detail and efficiency?	4	3	2	1
12. How well do we handle our fees and billing procedures?	4	3	2	1
13. Are we available when you need us?	4	3	2	1
14. How do you recommend our quality of care to friends and relatives?	4	3	2	1

Chapter Eight

Growing in

Choice

"I am now giving you the choice between life and death, between God's blessing and God's curse... Choose life" (Deuteronomy 30:19).

Why did I select a picture of a heart on a computer screen to represent this important subject of choice? I can think of no better picture to represent the fact that our choices are made up of two components, head and heart. The computer illustrates the cognitive element of our choices, while the heart portrays the sensitivity that needs to temper our decisions.

Aldous Huxley speaks of our choices as guided by an inward fire:

> The choice is always ours
> ...to tend and feed and fan
> that inward fire
> whose small precarious flame
> kindled or quenched
> creates the noble or ignoble men we are
> the worlds we live in,
> our very fates,
> our bright or muddy stars.

Each of us needs an inner flame that gives us a sense of our destiny. Our destiny is not some mysterious force but is created by our choices. Our choices, either positive or negative, will predetermine our acts, habits, character and destiny.

In order to live a fruitful life, we must learn the necessary processes for making choices toward our desired goals. We each are on a journey to someplace. Whether we actually arrive at our destination will depend upon more than chance or circumstances; the key ingredient will be our choices.

We may be likened to a seafaring sailboat. The winds provide us with power, but the secret of success will be how we set the sails, read the compass, weather the storms and steer the rudder. Also, in every ship there needs to be some weighty center under the water, the keel, to keep us from tilting over or slipping off course. Our lives need a keel like this—the subconscious value systems that bring stability and perseverance to our lives. Many people, however, are unaware that they are drifting from their destiny. Unless they wake up, they will never reach their intended destination.

Airplanes provide a similar analogy. Most people who fly commercially just trust the pilot to make the complicated choices, and we have a high degree of confidence that we'll arrive at our destination, barring a rare mishap. However, private pilots like myself realize the numerous decisions that must be made in order to get off the ground, fly straight, and complete our journey. Flying is an exhilarating experience for me. I get turned on as the endorphins kick in, giving me a high that keeps me coming back in spite of the challenging complexities of flying.

For every flight, the pilot must file a flight plan. This involves making numerous choices, taking into account such things as winds, temperature, weather, fuel, baggage and weight. Preflight inspection is also necessary, requiring many choices necessary for the safety of the plane and its occupants. Once we take off, we make many additional adjustments on the instrument panel, the radios and the communications system. Most of all, we have to choose our compass setting properly, so we can head for our destination. Many planes have auto-pilots which steer by our settings.

In flying, as in all of life, "attitude" is everything. A plane's attitude is defined as the precise angle of attack as it pierces the air. In aviation terms, "angle of attack" is the angle between the ground and the direction of flight. A pilot who ignores the proper attitude of his plane runs the risk of stalls and even death. Whether taking off, flying straight, or landing, a plane's attitude is of the utmost importance. In the same way, setting the attitudes of our hearts is like a plane's auto-pilot that faithfully directs it to its destination.

Attitude is one of several key words that are involved in our choices:

- ▶ Habitudes
- ▶ Heart
- ▶ Decision-making
- ▶ Values
- ▶ Conscience – soul
- ▶ Ethics

Attitude

Pastor and author Charles Swindoll makes this observation about the impact that our attitudes will have on every area of our lives:

The longer I live, the more I realize
the impact of attitude on life.
Attitude, to me, is more important than facts.
It is more important than the past, than education,
than money, than circumstance,
than failures, than successes,
than what other people think or say or do.
It is more important
than appearance, giftedness or skill.
It will make or break a company...a church...a home.
The remarkable thing is, we have a choice every day
regarding the attitude we will embrace for that day.
We cannot change our past...
we cannot change the fact
that people will act in a certain way.
We cannot change the inevitable.
The only thing we can do
is play on the string we have,
and that is our attitude...
I am convinced that
life is 10% what happens to me
and 90% how I react to it.
And so it is with you...
we are in charge of our attitudes.

I define attitude as the powerful, changeable mindset which pre-determines our actions, either to react or respond to circumstances and stimuli. Setting our attitudes is a lot like setting the channels on our TV: Only as we find the proper channel will we get the program and picture we want. Our preset channel numbers will predetermine the programs we receive.

Similarly, the computer mouse and selection keys predetermine our choice of software programs. What goes into the computer is predetermined to also come out, and the same is true of our brains. In both the brain and the computer, the programs can be changed by our choices. Our attitudes and choices are the crucial ingredients in our brain activities and our ultimate lifestyles! We can program success or failure, excellence or mediocrity, positive or negative living, just as we can for televisions and computers.

Attitude: that changeable, reprogrammable, restructurable, renewable pattern of our thoughts, which makes growth possible; the powerful, changeable mindset which predetermines our actions, either to react or respond to circumstances and stimuli.

As in flying and sailing, the secret is in discovering how to create the most effective attitudes. How can we do this? Take a look at the process that determines our destiny:

Our *destiny* is predetermined by our *character.*
Our *character* is predetermined by our *habits.*
Our *habits* are predetermined by our *actions.*
Our *actions* are predetermined by our *attitudes.*
Our *attitudes* are predetermined by our *thoughts.*

Many persons are not aware that their attitudes and their actions are merely reactions to stimuli or circumstances. Their attitudes are set, and something triggers a reaction. Perhaps the reaction is good, but often times it is bad. There is often no choice involved, since attitudes reside in the subconscious. Even though we are not aware of them, our attitudes shape our actions.

The 12 essential inner nutrients of growth (EINGs) are not just a nice theory, they are a very practical and workable model for maturity. Starting with awareness and freedom, the EINGs help us in the construction of healthy attitudes. These attitudes, in turn, enable us to act in a new way. These new actions are characterized by *responding* in an adaptive-proactive way rather than *reacting* without conscious choice.

The EINGs interact to provide us with a framework of action in the circumstances where choice is demanded:

1. Awareness – Become *aware* of our internal and external environment.

2. Freedom – Seize the *freedom* of choice and the other EINGs.

3. Think – *Think* things through and use our intellectual powers to begin programming or reprogramming our thoughts.

4. Feel – Reorganize and manage our *feelings*, allowing the positive emotions to overcome the negative.

5. Desire – Understand what our *desires* and creative imagination see as our destiny.

6. Purpose – Adjust our goals to be in harmony with our *purpose* and the good of others.

7. Priorities – Clearly set down our *priorities* and values, ranking them in order of importance.

8. Choose – With the foundation of the other EINGs, we become free to *choose* from the order of priorities.

9. Act – Once our values and purposes are clear, we can *act* with confidence.

10. Persist – Our actions will not always bring immediate results, and this will leave us with the choice to either *persist* or quit.

11. Response-able – Whether we are able to become *response-able* rather than react/able will be predetermined by our processing of the previous EINGs.

12. Change – We must *change* the programming of our attitudes so we can adapt and grow toward our destiny.

If these EINGs are implemented, we will be empowered to:

1. Make wise choices
2. Get a sense of our destiny and purpose
3. Get a new sensitivity to proper ethics
4. Aspire to harmony, unity and balance in the human family.

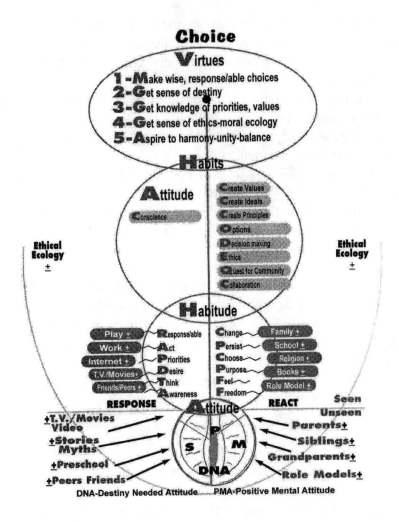

Habitudes

Having the proper habitudes will have a profound impact on our lives. These habitudes can be expected to help us:

1. Create...
    ...values
    ...ideals
    ...principles
    ...conscience.

2. Become aware of options.

3. Make wise decisions, choosing the best options.

Habitude: an attitude in process of becoming a solidified habit.

Conscience

One serious defect in both computers and TVs is that they are lacking in emotion and conscience. Both of these electronic gadgets are intrinsically void of these two great qualities of the human species. Some people, likewise, show little indication of emotion or conscience. Since these positive emotions elevate the human species above all other forms of life, people devoid of emotion are practically in a non-human state. In the same way, conscience is an indispensable quality that unifies the human race and keeps it from total disaster.

Conscience: stemming from two Latin words, con (with) and science (knowledge), this is inner awareness of our passions, perceptions, principles, priorities, purposes and the freedom to choose.

Having previously defined emotions, I would now like to define conscience. Our English word "conscience" comes from two Latin words, *con* (with) and *science* (knowledge). Conscience can be defined as that inner awareness of our...

...passions
...perceptions
...principles
...priorities
...purposes
...and the freedom to choose.

Conscience is an integral part of our soul—a distinctly human characteristic. In order to grow, we must develop an awareness of our conscience, our inner self. Although conscience is developed as a compartment in our brain, it is distinct from such things as our intellect, special senses, and motor skills. Conscience must be learned and developed like any other process of growth, in harmony with the 12 essential inner nutrients.

Conscience gives us our sense of right and wrong. It is the inner flame or inner light often hidden from ourselves and others. It is only when we observe the actions and attitudes of those around us that we begin to understand their conscience. It is an integral part of the soul.

When people speak of "matters of the heart," they ordinarily are not referring to the powerful, pulsating pump in our chest. However, in past centuries people may well have experienced palpitating chest sensations and considered the heart to be the source of passions and feelings. Before the age of modern science, people typically thought that emotions came from various organs below the head, such as the heart, liver, gall bladder or intestines.

When we "speak from the heart," we communicate our passions, emotions, desires, ideals, principles, inner treasures, values, goals, thoughts and attitudes. Instead of originating in our hearts, these expressions come from deep within our brains. Our attitudes and actions reveal what is going on deep in our brain—our conscience.

Although I realize it would be an uphill battle to change this common metaphor, I wish we could find a more accurate description than saying we are speaking from our heart. Though not as poetic, it is certainly more precise to say, "I am speaking person to person from my deepest, most private treasure chest." I view conscience as my "wisdom box." It is something very personal, containing the inner programming of my brain, a product of my learning and growth. It is my character.

As mentioned before, Virginia Satir, in her book, *People Making,* says she thinks of this "wisdom box" as deep inside us, somewhere between the heart and stomach. We can all relate to this in times of deep emotion and expression, saying we feel it "in our guts." As much as these visceral sensations may seem to flow "from the heart," in reality these result from deep within our brain.

Not only do we need to grow intellectually, socially and physically, but our spiritual growth also needs nurturing. This is how we achieve growth, harmony, unity and balance: by controlling our passions and feelings, becoming aware and free to choose, and wisely choosing the ideals and principles that will guide our lives.

Whenever someone talks about matters close to their heart, I try to look to their attitudes and the things in their wisdom box that created those attitudes. When I read in the Scriptures of things relating to the "heart," I again think primarily of attitudes and conscience. A change of heart means a change of attitudes. Jesus spoke very directly to this in Matthew 12:33:

> "Either make a tree good and its fruit good, or else make the tree bad and its fruit bad; for a tree is known by its fruit. Brood of vipers! How can you being evil speak good things? For out of the abundance of the heart the mouth speaks. A good man out of the treasure of his heart brings forth good things, and an evil man out of the evil treasure brings forth evil things."

Negative thoughts make for negative attitudes, actions, habits and processes. As Jesus instructed His disciples, "Where your treasure is, there your heart will be also" (Matthew 6:21).

Choice and change go hand in hand as two of the most powerful processes in human growth. They are the equivalents of the right and left hands working together in unity in order to create a new conscience, attitude, habit, character and destiny. This wonderful capacity for choice and change has been demonstrated in humankind for centuries. These powerful processes are open to anyone who desires to grow and reach full potential.

Values

Industry consultants and authors, Blessing and White, have done extensive studies on the matter of values in the workplace. Their main focus has been the manufacturing sector, and I'm not sure how much they have been called upon by physicians and hospitals for their consulting. However, the health sector has a great need in this area. It is time to clearly consider our value systems and develop corresponding mission statements. At times our individual values will be in conflict with those of others—if, indeed, we feel passionately about them. We will need guidelines about how to resolve these conflicts when they occur.

Blessing and White emphasize the importance of a clear system of values:

> A firm values framework is at the very heart of our making decisions. Without it, we lose confidence in our decisions. People who don't have a values framework tend to be apathetic, indecisive and inconsistent. Our decisions are always based on our beliefs, attitudes and values.

I might add that without a set of values and beliefs a person is flying or sailing without a compass. They don't know where they are or where they are going. Many today are flying upside down, without awareness, as in a cloud with no instruments to tell them which way they are headed.

Values may be defined as what a person (or institution) prizes, places as top worth, and prioritizes in order of importance. Values must be set in many different areas, such as material, spiritual, ideals or goals. Scrutinizing our own values is hard work. As Norman Cousins warns, there are consequences of this quest: "The moment we accept the importance of values in the study and practice of medicine, we also accept an obligation to deal with the philosophical issues."

Values: what a person (or institution) prizes, places as top worth, and prioritizes in order of importance.

Blessing and White, on the other hand, remind us of the benefits of values clarification: "Clarifying personal values is the essential first step toward a richer, fuller, more productive and satisfying life." We may also be compelled to ask, "How can we assist our patients in clarifying *their* values unless we have clarified our *own*?" Many professionals have been oblivious to this wise exercise. "Know thyself" is often quoted from Shakespeare and Socrates, yet it is seldom heeded.

The medical field as a whole would benefit from a clarification of its values, which hopefully would include many of those advocated in this book. True, every physician would have a somewhat different list, and the items would vary in order of importance. However, isn't it possible to find common ground on at least a few important values? Wouldn't our patients appreciate this kind of clarification? Wouldn't both physicians and patients benefit from a quest for universal values?

This is one of my primary objectives in writing this book: to find common values. I shall list some of these considerations, but be assured that many others could be added to the list:

- Excellence – success
- Creativity and growth – 12 EINGs
- Communication
- Conflict resolution – peace – harmony – unity
- Confidence – trust – respect – hope – joy – faith
- Compassion – empathy – caring – sympathy
- Carefulness – risk management
- Concern – service
- Choice – freedom
- Change – flexibility – adaptability
- Control over stress – effective management
- Control over business – management – leadership
- Control in family – unity
- Inner freedom – awareness
- Health
- Relationships – partners with Creator and community
- Effectiveness – power
- Interdependence
- Balance
- Harmony
- Response-ability
- Positive mental attitude

These values comprise a small but high priority list, reflecting issues that should be common ground for both patients and physicians. These are truly powerful treasures, important not only to learn but also to implement. We need only be clear in our perceptions and definitions. Can you list your perceived values? Have you stopped to consider what you treasure the most?

Ethics

This word "ethics" has always been difficult to define. It has a mystical vagueness unless we really study it. Ethics can best be defined as the community collaboration concerning the highest standards of human behavior and moral values; the highest good. Since there is a wide spectrum of personal values in the human race, it follows that there will always be ethical conflicts. In medical practice, for example, we inevitably confront conflicting values on a wide variety of topics. To resolve these issues of differing value systems, a process needs to be developed. This is ethics.

Ethics: the community collaboration concerning the highest standards of human behavior and moral values; the highest good.

John C. Fletcher, Ph.D., has edited two great volumes with the input of a select number of physicians, nurses, lawyers and ethicists. They are a collaboration of medicine, law, religion and social science, along with patients and families who attempt to solve many new ethical controversies involving sickness, treatment or death.

Right and wrong is not always black and white. The struggle to find the highest standard possible is a process of weighing competing priorities and values. There are a number of current areas in medicine that will require the wisdom of Solomon to successfully resolve:

1. Confidentiality and privacy
2. Disclosure
3. Individual capacity
4. Informed consent

5. Refusal of treatment
6. Life-prolonging procedures
7. Death and dying – assisted suicide
8. Abortion – birth control
9. Justice
10. Cost containment
11. Homosexual marriages
12. Population control
13. Capital punishment
14. Censorship

New technologies such as in bioengineering, cloning and genetic testing are adding new and colossal quandaries. We are entering uncharted territories, boldly going where humans have never gone before. Will we be up to the task of sorting out these ethical dilemmas?

Ethical Ecology

I am not raising the subject of ethics in hopes of finding instantaneous answers to these puzzling ethical questions. The answers are likely to require much time and consideration. We must implement sound processes for the resolution of value conflicts, even before they arise.

Ethical logjams are best handled by collaboration rather than legislation. The law books are already filled with plenty of confusing rules and regulations. Legal processes are typically adversarial, but our need is for more mechanisms that can mediate, contemplate and collaborate on these issues. The power of choice is best served when medical minds are married to spiritual principles—those which bring harmony, unity and balance in the family of man.

Ethical ecology: the moral climate, community conscience, and sum total of all forces outside of ourselves—good/evil or positive/negative—which impact our thoughts, behavior, character, growth, harmony, unity and balance in society and the individual.

Often our quest for excellence in the science of medicine is burdened by the tough ethical choices we face. Resolving these issues will require a community conscience and moral environment—what I refer to as an "ethical ecology." This can be defined as the moral climate, community conscience, and sum total of all forces outside of ourselves—good/evil or positive/negative—which impact our thoughts, behavior, character, growth, harmony, unity and balance in society and the individual. Developing this ethical ecology is an uphill battle. In a society flooded with violence and sexual expression on TV, videos, movies and books, it is inevitable that unhealthy attitudes will be created in children and adults with impressionable minds.

It is no coincidence that violence and sexual crimes have multiplied significantly all over the world since the advent of TV, videos and the Internet. If we nurture fantasies of adultery and rape, we are setting ourselves up for a society filled with infidelity and sexual assault. If angry thoughts aren't processed positively, we tend to become violent and uncontrolled in reaction to stress or when under attack. Today's media only fuels this negative fire.

We in the medical profession have a wonderful opportunity to be positive influences in the ethical ecology of our society. While this cultural battle may seem difficult or even hopeless, we should be encouraged by the realization that even a small light can overcome the surrounding darkness. Our small, random acts of kindness and service can create a mighty ripple effect that will positively impact the ethical atmosphere around us.

Sin and Evil

It is beyond the scope of the medical profession to deal with sin and evil. That is best left with the spiritual leaders. However, as we have already seen in this chapter, value systems and choices of the soul are bound together. Doctors deal frequently with people who are loaded down with guilt and other consequences of wrongdoing. This places us in very uncomfortable positions, for our training focused on medical issues, not moral or spiritual ones.

The least we can do is clearly define our own concept of evil and sin. While I would prefer to focus on the positive side of life, it is impossible to ignore the reality of evil. You don't have to be a historian or theologian to conclude that humans are all too prone to choose destructive and sinful ways.

Evil can be defined as any force, attitude or act which violates the harmony, unity or balance in the family of man and our environment. Evil is, by definition, at cross purposes to the amazing plan of our Creator. It unleashes negative forces and processes that oppose the good and positive forces and processes. This war has been waged since the Garden of Eden, when man and woman first became aware of good and evil—and exercised their free will to choose evil.

Sin can be defined as any choice, attitude or action which violates a trusting, positive relationship between persons, our Creator, or our potential for growth. Some acts of sin are blatant violations of trusting relationship, such as disregard of the 10 Commandments. This timeless code of ethics is still well known to many in the modern world. Most physicians are more familiar with the 10 Commandments than with the principles of behavior espoused in the Hippocratic Oath. These are value systems of time-honored, tested truths.

Evil: any force, thought, fantasy or attitude which violates the harmony, unity or balance in the family of man and our environment.

It is my conviction that members of the healing community will best serve our patients if we develop an awareness of proper and improper attitudes. A new oath and commitment to positive attitudes and processes could serve as a guide to higher professional behavior.

Sin: any choice, attitude or action which violates a trusting, positive relationship between persons, our Creator, or our potential for growth.

Moses Maimonides' prayer for guidance in his healing work, written around 1200 AD, seems to me fuller and richer than the Hippocratic Oath. It could serve as a model for composing a twenty-first century commitment by healing practitioners to those who suffer.

> God grant that I may be filled with love for my art and for my fellowman. May the thirst for gain and the desire for fame be far from my heart, for these are the enemies of pity and the ministers of hate. Grant that I may be able to devote myself, body and soul, to Your children who suffer with pain. Preserve my strength that I may restore strength to the rich and poor, good and bad, friend and foe. Let me see in the sufferer the man alone. When wiser men teach me, let me be humble to learn, for the mind of man is so puny and the art of healing is so vast. Let me be intent upon one thing, oh Father of Mercy, to be always merciful to Your suffering children.

There are quite a number of subtle sins which affect our potential for healing, growth and trusting human relationships. I mention only a few which seem to inflict all of us at times:

• Fear	• Gluttony
• Anger	• Hating
• Addictions	• Isolation
• Apathy	• Jealousy
• Arrogance	• Loneliness
• Anxiety	• Self-centeredness
• Lust	• Blaming
• Criticizing	• Defending
• Envy	• Greed

The choice is ours to find a way to replace these negative attitudes and emotions with positive ones. Instead of nursing the negative, we can change the channel, get new headings, set the compass, and flip the switch—all by understanding the processes of choice and change of attitudes. We can put the "heart" in our TV set, our computer, our brain. This is commitment to choice.

Religion

Among physicians and healers there is wide diversity in matters of religion, but healing in medicine is inextricably bound to religion. Religion can be defined as a system of values, traditions and spiritual practices which aspire to the highest good for man, inspired by the Creator of the universe.

In spite of the diverse forms of religious traditions and practices around the world, there are some universal values that the major religions have in common. The all-important thread that binds religious and spiritual minds together is the concept of a Supreme Being, Creator, Master Intelligence or Benevolent Guide. This Being has been referred to with such titles as God, Father in Heaven, Allah and Krishna. Whatever the title may be, nearly all major religions acknowledge that God is love. Difficulties abound, however, when we try to define love and behave in loving ways.

Religion: a system of values, traditions and spiritual practices which aspire to the highest good for man, inspired by the Creator of the universe.

I have worked hard in my medical practice trying to respect the viewpoints of others, especially their religious practices and beliefs. This requires a commitment to facilitate healing and the common good, working for unity, peace and joy for all. Doctors today not only face questions about ancient religious values and truths, but also a vast array of unanswered scientific questions about disease and disease processes. In facing these questions, medical science is enriched by a commitment to spiritual and ethical considerations.

Rather than providing simplistic answers, true religion will enable us to face the difficult ethical dilemmas of our day: genetic engineering, abortion, homosexuality, capital punishment, distribution of wealth, public aid, conservation, environmental purification, etc. Political savvy will not be successful if left to its own uncreative, negative, adversarial processes.

Science needs spiritual wisdom and religion needs scientific enlightenment. Both need the wisdom and simplicity of Albert Schweitzer's famous value system: "reverence for life." This insight came to Schweitzer suddenly, and meant for him that not only human life, but all life on earth, should be respected. Schweitzer, a compassionate physician, was also a noted philosopher, theologian, musician and missionary. Seeking to preserve both the physical and ethical ecology, he realized that this could never be done unless modern knowledge, technology and scientific advances are combined with the wisdom and values of ancient spiritual truths.

We also should be challenged by Immanuel Kant's dictum *"Sapire aude"*—Dare to know. Robert Hilary Kane of Texas University adds a cogent word to Kant: *"Sapire aspirare aude"*—Dare to aspire to know.

Questions for Partners Regarding Choice

1. Does your physician seem to respect and honor your belief systems, values and religious views?
2. Does your physician give you the choice of your specific goals, plans and options?
3. Does your physician give you the choice of consultants?
4. Do you feel unduly pressured to do whatever your physician advises, without question?
5. Do you feel you are offered adequate explanations and options regarding difficult ethical questions?
6. Do you feel freedom to express your own preferences and options?
7. Are the medical options outlined clearly by your physician?
8. Do your physician's "informed consent" procedures respect your choices?
9. Are both the risks and benefits of proposed treatments discussed?
10. Does your physician seem to have a reverence for life?
11. Does your physician give you the option and freedom to change?

12. Do you feel unrestricted in your freedom to choose your insurance plan?
13. Do you have adequate freedom to choose your healthcare providers?

Chapter Nine

Growing in

Change

"Do not be conformed to this world, but be transformed by the renewing of your mind" (Romans 12:2).

There is nothing so constant in life as change. There is also nothing quite so exciting or risky. The universe is filled with the dynamic of motion, energy, rest, growth, decay, creation and restructure. These processes are discovered throughout the microcosm, the orbiting electrons in the atoms undergirding all life and substance.

The same is true in the macrocosm. Change is everywhere, reflected in such things as black holes, the expansion of the universe, dying stars, and similar phenomena. Although these radical changes are beyond our comprehension and awareness, they are occurring each day at a dizzying pace.

Change is also a prevalent force in our social relationships. Our cities, communities and daily lives are regularly confronted with untold trillions of changes. These changes demand an increasing awareness of how we must respond, react, adapt and integrate. The changes we face are often chaotic, unplanned and disorderly. The natural world, by contrast, generally exhibits an amazing orderliness and predictability in its changes. Becoming change-masters in the civilized world involves a challenge to match the model of excellence found in the natural world.

Several key words are involved in this process of change:

▶ Status quo   ▶ Renewal
▶ New possibilities   ▶ Restructuring
▶ New processes   ▶ Transformation

One of nature's most beautiful and inspiring examples of change is the monarch butterfly, which I have chosen for the opening page of this chapter. The life of a monarch begins as a tiny egg fertilized by union of male and female. Eggs are laid under the leaf of a special plant, the milkweed. This one-celled egg grows into an attractive caterpillar with concentric stripes of green, yellow, white and black. Its voracious appetite, feeding on milkweed leaves, reminds me of the feeding of our teenagers till they reach adulthood.

Upon reaching full size, the caterpillar forms a shell around it and attaches itself by a thin stalk to the milkweed. Again, the pupa stage reminds me of an adolescent—with a hard casing on the outside but a mass of soft, jelly-like stuff on the inside. Like a growing teen, the butterfly gradually forms its own identity. It transforms the goo into skeleton, and the intricate parts of a mature butterfly are packed neatly within this chrysalis. After a period of two or three weeks there is a break in the hard shell. The adult monarch emerges and dries its crinkled, unfolded wings. In a couple of hours it flies— another miracle of change. The miracle continues as it instinctively joins other adult butterflies to fly hundreds of miles across uncharted oceans to their destiny—a place they have never been before.

What is so wonderful and mysterious is the innate instinct—creative force—which guides them to an area two miles square in the mountains of Mexico. Similarly, the painted lady butterfly sojourns from California to Hawaii. This miracle of change occurs year after year, perhaps for thousands of millennia.

The processes of change are no less amazing in human growth and development. We change not only physically, but also mentally, emotionally and in our character development. While physical change is a fact of life to be accepted, understood and cherished, character development generally is not so predictable or dependable. Choice and change go hand in hand in determining our character and destiny. It is sad that not everyone is successful in adapting to all of the changes thrust upon them.

In his prophetic book, *Future Shock*, written 20 years ago, Alvin Toffler outlined the enormity of problems we all must face as a result of the accelerating pace of change in our society. The choice is ours whether to simply react to these changes or whether to respond and become response-able. We can view change as either a positive or negative force. We can resist or adapt. We can use change as a force for growth or an excuse for stagnation and decline.

In the practice of medicine there are ever-accelerating changes in scientific knowledge and technology. This requires a constant effort to absorb, adapt and integrate the new. There is a constant need to renew and update our data bank. Right when we think we understand something, new evidence surfaces to change our thinking and approach to a disease.

Not only do we face changes brought by scientific progress, we also are confronted by constant modifications to the healthcare delivery processes. Corporate structures, insurance guidelines, and government regulations change at a frantic and frustrating pace. In both our personal lives and social institutions, we have too often reacted instead of responding to the changes thrust upon us. In order to adapt positively, we must first understand change and the processes necessary for a successful outcome.

To become change-masters who personify the virtues of commitment to innovation, renewing, restructuring and transforming, we begin at the bottom of the growth paradigm. To develop the attitudes which make for success in change, we can begin early in life, even at age six. We must begin with the foundational microprocesses, the 12 essential inner nutrients for growth.

Habitudes of change begin with the *awareness* we all have to change when we:

1. Become aware that something needs to be changed.
2. Freedom to change.
3. *Think* about the possibilities for change.
4. Search our *feelings* as to whether we are ready for change, positive or negative.
5. Clearly define the changes we *desire*, beginning to imagine that the possibilities are a vivid reality.
6. Think about the *purpose* for change, and begin to plan specific goals.
7. *Prioritize* which changes need urgent attention and which can be put on the back burner.
8. *Choose* those changes with deep commitment
9. Begin to *act* according to these priorities and choices.
10. *Persist*, hanging in there regardless of the opposition or difficulties.
11. Have confidence that, having done all the other microprocesses, we can become *response-able* to change, rather than merely reacting.
12. Positive *change* is the outcome—a habitude that occurs when we repetitively engage in these processes of growth.

In their book, *The Leadership Challenge*, Kouzes and Posner provide a great outline of choices and actions which will bring about successful change. They point out five traits of effective leaders:

1. **Challenge the process.** True leaders are not satisfied with the status quo. Restless for change, they are constantly looking for opportunities to grow. They propose new possibilities to make things better, even when risks are involved. Effective leaders avoid being smothered by routine work, and they regularly take time for creative planning.

2. **Inspire a shared vision.** With clear purpose and goals, good leaders create and communicate a shared vision or dream. They have sincere enthusiasm for the vision and are able to inspire commitment in others.

3. **Enable others to act.** Successful leaders realize that their effectiveness is dependent on a team effort. They develop a sense of teamwork and ownership in those around them, always pointing people to their common purpose. As they share information and power, the organization becomes increasingly marked by positive and trusting relationships.

4. **Model the way.** Effective leaders not only have detailed plans, but they also practice what they preach. Their words are matched by their deeds. The organization's values are exemplified in the conduct of its leaders.

5. **Encourage the heart.** It is crucial for leaders to celebrate accomplishments and recognize individual contributions.

With the foundation of the EINGs, we can implement the leadership characteristics suggested by Kouzes and Posner. Some wonderful changes in healthcare delivery systems can evolve if patients and physicians become committed to the processes of change.

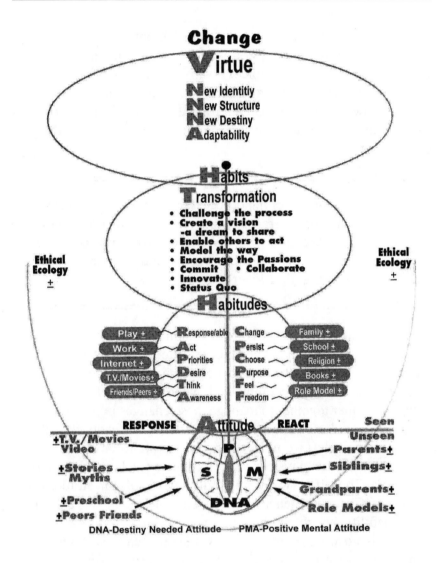

Change

Change can be defined as the powerful process of renewing, replacing, restructuring or transforming, which yields a new direction, identity and destiny. If we can learn to apply the growth paradigm toward change in our personal behavior, we can then apply the same principles to bring transformation in our homes, schools, churches, hospitals and government.

Once we have learned and lived these lessons personally, we will be amazed with the miracles of change possible in our institutions. However, this requires a choice. Positive change only occurs when we make a clear decision to grow. If we merely react, there is usually no growth; if we respond appropriately, there is great potential for growth. That means being committed to excellence in the processes of change.

Change: the faculty of mind necessary to renew or restructure our attitudes, transforming our person into a new identity and direction of growth; the powerful process of renewing, replacing, restructuring or transforming, which yields a new direction, identity and destiny.

Our patients play a vital role in helping us respond to all the changes taking place in the healthcare system. Patients are often the victims of processes that are poorly planned and delivered. But great things can be accomplished when we, as physicians and patients, partner together to manage these changes in positive ways.

Patients can do some things we can't do. Their feedback and participation can help give us power and motivation for change. Their perceptions about a physician's performance can be vital in helping him grow. Too often, we are not fully aware of our attitudes and behaviors. Changes often are needed, but unless someone calls us to accountability, we go on doing things as usual.

There is no way to grow socially and spiritually without undergoing the process of change. If we are truly striving for excellence, we will be *eager* for personal growth. Patients are not aware of how much effort most physicians exert in keeping up in our intellectual growth. Yet, as important as this is, our patients are entitled to something more: They want us to also grow in our capacity for human relationships, our ability to treat them better as persons.

In this joint venture between physicians and patients, we can spur one another toward the possibilities for change. However, one thing must be clear: It is not the patient's responsibility to change his physician. Nor is it the responsibility of a physician to change his patient. Each is responsible for changes within himself. Attitudinal change is an internal mechanism. That is a cardinal principle in this whole process of change. We must change ourselves first and then let the change in our attitudes facilitate the change in others. If we positively restructure our own attitudes, there will be positive results in those around us as well.

Most of us have learned this same lesson as husbands. We have discovered, usually the hard way, that when we set our minds to change our wives the results are disastrous. Likewise, we usually just dig in our heels when our wives try to force us to change. The conclusion is this: If we desire to change any other person, we will be most effective in looking inward to our own attitudes, seeking to change ourselves first. Sometimes the needed change is simply a more empathetic attitude, an openness to listen, or a willingness to forgive.

Not all change is positive. In fact, change for the sake of change is an immature, reactionary position. Change should be directed toward a beneficial purpose: to make things better, adapt, grow, become healed of old hurts, and get closer to our destiny.

Status Quo

There is almost always resistance to change. The status quo is a mighty rock to move out of the pathways of progress and growth. Marcus Aurelias of ancient times recognized this, asking, "Is there any man not afraid of change? Yet what progress can ensue without it? Can anything that is useful be accomplished without change?"

Changing our attitudes often seems about as difficult as moving mountains. Yet, when we become familiar with the processes of change, we can discover the remarkable truth that "if you have faith as a mustard seed, nothing will be impossible" (see Matthew 17:21). The status quo, stubbornly resistant to change, will finally give way to the force of faith and persistence.

James Russell Lowell superbly applied his wisdom to transforming the status quo:

New times demand new measures and new men. The world advances and in time outgrows the laws that in our father's day were best. And doubtless after us some purer scheme will be shaped out by wiser men than we, made wiser by the steady growth of truth. The time is ripe, and rotten ripe, for change. Then let it come!

We all know that our lives could be changed for the better. However, we often lack a clear vision of the specific changes that are needed. In *Man of La Mancha*, Don Quixote says, "Too much sanity may be madness, and the maddest of all is to see life as it is and not as it should be." In a similar thought, George Bernard Shaw relates in *John Bull's Island*, "Some men see things as they are and say, 'Why?' I dream of things that never were and say, 'Why not?'"

A century ago, Dr. William Osler identified some of the necessary elements for positive change to occur. Osler said the progress required "the open mind, the free spirit of science, the ready acceptance of the best from any source, the attitude of rational receptiveness, rather than antagonism to new ideas."

Phil Crosby, a consultant in the manufacturing sector, once made a powerful statement that applies to the changes needed in the healthcare systems: "The culture we now have...we don't need to condemn it...All we have to do is describe the future as we would like to and then march down the yellow brick road." Understanding the power of vision, Crosby points out that there is a road of destiny marked out for us—as the road Dorothy found on her way to the Wizard of Oz.

There may be many things we don't like in ourselves, in others, in our circumstances, or in the practice of medicine. Although some of these things may be impossible to change, we can always change our attitudes. Life involves many choices, but often the only choice available is our choice of attitudes.

M. Goodman's poem is good for all ages in a moment of frustrating circumstance:

Find a Rainbow

It really doesn't matter
If the day is dark or bright,
I can always make it better
If my attitude is right.

Sometimes clouds obscure the sunshine.
That's when faith comes shining through;
For I know there is a rainbow
Just beyond my point of view.

So I've learned to keep on trusting,
Even in the darkest day,
And I always find a rainbow
That can drive the clouds away.

Change can occur even when the 12 microprocesses (EINGs) are not all present. Personal change may be sparked by a role model, a lecture, a line from a book, a sermon, a story, a friend or even a character-building movie. Such things are frequently a catalyst for change, providing new insights and beckoning us toward our destiny. Changing a culture involves a similar process, requiring the changing of our values, desires, thoughts and role models.

Psychologist William James argued, "The greatest discovery of my generation is that human beings can alter their lives by altering their attitudes of mind. If we act as if something is real, something magical will occur—it will *become* real. The matter that we focus our attention on will gain such a connection with our life that it will come to pass, just as we imagined."

In her book, *People Making*, Virginia Satir writes: "There is always hope that your life can change, because you can always learn new things. Human beings can grow and change all their lives. It is a little harder as we grow older, and it takes a little longer. But knowing that change is possible and wanting to do it are the two first big steps." Our mindsets, our mind pathways, and our attitudes can be renewed, restructured and transformed into a new identity and destiny.

Satir aptly likens changing our attitudes and behaviors to the remodeling of old houses. It is amazing how old houses can be transformed by rewiring, new carpet, updated drapes, modern plumbing fixtures, and applying new wallpaper and paint. In the early years of my medical practice, I had the challenge of adapting three old residential houses into my first three offices.

In *Man of La Mancha*, Don Quixote points out that the number one enemy of change is our hard-core self-satisfaction. The status quo in most medical schools prevents them from attempting to teach about proper attitudes. In fact, during my entire schooling, I was never taught about the relationship between attitudes and needed change. Yes, I did have some positive role models in my family, church and schools, but I was never given an understanding of the processes of attitudinal change.

From 1987 to 1992 I taught in the family practice residency-training program at the University of Illinois at Peoria. I was well acquainted with the educational processes in the program to train physicians: hard-stuff knowledge and technology dominated the curriculum. Behavioral scientists, rather than doctors, tried to address the residents' attitudes and need for personal changes. The curriculum was too filled with technical knowledge to have time to address the processes of needed attitudinal changes. In fact, there was an expressed opinion that attitudes, values and character could not be taught.

At the same time, many negative, maladaptive attitudes were visibly apparent, but they were allowed to slip by. We really didn't know "how to" change these young physicians' attitudes or show them the necessary processes for change. Nor could we equip them to help their patients who had negative attitudes.

I found this situation frustrating. Some of the residents had attitudes that predictably would impair their success. Some of the attitudes may even have resulted in a danger to the public. These residents were, however, passed on through the system and graduated. They were deemed ready for practice, simply because they had sufficient knowledge to pass the written exams. Character growth was not an issue in this training, nor would it be a goal for physicians after they began the rigors of practice.

Education is a lifelong process. True education brings change in our intellectual, social and spiritual dimensions. Most of our educational programs are just that—a program, ending with a diploma. Those who strive for excellence, on the other hand, will continuously pursue intellectual and character growth. A wise philosopher said, "When you are through changing, you are through"! Wilferd Peterson writes in his book, *The Art of Living Day by Day*:

Change is life's makeup artist. Our faces are changed according to the experiences and influences we seek, the manner of our day by day living, the quality of our thoughts and emotions, the way we respond to crises and challenge, the dreams and ideals we strive toward, the spirit in which we meet suffering and defeat. We are responsible for our faces.

The countenance of our face reflects our soul, attitudes, wisdom and commitment to change. We always have the freedom to choose our attitudes, restructuring them in a way that transforms our direction, identity and destiny.

Medical Licensing Boards

During my 48 years in the practice of medicine, I have seen numerous ideas, actions, organizations and government regulations intended to improve the quality of medicine. Since the Flexner Report in 1910, state medical licensing boards were created to legislate the safe practice of medicine for the public. The Flexner Report succeeded in awakening the public to the poor practices of medicine at that time.

The list is long of organizations—state, federal and private— whose existence is devoted to improving the quality of physicians and hospitals. They have helped increase the quality of medical practices and standards over the years. However, while medical care in America deservedly enjoys a sterling reputation throughout the world, most medical practitioners agree that changes still need to be made. Yet, the needed changes will not come about because of further rules and regulations. Instead, we need new processes in our medical schools, residency programs, and credentialling bodies. These new processes will recognize that a diploma and certification by a school, state or specialty board does not necessarily indicate competence or excellence.

Ultimately, the power to change the quality of medical care rests with the *attitudes* of physicians, nurses, hospital employees, and other healthcare workers. This can result in excellence, though not perfection. The public's expectation of perfection is not only unrealistic, but it promotes adversarial situations. Instead of being adversaries, patients and members of the medical profession must become partners in nurturing character growth. This is the only road to true accountability and excellence.

When I served on the medical licensing board of Indiana, I discovered that most states have a statement in their rules and regulations that a physician "shall be of good moral character." However, the legal system is incapable of defining "good moral character." Consequently, there is no way to enforce that most important determinant of the excellence to which we aspire.

Licensing boards have many hurdles to overcome in achieving their objective of trying to enforce excellence in the medical profession. They are constrained by a lack of funds, personnel and time. With legal processes guided by an obsession with "individual rights," the medical licensing boards often fail to prosecute physicians who have obvious attitudinal and character disorders.

In their defense, the licensing boards are hampered by our present adversarial legal processes. As a result, very few physicians who need character and attitudinal restructure are adequately confronted. Even when much public grief and dissatisfaction has been caused, only a few of the offending physicians are censured, suspended or have licenses taken away. Usually such discipline only occurs when there has been a clear violation of laws, rules or regulations. This leaves many attitudinal problems unresolved.

The public must see the folly of relying on legislation, rules and regulations to inspire excellence on matters of character. Heaven forbid that legislators ever be given the power to mess with our minds. But to whom is the physician accountable then? I say to our patients—our partners who know us well: "Observe our behavior and attitudes." Unfortunately, this partnership is generally not strong, accountable or effective in America today. Yet this is the last hope of bringing about excellence in medicine.

Excellence cannot be defined or learned except in the context of character change and growth. We must restructure, renew and transform our thoughts, feelings, desires, purposes, priorities, choices and actions. This brings us right back to the growth paradigm for change, a venture that is both spiritual and social in nature.

Report Cards

Can physicians be changed by giving them report cards? Some managed care and governmental systems are advocating that. Though it sounds like a good idea, something about it makes me shudder. I am concerned about what data is being used, who is accumulating it, and the question of whether a simple grade reflects the complexity of a physician's character and performance.

While the idea of getting feedback is important for nurturing a physician's sensitivity to his patients, most questionnaires for patient satisfaction are far too simple to be of real value to patients in evaluating physicians. I have devised a patient satisfaction questionnaire that I regularly use in my office, chiefly for the purpose of getting ideas for growth and making things better in my office. It is a useful tool that invites my patients to help me improve my services. I am grateful to the patients who have carefronted me when I haven't lived up to their expectations. These experiences have been a great source of growth.

However, constructive patient feedback is altogether different from a report card that comes from an insurance company, HMO or governmental agency. Such a report card, based on organizational mechanisms rather than relationships, would be reprehensible to me. There are too many conflicts of interest. Credentialling based only on financial considerations is already rampant in many health-care delivery systems. Many physicians who practice with excellence are being denied positions in managed care systems because they aren't sufficiently productive, efficient or income-generating to satisfy the business managers. All too often, profit motives such as these override considerations of service and excellence.

Accountability

Change is possible only when we are in a relationship that holds us accountable to indications of change. It may be a generation or two before patients realize the power they have in bringing us physicians up to standards of excellence. For too long we have expected the state or federal government to devise legislation to achieve excellence. The sacred doctor-patient relationship must regain its trust and enormous value by partnering—not by legislation.

Doctors should be primarily accountable to their patients, not government, insurance companies, or HMOs. Only the patients can help doctors preserve the long tradition of serving with excellence. There is no way that healthcare providers can achieve this excellence without the help of the patients. We need partnering—not patient adversaries.

We physicians, however, must provide the leadership for partnering. Though our patients play a crucial role, we doctors must provide the inspiration to change our processes. We should empower our patients to do what we can't do. For too long we have used our authority and position arrogantly, without recognizing the vital role of the patient.

Where a partnership lacks trust, the parties will continually be wary or on the defensive. As we do in our families, we who are healthcare providers need to build trust through regular collaboration with our patients. We need to be aware of the forces and factors that weaken partnership, accountability and growth.

Most physicians enjoy and take pride in their profession, serving their patients for cures, healing and help with difficult circumstances such as sickness, sorrow, stress, pain and brokenness. However, we are weary of the legal processes which penalize the entire profession. These processes are intended to address a small minority of healthcare providers—the rotten apples, who behave badly because of negative attitudes or serious character defects. Certainly every doctor, being human, will be in need of some kind of attitude adjustment from time to time. However, is the legal system our only redress for accountability in such situations? To this I soundly say no, it doesn't have to be.

Together, and only together, we can come up with new systems and processes of how we change our minds, relationships and practices. Aldous Huxley poetically spoke of changing "our very lives and fates, our bright or muddy stars." Following principles such as those Kouzes and Posner have suggested, health delivery in America can be radically changed for the better.

Let's respond—not react—to all the changes clamoring around us. Let's become change masters. As someone has well said, "Changing things is mighty risky, but not changing things is worse—that is, if you can think of something better to change to."

Power Questions for Partners

1. Are we responders rather than reactors, having a positive mental attitude when faced with change?

2. Are we encouraging each other to new possibilities for change and growth?

3. Are we keeping up with the changes in our society?

4. Do we provide for adequate collaboration with partners about what needs changing?

5. Is there evidence of a desire for innovation and successful risk management?

6. Is there a freedom to acknowledge mistakes and learn by them?

7. Is there evidence of flexibility and adaptability in new situations?

8. Is there evidence of efforts to continuously make things better—to improve the processes?

9. Is there a vision to meet changing needs and circumstances?

10. Is there a clear statement of missions, values, and goals which bring about changes?

11. Is there an enthusiastic commitment to change?

Chapter Ten

Growing in

Control Over Stress

*"We are greater than anything
that can happen to us.*

— Anonymous

We live in one of the most stressful periods in history. Because of this, understanding and controlling stress is one of the most crucial tasks of both physicians and patients. Failure to master this area will result in negative consequences to our physical, emotional, social and spiritual health.

What does it mean to gain control over stress? Controlling stress can be defined as managing the thoughts and circumstances which challenge us to adapt either positively and pro-adaptively, or negatively and maladaptively. An important part of our medical practices is consumed with evaluating how stresses impact our bodies, social interactions, and living conditions.

In medical school we studied a great deal about the processes of stress and disease. Specifically, we learned about the chemical changes that are triggered by stress. This field was pioneered by Dr. Hans Selye, whom I call the father of stress understanding and management. His inspirational book, *Stress Without Distress,* was written in 1974, near the end of his life.

Controlling stress: managing the thoughts and circumstances which challenge us to adapt either positively and pro-adaptively, or negatively and maladaptively.

Selye's book stemmed not only from his huge scientific understanding, but he also spoke very personally about how to apply the principles of stress management to our behavior. His book is even more relevant today than when it was written. Even though our scientific knowledge has expanded greatly in the past 25 years, we are all still groping for a better understanding of how to take control over our thoughts and circumstances—so that they don't control *us*.

As a family practitioner, dealing with stress is a part of almost every patient encounter. Whether physician or patient, we all have stresses in one form or another. Physicians are called upon to help patients and their families manage a long list of circumstances that commonly trigger excessive stress:

- Death
- Divorce
- Marital conflict
- Financial distress
- Job changes
- Child behavior problems
- Sleep deprivation
- Lack of energy
- Separation
- Sexual difficulties
- Conflict in the workplace
- Chemical dependency
- Isolation and loneliness
- Over-commitment
- Poor nutrition
- Worries, anxieties

While excessive stress can be destructive, we need to recognize that there are also many positive, exhilarating, stressful experiences that add joy and spice of life:

- Marriage
- Work promotions
- Graduation
- Helping a neighbor
- Holidays and vacations
- Geographical moves
- Birth of a new baby
- Community involvement

Our patients may wonder what kinds of stresses we physicians have, and how we are managing them. As a teacher in a medical school for five years, I observed that medical students, residents and physicians are generally left to their own devices in this area. Yes, there was token appreciation that becoming a physician involved unique stresses. However, we needed vastly more understanding of *how* to manage our own stress and help our patients manage theirs.

Many medical students and practicing physicians have not yet mastered or taken control over the stresses of their own lives. Patients are often unaware of these stresses, thinking that doctors must have a pretty easy life. However, physicians face some unique stresses, and here are a few cogent examples:

1. *The adversarial climate of legal processes in our society.* The legal profession has spawned a plethora of laws and legal processes that intimidate the entire medical community. Doctors are perceived as "deep pockets," easily vulnerable to claims of "malpractice." Few people realize that 90% of all malpractice claims against doctors are frivolous and have no basis for recompense.

I know that *most* lawyers are good people; not all are intentional shysters. However, the system and processes in which they operate tend to make their lives focused on winning the case at any cost, regardless of the merit of their client's claim.

Will this ever change? Not likely, since exorbitant money is to be gained in a system where legal fees are not limited by law. Contingency fees are still attractive motivators, and it will be an uphill battle to change our state and federal laws to bring some sanity to this situation.

This litigious climate has been the source of considerable stress in the lives of physicians, hospitals and the entire medical community. Many physicians have quit their medical practice or retired early because of the enormous fears engendered by this hostile atmosphere—not to mention the high premiums for malpractice insurance. It is no wonder that malpractice premiums have soared, since few physicians have avoided being dragged through the legal morass at one time or another. Even though 90% of the stressful legal ordeals are decided in favor of the physician, an enormous price is nevertheless paid: emotional distress and a waste of valuable time, money and resources.

In the name of "free rights," America has weakened its moral fiber by providing a nearly unlimited license to sue. As has been done in England and many other countries, there should be severe consequences for those who make frivolous claims. Certainly there should be just recompense for patients who have been wrongfully treated or truly the victims of negligence. However, patients need to understand that bad outcomes are found every day in medical practice. Most of these occur under the best medical care that can be provided. Sadly, though, many patients or family members have unrealistic expectations, assuming that all poor outcomes are the result of incompetent treatment. People sometimes die in spite of having received excellent medical care.

2. *The plethora of governmental regulations.* Coding has come about since that onerous day in October 1984 when our government initiated "DRG"—diagnostic related groups. These were new rules legislated to control costs and put the brakes on spiraling fees for hospitals and physicians. Unfortunately, the regulations had many unforeseen negative consequences. The complexity of coding and reimbursement has become an enormous and stressful burden on physicians and hospitals. The government has focused on trimming the fees of doctors and hospitals as if that is the *only* way to trim the budget.Our patients usually have no idea how difficult it is to deal with the 100,000 different diagnostic codes and procedure numbers now required in order to get insurance reimbursement. The public would be astonished to see how thick and ludicrously complex the code books are. Sometimes I have shown these to patients who want to understand the stresses and frustrations encountered by today's doctors.

This onslaught of administrative complexity has tended to dehumanize the art of medicine—reducing physicians to the level of artists who paint by numbers. The intimidating government rules and regulations have made it very difficult to practice medicine with the freedom to concentrate on the patient. This stress has caused many physicians to give up medicine and has discouraged young people from pursuing medical careers. Many have been dissuaded from going into medicine, because they've heard doctors' frustrations echoed in homes, hallways and highways. Meanwhile, increasing numbers of young people see the legal profession as the last bastion of freedom from excessive governmental control.

3. *Managed care.* When first inaugurated, managed care seemed to be a great idea and noble experiment in America's healthcare delivery system. Now, however, it is apparent that it has created a monster—a system that often appears to be on the edge of collapse. In recent years managed-care companies have been formed by the hundreds, offering American consumers and industry a highly touted cost-containing system of care. Many of these organizations have become gigantic. While creating an enormous administrative infrastructure, they have cut the income of those who actually provide the medical care—physicians and hospitals.

There have been many unfortunate consequences of this experiment. Patients have been deprived of their choice of physicians and hospitals, hospital days have been cut too short at times, physicians have been removed from the decision-making processes, preventive care has been only half-heartedly pursued, and the overall healthcare system has been dehumanized. Total commitment to preventive care by patients, physicians, hospitals, insurance companies, and government is the only sure way to keep long-term medical costs from escalating. Managed care makes sure that we continue to reward careless people by insuring them regardless of their lifestyles.

4. *Unrealistic expectations of patients regarding the standard of perfection for healthcare professionals.* We might well celebrate the beauty and perfection in the works of creation—in nature and the universe. We can stand in awe, wonder and great reverence before the majesty of the natural world. However, patients make a colossal mistake when they regard their physicians, or any human, with this kind of accolade. No matter how knowledgeable or careful we are, we are human and will make mistakes and errors in judgment. The art of medicine is limitless in its scope and knowledge, and no one can claim complete mastery of its complexity.

5. *Stresses within the medical community.* While many people feel stressed out in our fast-passed society today, physicians face a variety of situations that are uniquely stressful:

- Long and irregular hours, with particular risks of sleep deprivation to interns, residents and medical students.
- Over-commitment to medical practice, with disregard to the needs of our family, friends and personal growth.
- Lack of autonomy to make decisions, especially with managed care and government regulations.
- Lack of behavioral skills or training in conflict resolution.

For centuries there have been turf wars and competitiveness in the medical field. Especially in academia, there are interdepartmental and intradepartmental conflicts which are managed on a primitive level. Conflict resolution skills are not modeled or taught in medical schools or any training program. This lack of attention to relational skills is reflected both in the conflicts that arise with our patients and in the flawed peer-review mechanisms we use.

My paradigm for control over stress is constructed in conjunction with the other basic commitments to growth. As we become aware of the process of control over stress, we will adapt positively, becoming pro-adaptive rather than reactive.

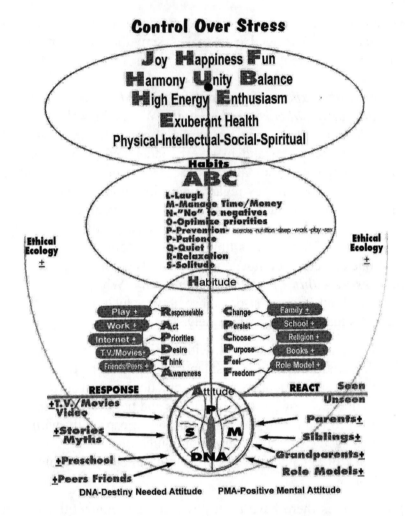

Hundreds of thoughts, circumstances, events, persons and influences impact our lives. These have a potential for either good (positive) or bad (negative) consequences. Yet the outside circumstances or influences aren't what makes the real differences in our lives—it is our attitudes in response. It is how we handle the influences that come our way. The difference is in our decisions, how we process our thoughts, perceptions and circumstances.

You, the patient, can help us physicians grow in our stress-management skills. This will happen as you consider this paradigm of the process. In particular, we need to agree on several statements:

1. Stress and problems are not necessarily our enemies, but rather are essential for growth. Every adversity or stress presents us with the potential for either growth or demise.

2. We all have enormous powers for handling stress. Instead of seeing ourselves as helpless victims, we need to realize our potential to be overcomers.

3. Outward circumstances and stressful situations do not determine our destiny. The key is how we process these situations internally, restructuring our attitudes toward the stressful events and thoughts.

4. Successful outcomes are most likely to occur when we employ positive thoughts and processes. Adversity often requires changes, and the more positive our attitudes are, the more positive the changes will be. Although it is sometimes appropriate to simply react to danger, fear or calamity, we will be better served by learning to respond in positive ways.

All forms of life originate from a seed. From the initial seed, growth occurs, which requires a continuous internal restructuring of our attitudes. The above paradigm shows the growth processes required in our attitudes if we are to successfully manage the stress in our lives.

This internal restructuring begins with a choice of whether to react or respond. If we react, it will be either by *fight* (striking back) or *flight* (removing ourselves from the event or situation). On the other hand, if we choose to respond and become ***response-able*** (EING #11), we use our analytical powers to get a clear perception of the circumstance or stimulus. We recognize the enemy. We read books, prepare pro-con lists, and take other actions that promote health and growth.

Next, we get in touch with ***feelings*** (EING #4). We begin the healing processes, especially with our support systems in family, friends and counselors. We work through the anger, bargaining and denial, accepting the stress as a fact to process. The successful culmination of this process is that we will become victorious over stress.

In our ***desire*** (EING #5), we begin to visualize the desired outcome, beginning to see some possibilities for our good regardless of the outward circumstances. A glimmer of hope will creep in, and we may well find that adversity, sickness, loss, pain or brokenness have stimulated us to a new lease on life. This new *purpose* (EING #6) may be different than our previous purposes, but it will be a wonderful development, the result of positive growth.

A tragic happening in our life, such as an accident, sickness, earthquake, flood or tornado, will often give us pause to reexamine our *priorities* (EING #7). As some of the things we have treasured are lost, perhaps we will come to see it as good riddance—a blessing in disguise. At any rate, setting priorities is essential for growth in stress control.

Continually *choosing* (EING #8) those priorities will guide our actions and spell out our future happiness. Positive choices must lead to positive *actions* (EING #9). We must devise a specific plan of action for handling stress. This means being pro-adaptive, organizing the things we can so that negative stress is minimized. This is shown by my "LMNOPPPQRS" outline in the previous paradigm.

Persistence (EING #10) is often overlooked in our quest to handle stress. One of the greatest positive attitudes in fighting disease is to never give in to an adverse diagnosis or stress. None of us has the wisdom or knowledge of how to overcome every negative circumstance, but there is a providential wisdom higher than ours. Keeping a hope-filled attitude—persisting with all our strength—is the surest predictor of success in dealing with stress.

After we employ all the other essential inner nutrients for growth, we are well on our way to becoming *response-able* people who can manage stress (EING #11). This inevitably brings about positive *change* (EING #12) in our identity, direction and destiny

Resources and Plans

There are many excellent books that can activate and facilitate our ability to control stress. Some of the books apply to specific kinds of stress-filled circumstances. Daily actions are prescribed that will create positive habits and reinforce attitudes conducive to growth.

Nathan, Staats and Rosch compiled many "how to's" in *A*

Doctor's Guide to Instant Stress Relief. Dr. Paul J. Rosch was the dean of the American Institute of Stress. This book has a marvelously simple biofeedback tool to identify and reduce our levels of stress.

Dr. Peter Hanson, a family practitioner, has had a very special interest in stress management. His book, *Stress for Success,* followed his first book, *The Joy of Stress.* In both books he offers some very practical, positive plans for choosing a successful outcome over stress and adversity.

Managing stress, however, requires more than some kind of simple 1-2-3 formula. Each person must dig, devise and defend his own plan of action. A lot of the tranquilizers, anti-depressants and anxiolytics prescribed today would become unnecessary if specific stress-management plans were implemented. I have devised such a plan for myself, and I believe that it would prove useful to others who are pursuing control over stress. In a nutshell, my plan involves cultivating the habits of joy and equanimity (peace of mind).

My paradigm (on a previous page) involves the following powerful habits designed to help us achieve our desired outcome in managing stress:

L - laugh
M - manage time, money and circumstances
N - say no to negatives
O - "optionize" priorities
P - prevention
     nutrition
     exercise
     rest
     work
     play
     sex
P – pro-adaptive
P - patience
Q - quiet
R - relax
S - solitude
S - success (positive mental attitude)

Laugh. Norman Cousins, the author of *Anatomy of Illness,* recounts his experience with laughter, which he gives a large measure of credit for his recovery from a serious illness. Medical literature is quite clear that the laughter-induced endorphins liberated in the brain affect the immune system "T cells" in a positive manner. Laughter also puts things into perspective and often can lift our attitudes out of depression.

Manage. Our time, money and circumstances are all precious gifts that must be carefully managed. In his book, *Margin,* Dr. Richard Swenson has given us great pause to rethink our margins in time, money and many other areas. This incisive book is valuable in helping us to get the stress of time and money pressures off our backs. We physicians, like many of our patients, tend to get over-committed in both time and money, leaving very little of either left for family, friends, living and growing.

No. We need to say no to the many negatives that surround us in our society, our families and our workplaces. Negative influences permeate much of today's TV and other media. Our culture has been twisted by such things as pornography, gambling, chemical dependency, violence, dishonesty and other forms of moral deviance. However, if we keep thinking, identifying, championing and engaging in the positive, healthy, growth-inspiring stimuli, we will eliminate a huge amount of the stress we would otherwise incur.

"Optionize." Identifying and choosing the best of our options is a continuous process and is a crucial part of simplifying our lives. We need to take time to consider what we really treasure, value most, and are committed to. This should be where we spend the majority of our time and money. If we choose wisely, our lives will be much less stressful. That's the way of success: constantly growing and seeking excellence in every area of our lives.

Prevention. Though I have mentioned its importance throughout this book, preventive care deserves more detailed emphasis and explanation. In fact, an entire book could be written to explain the basic concepts of how to fix our healthcare system through preventive medicine. If you closely study my paradigm of "Integrated Care," you will see the 10 big killers that are responsible for millions of dollars in our nation's budget. Note that stress is just *one* of the enemies of health that waste our hard-earned dollars.

The most effective way to contain escalating costs in medical care is by empowering people to become response-able for their health. In contrast, our present insurance system actually *rewards* people for poor choices in their lifestyles. Too many people fail to care for themselves, yet expect physicians and insurance companies to fix their resulting problems. If people would take preventive maintenance of their bodies as seriously as they do their cars, healthcare costs would plummet.

Family physicians have been preaching prevention for years, but many patients are still not motivated to change their lifestyles. Why should they? Insurance pays the bills even when the costs stem from largely avoidable factors such as obesity, lack of exercise, smoking, excess alcohol, poor nutrition, or carelessness in sex.

Many diseases are preventable. Patients often suffer unnecessarily, because of their own misdeeds or negligence. Despite talk of a "Patient's Bill of Rights," legislators have not been committed to empowering people to exercise their response-ability to choose preventative behaviors. Our national healthcare is geared for *crisis* care, which is always more expensive. The old adage is true: "An ounce of prevention is worth a pound of cure!" The modern version of this could be stated: "Prevention Pays—Crisis Care Costs."

Are legislators fearful of calling the public to accountability in doing all they can to prevent illness? How can we change our lazy and shortsighted philosophy of assuming "Insurance will take care of it"? Insurance is not the answer! The only real way to achieve cost containment is to bring about a national change in attitude toward prevention. By fixing that attitude we will, in a large measure, fix our spiraling healthcare costs.

The 10 big killers—hypertension, cardiovascular disease, cancer, accidents, poor nutrition, chemical dependency, allergies, stress, diabetes, infections—can be cost-contained only if physicians and patients are highly committed to prevention. This will require insurance companies and government agencies to enact new policies that are geared to making prevention pay. Together we can make patients aware of how lifestyle changes can help prevent these 10 monstrous killers from devouring our healthcare resources.

• *Nutrition* – Nutrition in America is astonishingly poor, even in sectors where there is no financial reason for sub-standard diets. Teenagers, of course, head the list, but they are not the only ones whose diet is undermining their health. We could also mention business people who are too busy to eat right, obese people who eat too much of the wrong things, and the elderly who live alone.

Poor nutrition is not readily identified in our patients unless we request a food diary. In my years of practice it has become apparent to me that the "Mediterranean Diet," advocated by Dr. Walter Willette of Harvard University, is extremely helpful to most patients. Numerous illnesses, diseases and conditions are directly or indirectly related to a poor diet, and Dr. Willette's diet is my ideal for most people. Untold billions of dollars could be saved in the healthcare industry if people would just eat right.

• *Exercise* – The body tends to deteriorate if we do not regularly engage in vigorous activity. Countless problems are encountered by those who insist on continuing a sedentary lifestyle. Weakness, apathy, depression, high blood pressure, coronary artery disease, obesity, diabetes, cancer and many other conditions are often prevented or mitigated by vigorous exercise. The health and vigor of every organ in the body is positively impacted by regular, vigorous physical activity.

Dr. Ken Cooper's books about aerobics have inspired me and millions of other Americans to undertake a program of regular exercise. Cooper has given us the confidence that exercise and healthy lifestyles could make coronary artery disease an historical event relegated to the 20th century. This major scourge in America could be phased out of existence if we were merely willing to make changes in our lifestyles. Although it is tempting to blame insurance companies or healthcare providers for spiraling healthcare costs, the biggest culprit is simply the failure of consumers to embrace basic preventive measures.

• **Rest** – Insomnia and sleep deprivation are responsible for billions of dollars in healthcare costs. Numerous accidents on the highway, in the workplace and in the home can be attributed to sleep deprivation. We all need differing amounts of sleep, but physicians, residents, medical students, nurses, truck drivers, and adolescents are among the millions who typically don't get enough rest for their bodies. Although it is hard to accurately estimate the scope of this problem, it seems to me to be huge. This adds considerable amounts of stress to our lives, often unnecessarily. The situation is not made any better by the many enticements that keep us up at night and blur the value of a good night's rest—things like TV, videos, overtime, and three-shift work schedules. And, for many who live in apartments or college dorms, it isn't easy even to find a quiet place to sleep.

• **Work** – Unhealthy stress can result from either overwork or too little work. Both are serious issues in our society today. Unemployment is the source of great stress for approximately 4% of our population. On the other hand, however, workaholism is also a serious problem and is very much a part of our American ethic. In nearly every profession, we champion a workload that seems beyond reasonable limits. Workers often accept this as "normal," particularly because they crave the money, luxuries and sense of achievement that come as a result.
The European view of work is generally much different. Europeans tend to value a more relaxed atmosphere, with more time for vacations and recreation. In America the joy of life is too often wet-blanketed by excessive work expectations, which create undeserved stress, brownout, burnout and premature retirement.

• **Play** – Carl Sandburg once said, "It's not bad if one can grow old with a boy's heart." Although many books have been written on the value of play, we each have a different idea of what it is. Ideally, play is the time we take to recreate our energies and get a break from our work. We all need diversions. Unfortunately, much of our playtime is passive—TV, movies and spectator sports.

Happy is the person who has a hobby and is active in the pursuit of creating something beautiful or useful. Many people find great pleasure and renewal in their yards, gardens, workshops, crafts, paintings, crocheting, square dancing, singing, musical instruments or travel. Such "playful" activities are a great way to maintain our youthfulness, no matter what age we are.

• *Sex* – Although I could well have discussed sex in the context of play and recreation, it deserves some special consideration. Many volumes have been written to share its power in stress management. The *Gift of Sex* and *Restoring the Pleasure* by Clifford and Joyce Penner have done an outstanding job of putting sex in the proper perspective. While people often come to their physician with sexual problems, the real difficulty usually stems from relationship issues. Most sexual dysfunction is not a matter of physical limitations but rather a lack of communication and an inability to have a good clean fight.

Sex, in its loftiest expression, can only be attained by developing good partnerships: building unity, harmony and balance in sex and all of life. Sex is meant to be a fulfilling act of devotion and mutual satisfaction. On the other hand, an act of solitary sexual satisfaction brings only momentary pleasure, with no lasting joy. Solitary sex is stressful sex, lacking the joy and fulfillment of true intimacy.

Pro-adaptive. Stephen Covey, in his book *Seven Habits of Highly Effective People*, has defined the word proactive and explored its dynamic powers to impact personal and corporate habits. Most stress in interpersonal relationship would be preventable if we understood the process of becoming pro-adaptive instead of reactive. Becoming response-able, in my view, is similar to Covey's wonderful treatment of becoming pro-adaptive and responsible. These are fairly mature habits, achieved by many of us only after years of trying.

Pro-adaptive: a positive manner of adjusting to circumstances, responding rather than reacting.

How many marriages, partnerships and corporations would be less stressful if the persons involved would clearly define and share their unique perceptions, passions, needs, wants, principles, priorities and purposes? We can only understand the processes needed to get along in our relationships if we grasp this concept of being proactive and response-able. It takes much communication and empathy to understand each other's viewpoints. We don't have to let circumstances or events control our relationships. We have the power to stay on top of potentially disruptive circumstances.

Patience. Although this virtue is a time-tested stress reliever, it is sometimes hard to know when and how to apply it. The patience of Job is a renowned testimony of enduring hardships we are unable to prevent or do anything about. Likewise, Reinhold Niebuhr's "Serenity Prayer," quoted in a previous chapter, is a great stress reliever.

Quiet. Our immediate environment is often polluted with noise levels that are stressing our ears into premature deafness. Blaring radios, TVs, concerts, traffic noises, sweepers, machines, airplanes, crowds, factories, chain saws, sports events, and motor boats—these are only a few of the numerous sources of high noise levels in our society. This is stressful, even more so than we typically realize. The stress from excessive noise is not just a matter of annoyance to our ears, but it also has a profound effect on our nervous system and spiritual well-being. We need to seek relief.

Quietness is an essential ingredient in bringing our stressed-out nervous systems into true peace of mind and tranquillity. Where in our large cities can a person go to just enjoy the peace that comes from quietness? Even our hospitals, places where people go to find healing, are often affected by "noise pollution" from TV sets and noisy visitors. Not enough consideration is given to individuals who are seriously ill and in need of peace and quiet.

Personally, I have chosen to live on a farm. The quietness I experience there is a powerful anti-stress measure, very valuable to my own emotional health. After listening to complaints and problems all day, it is wonderful to let my trees talk to me, very quietly and in sweet, soothing noises.

Relaxation. Herbert Benson, M.D., has written the book, *The Relaxation Response.* which has gained wide acceptance in both medical circles and the lay press. The value of relaxation as an anti-stress measure has been known for years. However, it is easier to talk about relaxation than to achieve it.

Relaxation is a process of letting the tension out of mind and body. There is no question that the mind and body function more efficiently in a relaxed state. Relaxation techniques are now being taught in medical schools, something completely absent during my early medical training.

Hypnotism, though controversial to some, is probably the best technique to achieve a fully relaxed body. I first learned of the art and science of hypnosis under Dr. Milton Erickson in 1956. I was astonished to discover the enormous powers in the subconscious mind. Despite the amazing human potential that hypnosis can unlock, it took someone of Dr. Erickson's abilities to lead it out of the Dark Ages and into acceptance by the AMA in 1956. Hypnosis still is not a valued part of medical training today, but in my opinion it should be. Both medical practitioners and patients need to recognize it as one of the most powerful therapies to relieve the tensions and stresses that often cause illness.

Solitude. This condition, like quietness, is often difficult to find in our modern culture. Solitude should not be confused with loneliness. While solitude, or aloneness, is a valuable stress-relieving discipline, loneliness is a great source of distress to countless millions. Each of us would be wiser and stronger if he had a period of solitude each day, a get-away from the tensions and pressures of life. This could be a time to seek one's personal identity, asking questions such as:

1. Who am I?
2. Where am I going?
3. What is my purpose for living?
4. What are my values, interests and feelings?
5. What are the powers that propel me?
6. Who are my real companions and friends?

Seeking Spiritual Powers

As much as we as medical practitioners might try to offer excellent medical care, our own healing powers are clearly limited. We and our patients are wise to recognize the power of prayer as a source of comfort, strength and relief from stress. Billions of people of all faiths in the world's living religions have used prayer to change their attitudes in meeting stressful circumstances. Yet in most medical schools no one dares even to talk about prayer, in spite of its practice by many physicians in private. For some, it just doesn't seem to fit in with the science of medicine.

When will medical schools teach the science of prayer along with the science of medicine? Although this has been slow in coming, I sense that we are now on the verge of fantastic new discoveries in the spiritual power and discipline of prayer. Already, it now seems to be more acceptable in many circles for physicians to openly pray with patients and hear their prayers, petitions and passions.

So, what is to be the final outcome in this endeavor to control our stresses? Although ignored by medical schools, here are some words that depict the results of this crucial objective:

- Joy
- Happiness
- Peace of mind – equanimity
- Relaxed body and mind
- High energy
- A sense of humor

These qualities will not necessarily come easily or instantly. In fact, the full fruit of our labors in character growth may not come until late in life. But the process of striving for excellence is a worthwhile journey that is certain to bear good fruit in time.

My lifelong quest is to strengthen the partnership I have with my patients, sharing with them the key words, elements and processes necessary for growth and well-being. And not only do I share with my patients, they share with me—giving me valuable feedback that helps me grow as well. During the course of medical practice, numerous tensions arise, providing opportunities to help each other become masters over stress.

I have found that maintaining a positive mental attitude (PMA) is an important key to relieving stress and unlocking spiritual powers. A PMA helps to combat the stress that comes from worry, apathy, arrogance, fear, greed and many other negative thoughts and emotions. Many notable authors, such as W. Clement Stone, Norman Vincent Peale, Robert Schuller and Zig Ziglar, have written eloquently about the remarkable benefits of a PMA.

Excellent Stress Management Choices

Many factors go into the question of whether a person will be healthy or ill. Dr. Peter Hanson provides a good list of these in his book, *Stress for Success*:

1. **Good genetics:** You have "chosen" your ancestors well, and most of them have lived well past the age of 65.
2. **Sense of humor:** You can laugh with others, and at yourself.
3. **The right diet:** You eat a balanced diet that includes the right number of calories to maintain your ideal body weight.
4. **Alternate activity:** You have a balance of physical and intellectual activities in your life. You exercise at least three times a week and strive to maintain tone and flexibility in your body.
5. **Realistic goals:** You try to set clear, attainable goals regarding your work and your personal life.
6. **Stress skills:** You know how to identify stress in your life and are aware of what is happening inside your body during times of stress.
7. **Relaxation skills:** You sleep sufficiently well at

night to have full energy levels during the day. If you become fatigued, you have the ability to take a refreshing nap.

8. **Thorough job preparation:** You are fully rehearsed and mentally prepared to handle the routine stresses at work. When unexpected job stresses hit, you have some contingency plans and skills in crisis management.

9. **Financial stability:** You have the savings, insurance policies, and/or marketable job skills to protect yourself and your dependents should you lose your job because of changes in the economy or your health.

10. **Stable home and personal life:** You have an understanding confidant, a best friend, and a loving partner (even better if your spouse qualifies for all three). Your family is supportive, and your friends make you feel good about yourself, through good times and bad.

Chapter Eleven

Growing in

Control Over Practice

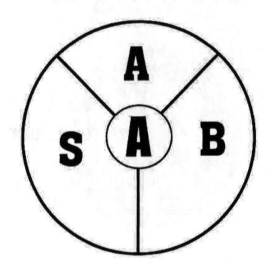

"Control your destiny or someone else will."

—Jack Welch, CEO
General Electric Company

Keywords

▶ Lead
▶ Excel
▶ Accountability
mission

▶ Challenge processes
▶ Adjust attitudes
▶ Unify – vision, purpose,

When I began the practice of medicine in 1953, I was poorly prepared for the flood of business decisions I would face in solo practice. My medical training was almost void of concepts and principles for making a practice successful. We concentrated mostly on the science of medicine, very little on the business side of things. Now most residencies have a relatively small portion of the curriculum devoted to practice management.

The evolution of the medical profession may be compared to the wonderful invention of the wheel. For centuries, beginning with man's initial search for ways to heal his hurts, the focus was primarily the *art* of medicine. Healing was sought from shamans, witch doctors and practitioners of folk medicine, using such things as herbs, incantations and sorcery.

The following diagram depicts the art of medicine, without the presence of the science of medicine:

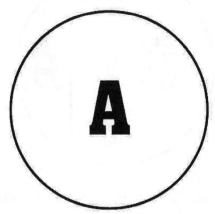

Only recently—mostly just in the past one or two centuries—did science begin to play an integral role in medical care. The art of medicine was still present, but science began to play an increasingly prominent role:

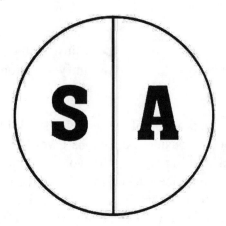

In the last century tremendous advances were made in discovering the causes of diseases. Paul Dekruif describes this transformation in his book, *The Microbe Hunters.* With the discovery of antibiotics such as penicillin and sulfa, the role of science began to expand exponentially, making the wheel better but often out of balance:

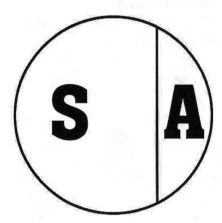

While we should all be grateful for the dramatic medical advancements of the past century, there is also a downside to the current trends. Some doctors are beginning to express regrets that science now has such an all-consuming role. They are sensing a need to bring back more of the art of medicine, the humanistic dynamics that make for a smoother, more efficient wheel. These are explained in previous chapters of this book.

Developments such as DRG (discussed previously) have created many changes in medical practice in our country. These changes require that we pay more attention to the business side of our profession. So we've added another new dimension to the wheel:

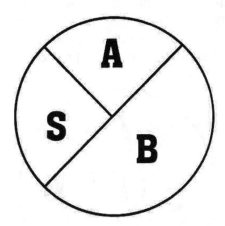

This wheel, like its predecessors, has tended to get out of balance. The new managed-care systems, HMOs and even solo practitioners are still not effectively balancing the dynamics of these competing aspects of medical practice.

Many medical care organizations are top heavy with business managers and office personnel who spend most of their time processing insurance forms. Hundreds of physicians have left the practice of medicine to go into management positions with HMO firms. Today more than 4500 physicians occupy positions far removed from a hands-on medical practice, often being paid far more than they could earn in giving direct medical care to patients. This new profession of medical managers in key positions could lend some beneficial values and perspectives to the insurance industry. Yet, it is sad that some expert physicians have left their medical practices because of frustrations that could have been avoided.

The new breed of medical administrators often fails to grasp the needs of people for continuity of care, freedom of choice, and individual consideration, all of which constitute the *art* of medicine. Of course, there are also good sides to this evolving wheel of medicine, the chief of which is greater accountability. When the medical profession could charge whatever the traffic would bear, with little competition, people frequently suffered either high fees or a lack of care.

We are at the dawn of a new era. The wheel is still evolving, and hopefully will ultimately bring all the aspects of medical care back together into balance and effectiveness. Yet this will not happen until the medical profession realizes the need for changes of attitude in our delivery of healthcare. Thus the balanced SAAB wheel:

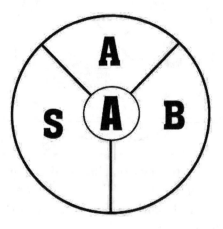

Attitudes are formed by our philosophy, values, ideals and principles. Aristotle was a man of science as well as a philosopher—a lover of wisdom. His thought and wisdom profoundly affected the ways of humankind for over 2000 years. Physicians and other professions were greatly shaped by Greek and Hebrew values, ideas and purposes. Many of the original physicians were philosophers, who integrated their art and healing with the wisdom of the ages. In fact, Aristotle's father was a physician and must have influenced his son to combine his scientific studies with the wisdom of Plato, his teacher.

And the whole matter of medical ethics and attitudes toward patients goes back to the Greek insights of Hippocrates.

However, for the past two or three centuries there has been an increased separation between science and philosophy. Likewise, science and religion have been divorced in the practices of many physicians. As scientific knowledge has grown, philosophy and religion have seemed an incompatible burden. In a battle with the provable, factual base of scientific knowledge, the "soft stuff" of values, meaning, purpose, goals and imagination is often discarded.

It is understandable that the science of medicine has prevailed, for that is what has produced the amazing achievements in modern medical care. The scientific approach distinguishes M.D.s from all the other professions who claim to be scientific healers, such as chiropractors, massage therapists, herbalists and naturopaths. Medical schools disciplined our minds to prove, test, discern, seek evidence, experiment and run controlled studies. The scientific method is indispensable in most curing, healing and prevention.

However, it is becoming evident that today's medical caregivers also need to bring back some of the spiritual and metaphysical elements of healing. Dr. William Osler is one of my role models in this quest to blend spiritual values with the scientific disciplines. Along with the intellectual "head knowledge" needed for sound medical practice, Osler spoke often of attitudes, things of the "heart and soul."

In the past century a number of physicians have endeavored to model that blend. Yet in medical schools there is still a chasm between the science of medicine and the art of medicine, with its stress on attitudes and values, compassion and caring. The balance depicted in the SAAB wheel is still missing. Although the wheel is spinning, it may take years to bring it into proper balance. We need more Schweitzers, Oslers and Selyes—men of faith who embrace the love of spiritual wisdom but also understand the scientific disciplines. This is not an easy task, for an Aristotle of our day would also have to deal with the business principles and economics of medicine.

Defining 'Control Over Practice'

Physicians today need to understand the concept of "control over practice." I define this as the powerful process of managing the science, art, attitudes and business in the practice of the medical profession. Those in our profession are bonded together by science, art, skills and knowledge in the prevention, curing and healing of diseases, illnesses and human hurts.

We should make it our objective to strive for excellence in living, serving and growing into our full potential. But how will we know if we have been successful? The fruit of our labors should be:

1. Medical care for all
2. Maximum development of partnerships with our patients
3. Maximum effort toward prevention
4. Increasing possibilities for curing disease
5. Attention to the skills of healing all human hurts

These desired goals will become a reality only if we reexamine the meaning of success and then gain an understanding of the processes needed to get there. Control equals good management, and good management yields success. Success, of course, has been defined in many different ways. Some of these definitions are simply an attempt to highlight one of the various facets of success. However, all too often we have had the wrong concept entirely. We have been seduced by the money, influence, position and power that we saw in the medical community. Medical school did little to clarify our values, for success during our training was mostly a matter of passing all the tests, board certifications, and other hurdles necessary to arrive at our intended financial oasis.

Control over practice: the powerful process of managing the science, art, attitudes and business in the practice of the medical profession.

If you have never taken time to evaluate your concept of success, I encourage you to do it now. There is a good chance that you will be surprised by your conclusions. According to George Sheeham, M.D., "Success is the knowledge that you have become yourself, the person you were meant to be...it is not measured by what you have accomplished, but by the obstacles you have overcome." Psychologist James Dobson adds, "Success can never be measured by bank balances. Money measures only prosperity, success is a matter of character."

Upon what are you basing your own sense of success and self-worth? Is your success based on solid ground or shifting sands? Louis Binstock warns us not to base our success on what we have, but who we are: "Success is finding a need and filling it. Material success is what a man *has*; spiritual success is what he *is*."

Freedom to Grow

Those entering the medical profession today face a vast array of negative forces and influences. Consider some of these symptoms of the culture of negativism that has often gripped our profession in recent years:

1. Complaints among medical practitioners that "The good old days are gone"
2. The demise of independent solo practitioners
3. An "us versus them" atmosphere of competition
4. Conflicts and turf wars
5. Governmental regulations
6. Greed, whether by physicians, patients, hospitals or insurance companies
7. Frivolous malpractice claims
8. Dehumanizing paperwork and procedures
9. Control by large corporate groups
10. A focus on technology rather than partnership
11. Lack of continuity of care

Despite these negative forces, there are also many positive voices calling for changes in the current medical-care culture. Movies and TV programs such as *Patch Adams, The Doctor,* or *Marcus Welby* point to values and attitudes that have the potential to restructure medicine in remarkable ways.

The process of restructuring our medical care-giving starts when we become *aware* of the need for change. In spite of all the negative cultural forces against us, we can continue to grow by gaining the *freedom* to think new *thoughts*, questioning our old ways of doing things. We begin to study subjects relating to the art of medicine, and get in our curriculums a more intense knowledge of human behavior, economics and business. We recognize our *feel-*

ings and natural reactions of anger, frustration, resentment and rebellion to the plethora of problems we face in our practices. We determine to respond rather than react.

We then should begin to express our *desires* to return to the original satisfaction we sought and found in medicine: helping people feel good, grow and overcome their diseases. We must all clearly set forth our *purposes*. Many doctors have failed to create and communicate a mission statement that they try to follow in their practices each day. Unless our patients understand our mission statement, how can they become partners with us, striving for excellence?

Priorities in medicine have traditionally been reserved for crisis care. Many physicians have responded superbly in crisis situations. Now that there is an overabundance of physicians most places, we have a sufficient work force to address both prevention and healing of the incurable. Financial priorities, likewise, must be sorted out in hospitals and physicians' offices. Is excellence truly our top value? Should money be the bottom line? Is service our true aim? Is satisfaction for our patients a high priority? Do we value effectiveness over efficiency?

Freedom of *choice* for both patient and physician is another value essential for growth. Any system of healthcare delivery which violates this basic freedom is surely doomed to failure and frustration. Individual consideration is vital because of the vast spectrum of variation in each person's needs, wants, expectations, principles, priorities and purposes.

Freedom to *act* is another essential quality in the medical profession. Much of the medical care we provide is dependent upon immediate action. This is contrary to most political bodies and businesses, which can afford to defer action or even take no action at all. Much frustration comes when physicians are forced by government or HMO regulations to play the game of "Mother may I?" as we did when we were children. Physicians and patients should have a high degree of autonomy in most healthcare decisions, unobstructed by delays and restrictions imposed by insurance companies. United Insurance is one company that has rediscovered this principle, and it is saving billions of dollars. Hopefully other HMOs will follow its lead.

Positive reformation of the healthcare system will not come without *persistence*. Tragically, the new managed-care systems have broken up many strong doctor-patient relationships. This is sad, not only because of sentimental reasons, but because it squanders the incredible healing value of support from trusting, continuing relationships. A persistence in relationships is sometimes the only way such things as chronic diseases, anxieties, fears or depressions can be successfully handled. Seemingly oblivious to this fact, the current healthcare system often requires those who change insurance companies to also change physicians. This is troubling for both doctors and patients.

Becoming *response-able*, rather than reacting, is the mature, positive way to process the pressures, stresses and adversities inherent in the science, art and business of medicine. There are enormous problems, far beyond our present capacity to solve. However, to continue reacting, grumbling, cursing or withdrawing will be maladaptive rather than constructive.

Freedom to *change* is the last essential inner nutrient for growth. But, as noted before, not all changes are good ones. While some things in our healthcare delivery system are getting better, many other things have stagnated or worsened. Something is wrong when 42 million people in our country are uninsured, financial resources are not prioritized, people are rewarded for poor lifestyles, and insurers are committed more to crisis management than preventive care.

Most of the changes that have occurred in the past 50 years have been driven by governmental and economic forces. While the medical profession has brought wonderful scientific advances, we have generally failed to bring positive changes in other aspects of our practices. Even our amazing new technologies have a downside, for they are one of the primary causes of spiraling costs. Meanwhile, physicians' incomes and hospital fees have been significantly lowered by government and private insurers, which seem to assume that such cost-cutting reductions can go on forever.

Courage will be needed by those seeking to shift accountabilities for the billions of dollars squandered each year to assist those who have chosen unhealthy lifestyles. Most of our medical-care costs are not related to unpreventable causes. Rather, many of our health problems are the direct result of wrong choices:

- Smoking and tobacco
- Alcohol
- Drug abuse
- Lack of exercise
- Obesity
- Poor nutrition
- Lack of stress prevention
- Violence
- Sexually transmitted diseases (STDs) resulting from unsafe sexual habits

Positive change will only come about when leadership from the medical profession become partners in the business of medicine through changing our attitudes. We already have far too many burdensome governmental rules, regulations and laws. More regulations are not the solution to leading our patients in pathways that will achieve our goals: medical care for all and successful prevention, curing and healing. Perhaps the following leadership acrostic will give some ideas to patients on how we can, together, achieve a better system of healthcare delivery.

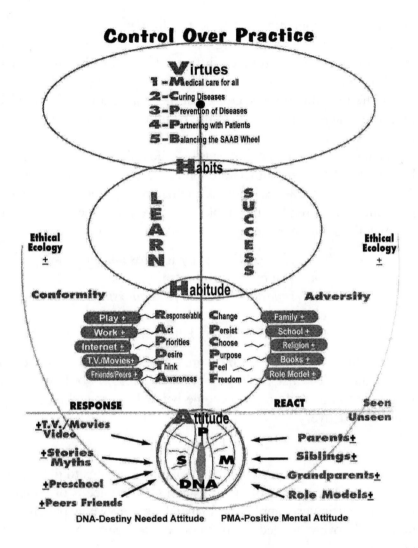

Control Over Practice

Virtues
1 – **M**edical care for all
2 – **C**uring Diseases
3 – **P**revention of Diseases
4 – **P**artnering with Patients
5 – **B**alancing the SAAB Wheel

Habits

L E A R N

S U C C E S S

Ethical Ecology ±

Ethical Ecology ±

Conformity

Habitude

Adversity

Play ±
Work +
Internet ±
T.V./Movies+
Friends/Peers ±

Response/able
Act
Priorities
Desire
Think
Awareness

Change
Persist
Choose
Purpose
Feel
Freedom

Family ±
School +
Religion ±
Books +
Role Model +

RESPONSE

REACT

Seen

Unseen

Attitude
P

+T.V./Movies Video
+Stories Myths
+Preschool
+Peers Friends

S   M

DNA

Parents±
Siblings±
Grandparents±
Role Models±

DNA-Destiny Needed Attitude   PMA-Positive Mental Attitude

Lead

We were taught in medical school that leadership means showing the patient the right medicine, surgery or procedure to follow, and then the desired outcome usually will happen. Often this leadership style was based on the physician's position of authority: "Take this," "Do this" or "Follow my advice" and you will be well. My characterization is oversimplified, but many patients and physicians find this directive leadership style easiest to follow.

However, there is a growing awareness that true leadership in medical practice is often much different from this directive model. Much of what I've learned about the qualities of leadership came out of the manufacturing sector—not medical schools. The service industries have trailed considerably behind the manufacturing sector in this area.

Much study has been done regarding the unique qualities of great leaders. Books on the subject are too numerous to list. However, in my search for excellence, success and personal growth, I have been particularly inspired by four books that have given me a glimpse of the magnitude of character growth needed to become a leader:

1. *The Leadership Challenge* by Kouzes and Posner
2. *Attilla the Hun* by Wes Roberts
3. *The 21 Irrefutable Laws of Leadership* by John Maxwell
4. *In Search of Excellence* by Peters and Waterman

The words below are action words that reflect the attributes of great leaders. The list could go on, but these few words will go a long way toward helping us become better leaders and partners in healthcare delivery.

Listen

This word is no stranger in this book, but it relates to the importance of healthcare practitioners listening to the needs of patients. Here this particularly applies to financial stresses. Many patients are uninsured, overextended, poor money managers, or even near bankruptcy.

Although I spend 98% of my time focusing on the medical concerns of my patients, I have learned that I must be sensitive to other needs as well. In recent years I have become increasingly aware that some patients cannot afford the medicine I would prescribe. As healthcare providers we must develop procedures that better identify those under financial duress. Good leaders are always listening to medical problems of their patients, aware of needs that poor leaders would overlook.

Excel

Providing excellence in medical services requires a commitment to a high quality of technology, office equipment, personnel and services. Our administrative procedures and business methods must be up to date, which means we will need not only sophisticated medical technology but also computers, copiers, e-mail and fax machines. It is no longer possible to practice with the old system of ledgers and hand-written insurance forms.

How will the new push for electronic medical records play out? I am cautious, because anything that might diminish the confidentiality of records could destroy some trust and confidences. So far, my office has stuck to written (dictated and transcribed) records. However, with insurance companies requiring a conspicuous, precise, numerical diagnosis on each billing, how much privacy can we preserve?

Become Accountable

For many years physicians were not held accountable to anyone. We did pretty much as we pleased, and we liked it that way. Except in cases of malpractice or totally bizarre behavior, we were practically above the law. Regulations and red tape were minimal, but so was accountability.

How can we have a proper degree of accountability, without adding even more cumbersome regulations? The only recourse is to have physicians lead patients to recognize the power they have to hold us accountable. As they observe our behavior and attitudes, they should give us feedback. While this is a relatively new idea to medicine, the process of giving constructive feedback has been a feature of family life for ages. We need to encourage our patients to speak honestly about their perceptions, empowering them to be open and candid if we are behaving in an annoying or unprofessional way.

On the other hand, the partnership must be a two-way street. Physicians need to call patients to accountability as well. This includes a variety of situations, such as when they request more sick leave than is medically necessary or want to lie on insurance forms.

Accountability does not occur automatically or easily. A strong partnership must be forged. By building a trusting, open relationship that inspires respect, courage and dignity, we must commit ourselves to a system of accountability that is more effective than burdensome regulations. We need to consider our ethical ecology.

Accountability can also be strengthened in other ways. For example, more refinement of the peer review processes in hospitals is required in order to stimulate professional and personal growth. Everyone involved in giving or receiving healthcare should take responsibility to participate in the processes of accountability.

Response-ability

Physicians in recent years have often abdicated their responsibility to become involved in the quagmire of legislative action. Instead of taking leadership on such issues, we have mostly sat back and complained. However, some doctors, including Dr. Otis Bowen, have been willing to do what they can to remedy such situations. Bowen's leadership has helped to restrain misguided legislative efforts that would have increased malpractice claims in the State of Indiana. As Dr. Bowen understood, the medical profession will not be improved by further legislation but by building excellence in character in medical schools and residencies.

Dr. Bowen was also 20 years ahead of his time when, as the Secretary of Health and Welfare, he made a valuable proposal to Congress. He urged Congress to pass a catastrophic insurance program that would make the entire population more accountable to health costs. The public expectation that insurance will pay all healthcare costs is simply unrealistic. We have deductibles on cars and houses, so why not health?

Another frontier in the area of responsibility will require a daring move on the part of leaders: We need to make the insureds more responsible for medical care claims directly related to voluntary behavior such as smoking or alcohol and drug abuse.

No to Negatives

Great leadership will never give in to negative forces. Physicians who understand their responsibility to lead will be aware of the large number of evil forces that impact the processes of character, growth, disease, illness and good relationships. For true leaders, passivity is not an option. We are not to be passive spectators of evil forces, but rather active participants in the battle to overcome them.

Evil, as already defined in chapter eight, is any act, attitude or force which violates harmony, unity and balance in the family of man or his environment. In the business of managing our practices, we encounter ample opportunities for evil actions, attitudes or forces. While the weak fall prey to pornography, gambling, drugs or violence, it behooves physicians of good character to join forces in fighting against the negative, while modeling the positive.

Serve

True medical leaders will seek to serve their patients rather than themselves. Physicians have always been recognized as members of society whose services are of high value. While the public is only partially aware of a doctor's sacrifices and responsibilities, most patients understand that their physicians should be well paid. However, in some cases this high rate of compensation has become twisted, motivated by greed more than service.

Not much is taught in our medical schools about Dr. William Osler's valuable warning to his medical students: "Medicine is a *calling*—not a *trade*." All too often, this is not the culture caught in the hospital halls and lounges by budding physicians. Instead of a commitment to service, they often see extravagant lifestyles and flaunted self-interests.

Most physicians are paid modestly, but well, in comparison to some other professions. There are professions in our society that receive much higher pay, especially in the past 10 years. Is there something wrong with societal value systems which honor the professional gamesters in baseball, basketball, football and golf so enormously? Doesn't this seem rather disproportionate compared to the compensation of teachers, ministers and physicians—those who shape the destiny of our children and our culture?

Unify

Real leaders understand the importance of unity in all of creation. This is especially true in medicine, where we see the importance of harmony among the 100 trillion cells in our organs and organ systems. It is one of our great privileges in medicine to study the wonder of the integrated systems and processes of the human body.

The unity of the human race is just as amazing. For example, isn't it remarkable that 20 million people living in a city such as Los Angeles could function together? Although every city has some pathological processes and some bad things happening, the human race as a whole desires to pull together in unity. The medical profession has always had its turf wars, jealousies and enormous differences of thought and values. Yet, despite our numerous disagreements, there is a desire to resolve the conflicts, find the common good, and grow in harmony.

There has been a long line of eloquent and outstanding leaders in the medical profession, but our independent tendencies have often left us a house divided. Recently there has been a movement to unionize parts of our profession. While I have always resisted the calls for unionization, I now have to acknowledge that they may be right on one key point: Lawmakers seem to only react to concerted pressure, rather than respond to apparent needs. If there is a continued lack of unity among healthcare providers regarding matters of public policy, physicians will continue to get the short end of the stick. As a result, the quality of medical care will suffer.

Challenge the Process

Our profession is forever trying to better understand the disease processes in the human body. As wonderful as that is, the world is now looking for medical leaders who also understand a different kind of pathology: the destructive processes taking place in the healthcare industry.

Deming and Juran, the prophets of due process in the manufacturing sector, have demonstrated that there is a need for medical leaders to understand similar but differing processes in medicine. However, some principles designed for excellence in manufacturing cars, phones or computers simply are not applicable to caring for humans. The human body is vastly more complex than even the most intricate human invention.

Just as the manufacturing and political sectors must be confronted from time to time, we need leaders today who will challenge unwise processes in the medical field. Excellence will be achieved only if we take periodic looks at how we can make things better.

Since our behaviors are predetermined by our attitudes, the highest form of facilitating change is by attitude restructuring. By challenging and nurturing changes in behavior, physicians have a powerful role to play in motivating patients to strive for excellence. This requires changing our language and culture in accordance with the processes discussed in this book.

Commit

The medical profession will achieve success and excellence only by a total commitment to exploring the powerful words and processes that can change our character. When we change our character, we change the face of healing, curing and preventing. As in any other enterprise committed to excellence, character makes a huge difference in the practice of medicine.

Encourage

All too often, our patients feel the sting of our criticism or attack. This usually isn't intentional, and frequently the criticism is communicated silently, with merely a disapproving glare. Our office workers, likewise, are sometimes belittled or blamed too readily. A physician who wants to be a leader should work to eliminate the ABCDs in strained relationships:

Attacking
Blaming
Criticizing
Defensiveness

As we try to avoid these toxic behaviors, we should follow Ken Blanchard and Spencer Johnson's *One Minute Manager* philosophy in giving messages of acceptance, praise and recognition to our office staff and patients. Rather than being quick to assign personal fault, we should recognize that mistakes are usually due to faulty processes. Instead of attacking the individual, we should devote our attention to remedying the process. As Kouzes and Posner enjoin us, we need to be quick to celebrate successes and good behavior. Was this taught in medical school? It certainly wasn't taught or modeled often enough.

Satisfy Expectations

As leaders to our patients and co-workers, we should strive to exceed their expectations. Each person should be treated as important, recognized for his or her uniqueness. He should be listened to with respect and dealt with carefully and compassionately. He should be given choices and the freedom to change. These are attitudes which reflect our highest values and thoughts.

Of course, we physicians would like to receive this same respect and courtesy from our patients as well. But, realistically, we should expect much less. Many of our patients are hurting and under stress. Even if they are normally patient and kind, they may not be during their visit to our office. As we successfully learn to manage our own stresses, we will be better able to absorb the testiness that inevitably arises from time to time in the course of our patients' illnesses, diseases, pains or circumstances.

Seek Change

Positive changes in the healthcare system are usually painfully slow. And, unless we have Pollyanna glasses on, we will have to acknowledge that some monumental changes will be needed to achieve the goal of providing excellent medical care for all. However, a good start would simply be to change our priority from crisis care to prevention.

One of the changes some would propose is the prudent adoption of some forms of alternative medicine. While some herbs or devices do indeed show promise, many others are worthless or even dangerous. Since the FDA doesn't require standardization and testing in this area, many alternative remedies are totally unproved empirically. Instead of just sitting back and watching the rapid developments in the field of alternative medicine, physicians need to take the lead in bringing some sanity back to the process of evaluating alleged cures and treatments.

Seek Opportunity in Every Adversity.

For years medical practitioners had a financial bonanza: an excess of patients, little competition, a steady cash flow, and little expense. However, the opposite is now true, and competition is a very real concern of many doctors. We need to see that competition can actually be our friend and not our enemy. It can make us better if we have a proactive, positive mental attitude in these times of seemingly dwindling opportunities.

Despite the challenges and obstacles, physician leaders with a clear vision can make the healthcare systems in America a phenomenal success. This is no small task, for to serve every person with excellence will require a plan and commitment of the highest order.

Loss of Control

We physicians practice under stresses that are often dehumanizing. Faced with these external pressures, it is easy to be fatalistic, feeling that we are helpless to do anything about them. Excellence is an anachronism under such circumstances.

We cannot legislate excellence. Attitudes cannot be coerced. Trying to motivate people by external means is usually based on punishment or fear. Instead, physicians can and must take control by demonstrating the processes of inner freedom, becoming responseable, and making changes both within ourselves and in the governmental policies that make for excellence.

Both politicians and physicians should strive to serve the people rather than themselves. Likewise, the patients must become response-able in their needs and demands. Physicians, lawyers and patients all must become aware of the tendency for greed to shape their desires and actions.

A successful healthcare system, stripped of mediocrity, will never be achieved by legislative processes. A milieu based on "my rights" and "your rights" will inevitability become adversarial. Only in an atmosphere of partnering can we establish excellence. Although Congress often seems clueless about the partnering process, patients have enormous powers that legislators lack. While most legislation is conceived in reaction to crises, response-able physicians, patients and legislators *can* find positive solutions. This doesn't have to be an impossible dream.

I challenge you who are patients to ask your physicians their feelings about the following questions:

1. Do you have the control and freedom you need to practice the excellence in medicine that you desire?
2. Do the stresses of imposed rules and regulations make you a better physician?
3. Do you struggle to interpret and keep up with the reams of new regulations that are promulgated every year?
4. Have you encountered times when the load of legislation has interfered with doctor-patient relationships and the overall quality of medical care?
5. Are the diagnosis codes and numbers required in HMO or government paperwork a serious source of stress and an impediment to the *art* of medicine?
6. Would you prefer a return to a "fee for service" system, with fee schedules devised and enforced by the medical profession?
7. Have insurance companies and government agencies been sufficiently committed to preventive care, which is the most effective way to reduce healthcare costs over the long term?
8. Do you feel dehumanized by the current limits imposed on your ability to practice medicine in the way that you see fit?
9. Do you feel that the present processes often dehumanize patients by limiting their individual choices, diminishing their trust, and undermining their continuity of care?
10. Would you enthusiastically encourage your children to become physicians or other healthcare providers of some kind?

I often find myself in despair when I consider the present system of negative external controls on medical practice. An increasing number of physicians are dealing with overt or suppressed feelings of anger, anxiety, frustration, apathy and helplessness. We are trying to adapt, but, too often, our joy and enthusiasm are gone.

It is wrong to assign the entire blame to legislators or insurance companies. The blame game is ultimately futile. Physicians, patients, insurance companies and legislators have all contributed to the present situation. As the Pogo comic strip proclaimed years ago, "We have met the enemy, and they is us!" Instead of casting blame, we each must take responsibility for our own role. Partnering together, we need to re-examine the processes and then find a way to fix the healthcare delivery systems.

Regaining Control of Our Destiny

Jack Welch, CEO of General Electric, has written a book with a very apt title that could apply to the history of American healthcare in recent decades: *Control Your Destiny or Someone Else Will.* Much of the dehumanizing quagmire of governmental control over the medical profession came upon us because we physicians did not adequately discipline our own members in our traditional fee-for-service system. While the vast majority of physicians charged fair fees, a greedy minority abused the situation.

Destiny: our vision of the end of life's journey.

When patients discovered that they had been ripped off by unscrupulous physicians, they were understandably irate. Their cries were heard by legislators, who took action to regulate *all* doctors, not just the ones who had abused the system. Because the medical profession was not ready to discipline its own members, the legislators did. The result, as has already been described, was the implementation of the messy new "diagnostic related groups" system (DRGs).

From my perspective, it would be better to scrap this burdensome apparatus and return to a fee-for-services approach. However, this time the medical societies would have to step up and bravely provide leadership in disciplining our fee scales. By providing account-ability and taking control of our own destinies, we could make gov-ernment intrusion largely unnecessary.

Would I encourage my grandchildren to go into medical careers under the present system of government regulations? NO! The issue most important to me in making this determination is not the money but the loss of inner freedom. As a profession we have become emasculated, indentured and kept under a system that steals our need for individual choices, priorities, purposes, desires, feelings and thoughts.

The present system has taken away, or at least distorted, our pro-cesses for growth and autonomy. Because of the negative ethical ecology that now permeates much of the healthcare system, I have to send a warning to those who are contemplating a medical career: Beware of letting any system, circumstance or person interfere with the processes of your inner freedom and growth. Our most prized possession is our capacity to think and act independently, with the goal of achieving interdependence.

I wish the wisdom contained in this book had come to me earlier. It is sad that I find myself at the end of my medical career when I am finally understanding its proper framework. However, it is my hope that hundreds or even thousands of young physicians can be impacted by these discoveries earlier in their careers.

In the remaining years of my life, I want to continue serving those who are in need of healing or counsel. But my focus will increasingly shift away from crisis care and high-tech medical equipment. Instead, I will emphasize prevention, helping people understand the processes that can keep them from unnecessary sick-ness, sorrow, stress, pain and brokenness. I will do this with joy and enthusiasm, largely unhindered by the oppressive restraints imposed by government and insurance regulations on traditional medical practices.

It is time for physicians to challenge the encumbering external forces that would destroy our inner freedom to grow into responsi-ble relationships with our patients. Hopefully the precepts and prin-ciples in this book will help reshape the ethical ecology for health-care providers and families. I pray that younger physicians and nurses will increasingly relate to patients with all 12 powerful processes that I've discussed here. In this way, we will reach our intended destiny: achieving excellence as we live, serve and grow into our full potential.

I am certainly not a political activist by nature. However, if there is ever a cause I can passionately champion, it is to deregulate the medical profession. We physicians slowly slipped into this messy, querulous quagmire because we didn't keep fees under control or discipline the greedy and incompetent doctors. We must now regain the leadership, throw out the unnecessary rules and regulations that encumber Medicare, Medicaid and entrepreneurial insurance providers, and return to a "fee for service" approach.

Deregulation does not mean that the medical profession can shirk its duty to identify and discipline the misguided or unfit doctors. This self-policing will be a crucial ingredient in our battle to maintain and improve the credibility of our profession. Deregulation is not an invitation to a sloppy or unethical practice of medicine. Rather, it will give both patients and physicians a welcome relief from the dehumanizing pressures of inept legislation. But it will require physicians to get back to freedom with response-ability, serving our patients more than ourselves.

How could deregulation ever occur in today's political climate? Only in response to well-planned, unified, nationwide action to get the message to government bureaucrats in Washington. What would happen if all physicians would bundle up the onerous stack of regulations and bring them to a huge gathering on the steps of Congress? There we would exclaim, "Enough is enough! We've had it! We confess our errors, but we protest the negative processes that will further harm our ailing healthcare system."

The thousands of gathered doctors could then toss their bundles into dumpsters dedicated to some useful recycling purpose. Perhaps then the public would realize what a waste of valuable paper goes into the production of these unattainable government expectations. I believe that most of our patients would applaud us when we return from our purifying pilgrimage to Washington.

Remember the first law of legislation: Excellence, attitudes and character cannot be legislated! Let's find ways to partner with our patients, serving them with excellence. Freedom and response-ability, two inseparable qualities, could then rise again to take control over the practice of medicine.

Chapter Twelve

Growing in

Control in Family

"By wisdom a home is built
And by understanding it is established
And with knowledge the rooms are filled
With all precious and pleasant riches"
(Proverbs 24:3-4).

It was in a college sociology course that I first studied the family in a scientific, behavioral way. There was a special course in family relations that stimulated my understanding of the dynamics in family life. In medical school, however, it was presumed that we had all the knowledge we needed, and very little thought was given to the enormous complexity in the life of a family. Whenever the subject of family problems arose during our medical training, it was quickly delegated to behavioral scientists or psychologists to work out. Meanwhile, we physicians dealt with the physical ailments and disease processes.

My perspectives have changed over the years, hopefully with greater understanding of one of life's most complex, challenging and important social structures. My wife and I have been married 50 years. We have nurtured six children from birth to their own marriages, watching them all establish homes of their own. With joy we have celebrated 18 grandchildren and a total of 150 years of wedding anniversaries in our family without a divorce. Our views on family are considerably different now from how they were at the beginning, and we are still in the process of getting greater wisdom of how to define family and understand its dynamic processes. Each day we learn a little more of "how to" strengthen the family and enable it to thrive.

There are a number of key words for us to consider in this chapter on family:

▶ Mission   ▶ Commit
▶ Praise   ▶ Communicate
▶ Grow   ▶ Intimacy
▶ Conciliate   ▶ Serve
▶ Unity and interdependence   ▶ Freedom and diversity

I define family as a unity of persons—ideally father, mother and child (or children)—committed to each other in loving relationships for growth and sharing of common needs, purposes and values. I realize, of course, that this ideal pattern is not always the case. There are families without children. There are single mothers and fathers. Grandmothers and grandfathers are frequently surrogate parents.

Today there are strong proponents of homosexual couples who would like to change the ideal paradigm that our Creator has designed for the human race. I agree with the vast majority of social and behavioral scientists—and the common sense of most people throughout the ages—that the structural unit of a husband, wife and child is the most durable form of family. It has stood the test of time.

Family: a unity of persons—ideally father, mother and child (or children)—committed to each other in loving relationships for growth and sharing of common needs, purposes and values.

Striving for excellence in family life involves serving each other for growth into our full potential as individuals and as a part of society as a whole. Though our society in recent years has witnessed an enormous failure to achieve this ideal paradigm of three hearts joined together in family, most people, it seems to me, still strive for that ideal. We want a long-term relationship which can provide maximum trust, security, love, joy, fulfillment, stability and mutual satisfaction.

So what are we to make of our astounding failure rate, with more than 50% of all marriages ending in divorce? This does not indicate an abdication of the ideal, but rather a failure to understand the basic processes in the complicated structure of marriage. Tragically, many young people grew up with no one to explain and model to them the processes and powerful words inherent in a successful marriage.

Our society is beginning to reap a dreadful harvest of suffering that inevitably attends broken homes and relationships. Think of the 1.5 million men and 800,000 women—many of them fathers and mothers—behind bars. Failure in the family has probably been the single most powerful contributing factor in their imprisonment.

Remarriages are evidence that people desire the hope of a second or third chance to be successful in the ideal paradigm. Seeking to recover and learn from their broken past, many people hope they have learned to do better this time. Although the failure rate for second and third marriages is even higher than for first marriages, some are successful in achieving the ideal. The marriage ideal shown on the three-hearts paradigm is, in my view, the ultimate evolutionary form of family structure. There is no other form of family life which so effectively serves the needs of the individual and society.

However, this paradigm has become very controversial in our day. Our media and legal processes have confused and weakened this time-honored premise. And while some churches and synagogues have been great champions of family values and integrity, others have failed to present a clear standard for family life. Many church members are hungering for more "know how" to achieve joy, peace, security and trust in their homes. Simply put, just talking about love, peace and joy in the family usually fails to achieve the ideal marriage. We must be committed to learning *how* marriage works, and this means acquiring an understanding of the processes involved.

Control

Webster defines control as:

1. Exercising restraint or direction over

2. Holding in check or curbing
3. Eliminating or preventing the spread or flourishing of something undesirable

These concepts of control are shared by most people. Control is viewed as an authoritative "power over others," most often practiced by parents, bosses or political leaders. If used exclusively, though, this concept is doomed to break down when applied to family relations.

Although there will be a need to exercise a certain amount of authority and restraint at times, we need "control" of another kind—inner control derived from the process of partnering. As shown by the Power of Partnership paradigm, the healthiest atmosphere comes when we all strive with all our powers to create harmony, unity and balance. In other words, each person in the family structure is working to maximize the powers of the partnership by becoming response-able. That is a whole new, positive way to look at control.

Commitment

Once we have defined the ideal family and understood control in its most positive form, all we need to do to have a successful family is to be committed. This is not easy for many of us. Selfishness and independence die a slow, painful death. Our culture is filled with influences that are destructive to family commitments. Marriage is the initial commitment process which helps us to choose attitudes and actions that will prove valuable in every area of our lives. Having learned commitment in the marriage relationship, we become more enabled to sustain steadfast loyalty to other people and to our principles, priorities, processes and purposes. We can maintain these commitments regardless of adverse circumstances.

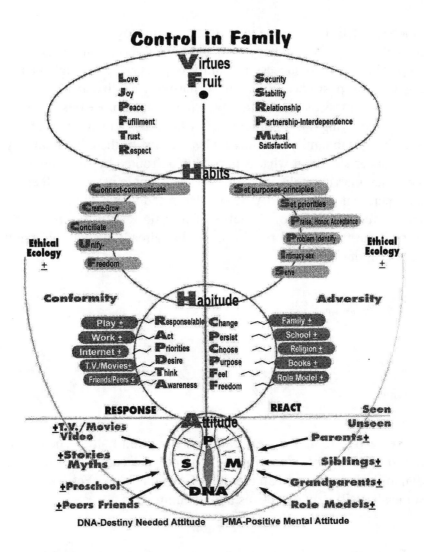

Control in Family

Virtues **F**ruit

Love
Joy
Peace
Fufillment
Trust
Respect

Security
Stability
Relationship
Partnership-Interdependence
Mutual Satisfaction

Habits

Connect-communicate
Create-Grow
Conciliate
Unify-
Freedom

Set purposes-principles
Set priorities
Praise, Honor, Acceptance
Problem Identify
Intimacy-sex
Serve

Ethical Ecology ±

Ethical Ecology ±

Conformity

Habitude

Adversity

Play ±
Work ±
Internet ±
T.V./Movies±
Friends/Peers ±

Response/able **C**hange
Act **P**ersist
Priorities **C**hoose
Desire **P**urpose
Think **F**eel
Awareness **F**reedom

Family ±
School ±
Religion ±
Books ±
Role Model ±

RESPONSE **REACT** Seen

Attitude

Unseen

+T.V./Movies Video
+Stories Myths
+Preschool
+Peers Friends

P
S M
DNA

Parents±
Siblings±
Grandparents±
Role Models±

DNA-Destiny Needed Attitude   PMA-Positive Mental Attitude

Politically Correct

Back to the growth paradigm. The growth of a family and marriage begins with a destiny-needed attitude (DNA)—a positive mental attitude that develops an awareness of structure, movement and processes.

When the wedding ring slips onto the finger, there is an implied commitment to unity, dissolving the former isolation, solitude and independence. Two unique individuals become aware that a positive mental attitude is necessary to begin a long-term, united relationship. The secret to success in family is preserving throughout life together our positive attitude, unity, harmony and balance.

An awareness of normal family dynamics and processes is essential to improving the conditions in our families. With all the stresses and changes in family structure and values today, there is a tendency to be uncertain about what is normal. Confronted by such things as same-sex marriages, live-ins, divorces and single parenting, there is a desperate need for clarifying standards and ideals. Otherwise, we will forfeit the awesome benefits of holistic family life, receiving instead the fragmented relationships that already plague too many people in our society.

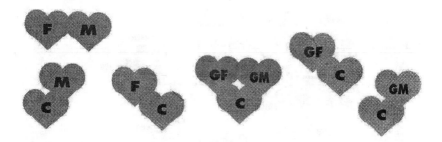

We need to rethink the ethical ecology of family life. The essential inner nutrients for growth here are basically the same 12 dynamic elements as in all the other Cs in this book. Yet, they have somewhat different objectives and commitments.

Freedom

This is the most basic element in successful family and interpersonal relationships. It creates an atmosphere of individual uniqueness, enabling us to accept and cherish the other person. We preserve their freedom to think, feel, desire, purpose, prioritize, choose, act, persist, respond and change in their own way. We also preserve our own freedom to express the "nutrients of growth" in our own way but in harmony with the other person's expressions—seeking unity through collaboration.

Many marital relationships have been stifled because of violating this most basic process. Without freedom, conflict and disharmony are the inevitable result. Conflict is not entirely a negative occurrence, for it is essential in the growth process of fusing out individual personality traits. Freedom does not imply selfishness. Families today have an urgent need to recognize that with freedom must come a commitment to response-ability. While it is easy to react negatively to the traits that make our mates unique, we need to instead learn to respond with love and sensitivity.

Freedom is a fragile quality, often under attack. Each person must prize and preserve it for ourselves, our mate and our children. This must be a resolute commitment, for it is the only way to maintain harmony and unity. However, although unity is the goal, that does not imply conformity. As we pursue harmony, we will encounter the process of growing from independence to interdependence, from solitude to partnership.

In medical school we learned a great deal about human physiology and anatomy, but almost nothing about what makes for good family relations. In fact, while there are many excellent examples of success in physicians' families, there is an appalling number of doctors who are dysfunctional in their family lives. While we were becoming more knowledgeable about how to handle disease, we were taught very little about how to keep our marriages together.

There are monstrous stresses in the medical profession, and they can't help but challenge the integrity and unity of our homes. Sadly, many physicians have never learned how to become partners. We haven't learned how to model freedom in our homes or in the workplace. As we learn to become better partners at home, we will also become better partners with our patients. Freedom is the quintessential inner nutrient for growth.

Thinking

We must read more books about healthy family life. Dr. James Dobson's Focus on the Family ministry is the most dynamic pro-family force in our country. For many years, Dr. Dobson has led the fight to preserve the unity and integrity of the family. Focus on the Family provides a wealth of excellent resources, such as pamphlets, audio tapes, videos, books and movies. Dr. Dobson and his organization have modeled the highest standard of excellence in how to overcome the brokenness, suffering and pathological conditions in our families.

Thinking: the faculty of our conscious mind that processes knowledge and experience by questioning, reasoning, problem-solving, assessing, analyzing, computing and compartmentalizing memories.

Just as Dr. Dobson and other family advocates have arisen in recent years, our families have also faced a massive flood of negative thinking and evil forces in our society. Yes, we are blessed to have a country that provides us with the freedom to think and read, but we need to discern whether the materials we encounter in books, movies, TV or Internet are truly beneficial. We need to be on our guard, for many elements of our culture are destructive and dangerous.

As we seek to care for illness and disease in families, we physicians need much more insight than we were taught in medical school or residency. We are confronted with family-life situations everyday, and often we are not able to just consign these problems to the schools, churches, social services, and legal processes.

My office includes a resource center designed and filled with materials from Focus on the Family. I have found these materials to have tremendous power to heal the hurts and brokenness in the family lives of my patients. A physician can only do so much, but we should do what we can.

Feelings

Physicians are not alone in their failure to recognize and share their feelings, emotions, passions, sufferings, anger, resentments, fears, anxieties, guilt, grief, isolation and self-centeredness. Like other human beings, we don't celebrate enough our love, joy, peace and need for fun—especially with family. However, by ignoring our feelings, we run into serious trouble. We need to have a place where we can openly share both our negative and positive feelings with someone.

My wife and children have been my greatest assets in life. They have always been there to listen, empathize and share my thoughts and feelings. There is no psychiatrist, psychologist or counselor who can match the power of an ardent and faithful lover. Nothing is more needed than one person we can trust to be a sounding board for our inner selves. This has been one of the greatest forces in my personal growth, and it has helped me develop trusting, long-term relationships with my patients.

Desire

Soul mates who can openly share their deepest desires, wishes and dreams are feeding their relationship with one of the essential inner nutrients for growth. Many marriages neglect this essential ingredient, rarely sharing their intimate wants and dreams. From time to time, every healthy marriage needs to ask questions such as, *What do we want to become?* and *Where would we like to be at the end of life?*

Do we take time to use our creativity and imagination? After all, the most powerful motivator in our life is our creative imagination. Most couples spend very little time in this growth nutrient. Many marital failures occur when this element of growth is ignored.

How many physicians are in tune with the wishes, desires and dreams of their patients? Do we take time enough to search for this personal trait? Are patients open to discussing this with their physicians? Do patients feel enough freedom and trust to share these things?

Relationships which include this positive sharing will create a unity of partnership that is truly inspiring and invigorating. However, it is unlikely that we will learn to share this phenomenon with our patients if we have never experienced it in our home life.

Purpose

While the vague and often nebulous powers of the imagination are important, growth also requires that we use our power to set more specific purposes. Each person in a relationship must become aware of a purpose for his or her life. In order to grow, we each must discover that purpose and then share it with our mate or friend. Even as a clear individual purpose is one of the most powerful integrators for our life, so is a shared purpose for a husband and wife.

Partnerships are much more likely to succeed if a mission statement is worked out by the individuals. A mission statement states our purposes and is a springboard for our plans of how to achieve our goals. Because this takes a lot of work, and often some difficult soul-searching, it is often neglected. But there is no shortcut in this area. We cannot just assume that the relationship will take care of itself. A life or a relationship that has no mission statement is like a ship or an airplane without a compass. Very few successful ventures are achieved without a clear statement of purpose, mission and destiny.

After the arduous work of espousing this mission statement, detailed plans are needed to carry out the stated purposes. Marriages and business partnerships both need to set aside enough time to unify and clarify purposes. This implies a great opportunity for differences and conflicts to be resolved. We should realize that the forging of interdependence often results in friction and crisis. Yet such conflicts, whether in homes or businesses, are a creative opportunity for growth. Again, as we learn to work through such things in our homes, we are better prepared as physicians to make mission statements and build strong relationships in our offices and hospitals.

Set Priorities

How much time do we spend as individuals or partners in setting our priorities and ordering their importance? As individuals we must first consider our needs and then our wants. Then we consider the things we value and treasure: persons, ideals, principles, purposes or possessions. This issue of what we treasure will have a profound impact on every other area of our lives. Take some time to ask yourself what you value the most:

- Possessions or people?
- Isolation or relationship?
- Partnership, unity and interdependence (our way) or independence (my way)?
- Addiction or freedom?
- Material wealth or being generous with others in need?

As with purpose, setting priorities begins with the individual and then proceeds outward to partnership or marriage. We need joint sessions with our partner or mate where we can set priorities and list them in order of importance. Many conflicts arise in marriage or other partnerships because of differing priorities: *How do we spend our money? How much time shall we devote to different areas of our lives? What relationships need to be shared with others?* Wow! What fertile areas for conflict. What great opportunities for adding adrenaline and zest to any marriage or other partnership!

As you may have already discovered, these matters are not easily processed. We all have a tendency to react negatively to the priorities of others. But it is crucial that we state, clarify and negotiate our priorities if we are going to achieve family unity.

Choose

Choice is almost a given where a family or partnership has done its homework in setting priorities together and making a mission statement of shared purposes, dreams, feelings and thoughts. However, choice is really biting the bullet—it means our mind is set. Choice involves setting the compass, selecting our course, and adjusting our attitudes. We are ready to act.

Act

Whether in our family or other partnerships, we are successful in growing together only if we act harmoniously. Having set our purposes and priorities, we follow through by positive action—going the same direction. We haven't surrendered our unique individuality but have gained greater power by giving up the attitudes that prevented harmony, unity and balance. We have learned the magic of synergy.

Marriage can be likened to two mighty rivers that are originally headed in different directions. Yet, at some strategic point, the rivers come together often with great turbulence and force. As the two rivers "become one," the resulting force contains all the elements contributed by each river. As individuality is lost, a greater power is found together.

However, humans are not rivers, so there is an important difference. It is not necessary to lose our identity in order to become partners and grow toward interdependence. A better analogy would be a redwood forest. Each giant redwood is an individual standing alone, yet they grow together in the forest. They could not stand alone against the storms of wind and snow, because they have no deep taproots. They stand as individual trees only because their shallow roots interlace and support each other.

A family is much like a redwood forest. Until hit with the severe adversities, storms and circumstances of life, an individual may be tempted to think he can stand alone. But, during such stressful times, the value of families and other support systems becomes very apparent.

The human body is another great example of interdependence. Each organ and process within that system is important for survival. The heart, brain, kidney, intestines, muscles, bones, endocrine glands, skin and reproductive organs are each wonderfully designed to contribute to the overall well-being of the body. What a wonder the human body is, with each organ doing its unique part, but with total regard for the unity and integrity of the whole. While similar harmony, unity and balance is displayed in all living organisms, the human body is by far the greatest of all of our Creator's achievements on the earth.

This model expands in ever-widening circles. Starting as individuals, we become partners and then parents. As parents we create the nuclear family, which becomes a culture, a country and finally a world community: the family of man. If civilization is to flower, it will only be as we grow into self-awareness, find our own identity, grow into partnership and interdependence, and then further the unity of all mankind.

We should trust that the processes of growth as individuals, partners and the larger community are just as complex as the body, or planets or galaxies. These processes are all so staggering in their wonder and immensity.

Persistence

With divorce rates soaring, something is clearly wrong in our approach to relationships. Many of these relationships could have been saved if only the partners were willing to hang in there and work on their partnership. Though the partners may have felt that they had tried "everything," they actually were ignorant of the powerful processes that could have helped them resolve their differences. They gave up too easily.

In almost every divorce or loss of relationship, there was very little thought or commitment to trying to understand the processes for healthy partnerships. Instead of finding solutions, the focus was merely on the problems. Some problems can never be solved by focusing on them. The key to a successful outcome, however, is our commitment to positive attitudes and responses. The twelve growth processes described in this book, if thoroughly studied and followed, would do away with the vast majority of failures in marriages and other partnerships.

The following powerful processes play a crucial role in determining whether a marriage can last or thrive:

- Creativity
- Communication
- Conflict resolution
- Confidence – trust, respect, hope
- Compassion – empathy
- Carefulness
- Concern – serving
- Choice
- Change
- Controlling our stresses
- Controlling our business and financial affairs

Of course, it takes both parties in a partnership to make or break it—no one person is solely to blame for a broken relationship. However, the traditional legal processes in divorce cases create an atmosphere that is basically adversarial, creating a shouting match about who is at fault. That is a no-win situation—only the lawyers win and neither of the partners is healed or happy.

"No-fault divorce" laws were an attempt to remedy this adversarial process. But these laws have serious shortcomings too, communicating the flawed perspective that marriages should be an "easy come – easy go" proposition. When will our legislators and court officials recognize the importance of facilitating mediation instead of divorces? Present laws and procedures seldom result in an ending that minimizes the destructive consequences for the partners and their children.

I fully realize that some relationships and partnerships are so toxic that they should be terminated. Sometimes just hanging together "for the children's sake" is hanging too heavy a load on everyone. Yet I am against making it too easy to get a divorce, and I am saddened that proper counseling is frequently not sought before the final break occurs. Couples who focus on the processes instead of the problems can often see remarkable restoration in their marriages. This is not an "easy fix," but is something that takes persistence.

Become Response-able

One of Stephen Covey's marvelous books is *Seven Habits of Highly Effective Families*. In this book, Covey concentrates on the habits which endow families with joy, harmony and other virtues. Although our paradigms might be a bit different, Covey shares my belief that becoming response-able is the process that underlies the habit of being proactive. I often wonder why the medical profession has been so slow to embrace the principles that Covey has outlined so beautifully.

We all tend to be creatures of habit, reacting rather predictably to almost every stimulus, circumstance or adversity. However, if we and our family members or partners became actively involved in the EING processes, we would be proactively creating a new habit—responding rather than reacting. Of course, there are some dangerous stimuli which call for an immediate reaction, such avoiding a violent blow. However, in nearly every situation we should listen to Covey's advice about this powerful process and habit of proactivity. Learning this approach is the best method to preventing ill-advised practices in human relationships.

Change

To grow is to change, and to change creatively and positively is growth. Yet there are many changes in our society today that are weakening the family. Alvin Tofler, in his book *Future Shock*, has outlined the enormous pressures that societal changes are bringing to bear on our families. In his book, *Margin*, Dr. Richard Swenson shares similar insights about the cultural changes that tend to jeopardize family unity.

Will the family look like this?

Or will the family look like this, with each member touching the others only barely or not at all?

Consider this chilling list of enemies to healthy family life:

- Financial stresses – reacting to pressures to buy more
- Over-commitment of time away from family
- Increased violence modeled and sold on TV and the Internet
- Increased distortion of sexual mores
- Lack of real intimacy
- Less face-to-face communication – overuse of the Internet and TV
- Increasing indifference to malevolent influences such as gambling and pornography
- Increasing affluence and self-indulgence
- Increasing divorce and family instability

How can we turn the tide in this battle to save our families? Are the negative changes in our culture inevitable? And, specifically, what is a physician's role in promoting sound families?

We physicians must first learn the dynamics of how to change things for the better in ourselves and our own families. Then we can become a force for good in the lives of our patients and those in our community. Like it or not, as physicians we are role models for our patients and our culture. We can bring valuable changes to our surroundings if we practice healthy processes in our own families and then become servant leaders to others.

We also can play a role in providing young couples with helpful books, such as Neil Clark Warren's *Finding the Love of Your Life* and James Dobson's *Love of a Lifetime*. Laying a good foundation in the early years of marriage is vitally important. Often there is a time in the first year or two of marriage when the partners are gripped with overwhelming disillusionment: "I made a mistake. I want out." Even at such stressful times, positive change is possible if the partners are willing to practice the processes for conciliation and growth.

Growing in loving relationships was not something I learned much about during my medical training. Only after a lifetime of searching and studying have I come to some wisdom that I would like to pass on to younger people. I suggest a few more words to which we can commit ourselves:

1. Praise. We need to liberally praise our spouses and partners. Spencer Johnson and Ken Blanchard, in their book *The One Minute Manager,* have successfully outlined the process of how to praise. They point out that people grow and thrive when given regular praise. Our partners could be starving for this kind of affirmation. We can all do more.

2. Honor. Author and speaker Gary Smalley has taught countless men the value of honoring their spouses. My wife is my most prized treasure—more than money or anything else in this world. But do my actions really affirm that every day in every way?

3. Acceptance. Do we accept our spouses, even with their idiosyncrasies and sometimes-irritating traits?

4.Respect. This is very similar to honor. Having an attitude of genuine respect for the other's worth and identity provides a good foundation for any relationship. We physicians often expect to be respected because of our position, knowledge and expertise. However, we will command more respect from our spouses and patients when we serve them, meet their needs, listen to them, and have compassion.

5. Recognition. As partners we need to celebrate the achievements and accomplishments of our mates, partners and children. We often overlook the heroes who do random acts of kindness or surmount enormous illnesses or obstacles. When we see patients grow in some area of their personhood, we should glow with satisfaction and be quick to recognize them. This same recognition should be conveyed to our spouses or children when they achieve something noteworthy.

6. Service. In a previous chapter I described how physicians need to be servant leaders to their patients. Medical practices where the doctor-patient relationship is built upon service will stand the pressures of any competition or changes in the marketplace. Likewise, a husband-wife partnership based upon serving one another will produce a home that is built upon solid rock.

Dissatisfaction in our marriages often stems from a failure to clearly define our gender roles. Wow! Have these ever changed since my wife and I began our married life! Until a couple takes time to work out their individual expectations, they are likely to experience a lot of conflict. And, since time and circumstances sometimes work to change our roles, we need to periodically reevaluate them.

7. Intimacy. After experiencing and studying about sexual relations, I know without a doubt that true intimacy comes about through a process. There is no quick, surefire key for "how to become intimate"—it comes by continuous improvement over a lifetime.

Yes, many teenagers today know "how to have sex." However, sex without intimacy is empty sex, never providing lasting satisfaction and never capable of creating harmony, unity and balance in a relationship. The sex act was designed primarily for procreation and pleasure, but true intimacy does more. It offers the foundation for a long-lasting, secure, stable, joyful relationship that leads to personal and partnership growth.

It is sad that things such as TV, movies, pornography and salacious literature prioritize and glamorize sex without regard for the process of becoming intimate. Achieving the best of sexual pleasuring is not obtained by a momentary thrill but a lifelong venture. Those who are successful know this. The wise can only pity those who cheapen sex and make it a self-centered, dehumanizing act. The unwise are not aware of how much they are missing until they go through one relationship after another, each with the same result: emptiness.

Clifford and Joyce Penner have written some of the finest books expressing the love and sexual intimacy we all have sought. Largely because of ignorance on this subject, only a small percentage of couples ever experience the joy and fulfillment that was intended for men and women in marriage. These books by the Penners are a great asset and should be in every home.

It is encouraging that new voices in our culture are pointing out that freedom in sex must be coupled with response-ability. We can, at any age, manage our sexual passions by the same processes of personal growth. We don't have to automatically react to the sexual stimuli that now are rampant in our society. Our teenagers can learn to be aware of their sexual feelings and process them with self-control. They can slow down, hold off, and wait for the sexual urges to get under control. The Penners have long championed the position that full sexual expression should be reserved for those in a committed marital relationship.

Joe McIlhaney, M.D., has presented some devastating facts about ill-advised sex, pointing out the grave dangers of teen pregnancy, STDs, AIDS, date rape, and a general loss of innocence. Wise are the relationships that choose abstinence while developing mature friendships. As a family physician I have lived through the days of sexual restraint, then the so-called sexual revolution, and now the dreadful harvest of consequences where there has been sex without response-ability. Many of those on this romantic roller coaster have found that true intimacy still eludes them.

Despite the great importance and timeliness of this subject, not much was ever taught in medical school or residency about sexual intimacy. In fact, most physicians don't have either the skill or the time for counseling in these matters. My definition of sexual intimacy is a union of mind, heart and sexual expression through the process of pleasuring and sharing our deepest wishes, dreams, desires, thoughts, feelings, values and purposes. Based on this definition, many relationships have a long way to go.

Sexual intimacy: a union of mind, heart and sexual expression through the process of pleasuring and sharing our deepest wishes, dreams, desires, thoughts, feelings, values and purposes.

Just as it is possible to have sex without intimacy, it is also possible to have intimacy without sex. This kind of intimacy involves the deepening of relationship and partnership. Intimacy without sex occurs where there is true friendship, something of lasting value.

Summary

Our primary commitments in our families and partnerships are to:

1. Processes of growth – creativity
2. Processes of effective communication – building bridges
3. Processes of conflict resolution – reconciliation
4. Processes of unifying – interdependence
5. Processes of freedom with response-ability

Our secondary commitments are processes of:

1. Clarifying and sharing our passions, perceptions, principles, priorities and purposes.
2. Praising, honoring, accepting, respecting and recognizing our partners
3. Problem identification, stress evaluation and becoming proactive
4. Becoming a servant – meeting the individual needs of our partners
5. Deepening our intimacy in friendship and appropriate sexual fulfillment

Caring for Our 'Garden'

For many years I have found enjoyment and inspiration in gardening. I particularly have developed an obsession with planting trees. I have planted fruit trees, fruit bushes, and nut trees. Almost every spring I also plant a garden of vegetables. In spite of my amateur attempts, our family has enjoyed the fruit of my labors. Every year we are able to fill our freezer and shelves with frozen and canned fruits and vegetables. Someday after retirement (or my vocational redirection) I will really get serious and become a better gardener.

Nearly 30 years ago, we began a family project of planting trees on our small farm. These trees now number over 35,000! They have been a great delight and a great learning experience. We have found that the trees must be thinned out periodically to make room for those left to grow into a grandeur and size that will be worthy to market.

Although most of the trees are now tall and straight, almost half the trees we planted either died, became deformed, or never outgrew their crooked tendencies. This happened in spite of all our attempts to prune and train them. They became the best that they could be. As we planted our vegetable garden and trees through the years, we did so with the expectation of growth and productivity. And we discovered that the more we learned about the processes of gardening and forestry, the better the resulting product.

Gardening and forestry have taught us one central lesson: A long-term commitment is required in order to ensure maximum growth. Farming, gardening and forestry demand a commitment to knowing and implementing the processes that facilitate growth. The more I've learned from my farm ventures, the more I've recognized the value of the essential inner nutrients of growth (EINGs) to growth in human character and relationships.

Creating a marriage and family is not a matter of a one-time decision, but rather a lifelong commitment to cultivating positive relationships. Although my family life has been an incredibly rewarding experience, it has also been the most risky, time-consuming, anxiety-producing, stress-filled commitment my wife and I have ever made. Our dream was to have six children (and countless pets, such as dogs, birds and horses). We envisioned them to be useful citizens, helping to solve problems and make this a better world. We hoped and prayed and held our breath that they would not become just another part of the world's problems—and they didn't.

We now have the same dreams for our grandchildren. We want them to find meaning and purpose in their lives. This now seems harder than it was for my wife and me and our children. Our grandchildren are confronted with a lot more negative, evil forces which threaten their growth and flowering into maturity. However, there are also powerful forces for good that can facilitate their positive development.

I hope this book has helped you to more clearly define the powers and processes of growth. The phenomenon of growth is, admittedly, so complex that our knowledge of it will inevitably be incomplete. Human growth and behavior will always be a subject of incredible mystery and wonder. So, despite my many hours of intense study, my attempts to define words I never really learned about in medical school are still somewhat of an enigma.

Would I go to medical school if I had it to do over again? Certainly. It is a profession filled with wonderful opportunities to serve an ailing, hurting and often misguided family of man. However, I hope the medical schools of the future can incorporate a greater balance, providing not only knowledge of medicine and technology but also the intangible but powerful dynamics that make us human beings a wonder of creation.

Epilogue

The Paragon of Excellence

*"Love the Lord your God with all your heart
and with all your soul and with all your mind
and with all your strength...
Love your neighbor as yourself"* (Mark 12:30-31).

This book can be summed up by the two key precepts spoken by Jesus of Nazareth: love God and love your neighbor. The essential inner nutrients for growth that I have described all find their ultimate roots in these two principles. If we set our hearts on loving God and each other, our priorities and purposes will be ordered in ways that promote health and growth. We will have the power to act response-ably. And, as our lives change, we will be able to bring positive changes to those around us.

The life of Jesus, and the principles He espoused, will be perceived differently and incompletely by each of us. But in my own life I have found that, as I continue to search for an understanding of His secrets, I am increasingly becoming the person I want to be at the end of my life. I have become a better physician, though far from perfect. Although I often fall short in my quest to serve my patients with excellence, I persist in striving for that excellence.

We can all learn from Jesus' example as a skilled and compassionate communicator. He modeled all the essential skills of communication: listening, speaking, establishing rapport, empathizing, forgiving, praying and healing. At an early age He was precocious in wisdom, and as an adult He shared truths that are still unsurpassed in simplicity and usefulness.

Jesus taught and lived the miracle of growth. Rather than accepting the status quo as an inevitable reality, He questioned everything. He never shied away from confronting the things that needed to be changed, even if they were firmly entrenched in the prevailing system.

He was curious, probing and always on the cutting edge of the new and controversial. Even though he was bold and unflinching in facing evil, He also was a gentle peacemaker. No one was more skillful in handling conflict, or more zealous to let conflict be a creative force for the well-being of others. Through the years, He has been my greatest consultant in conflict resolution.

He had high esteem, not only for His own worth, but also for those of every person he encountered. No one was just a number or statistic to Jesus—He was fortunate to live in an era before the advent of Social Security numbers—but He treated everyone as a unique individual, worthy of His full attention. He should be the envy of physicians today.

He embodied the attitudes and deeds of compassion and caring more than any other leader in human history. No one loved more deeply or suffered more completely in order to bring well-being to others. While He had a broad vision for the future, He also seized each moment to further His mission and share His message.

What an incredible example of service and leadership! Jesus motivated His associates, not by authoritarian demands, but by serving them and being attentive to their needs. The world has never seen a leader so inspiring and so free of self-serving. Instead of greed and acquisition, He relinquished His rights and sought to enrich others. His concern for the sick, the poor and the needy is a worthy model for all healthcare providers today.

Choice was a central part of Jesus' message. He probed the beliefs and values of those who came to Him, and He challenged them to choose for themselves. He promised that those who came to a knowledge of the truth would find a whole new realm of freedom and reality.

Jesus remains the single most significant, benevolent change-master in history. His life created a ripple effect that flows even to this present generation. He turned the rules for living and healing upside down, and the world has never been the same. His ultimate objective was to transform this world's pitiful, manmade conditions into a great new age where people all over the world become united members of a new community of lovers.

Who has ever faced greater stress than this amazing Physician? Who has ever handled stress with greater skill and control, coming out on top after carrying the weight of the world on his shoulders? Again, this is an example we need to heed.

This simple carpenter from Nazareth has been for me and countless other healers the one to model—the one who can lead us back to the basic attitudes and purposes of healing. I appreciate the ways I have been equipped with medical knowledge and technology, but I am also glad I can offer my patients something more. For I have also been equipped with an inner direction and consciousness of His presence, enabling some seemingly miraculous results.

What a privilege it is to be a part of a profession so blessed with opportunities to help heal the hurts, sorrows and miseries of this ailing world. Well aware of my human limitations and weaknesses, I acknowledge Him as the chief source of power in my life, in the healing profession, and in the writing of this book. He is the paragon of excellence.

THE END

Glossary of Definitions Found in This Book

Acceptance: an attitude which looks to the intrinsic worth of a person and values the potential of the inner person, regardless of status, intelligence, external dress, or obnoxious behaviors.

Action: to engage in a dynamic movement in reaction or response to stimuli and circumstances, predetermined largely by our attitudes and habits.

Altruism: a concern for meeting the needs of others, taking pleasure in enabling people to satisfy their needs.

Arrogance: an attitude of self-satisfaction, self-superiority and self-sufficiency.

Attitude: that changeable, reprogrammable, restructurable, renewable pattern of our thoughts, which makes growth possible; the powerful, changeable mindset which predetermines our actions, either to react or respond to circumstances and stimuli.

Awareness: becoming consciously circumspect and cognizant of our self and our circumstances; the conscious faculty of our brain which is alert and alive with all of our senses tuned to our internal and external environment.

Beauty: a perception of something that stirs the soul to smile, admire and desire.

Carefulness: the powerful process of becoming aware of risk, its potential and its pitfalls, by becoming thorough, vigilant and wary.

Caring: an attitude which is positive, warm, friendly and responsive to those who suffer, marked by a reaching out of our hand and heart to help.

Change: the faculty of mind necessary to renew or restructure our attitudes, transforming our person into a new identity and direction of growth; the powerful process of renewing, replacing, restructuring or transforming, which yields a new direction, identity and destiny.

Character: the stamp of individuality impressed upon a person by nature, education and habits; the inner core of one's being.

Choice: the faculty of free will which selects our options that are predetermined by our thoughts, desires, purposes and values.

Collaboration: defined by Webster's Dictionary as "working together."

Commitment: the choice of attitudes and actions which sustains steadfast loyalty to persons, principles, values, processes, purposes or things, regardless of circumstances or adversity.

Communication: the powerful process of listening and speaking to another person, sharing our thoughts and feelings about something and listening as the other person speaks their thoughts and feelings as well.

Compassion: the powerful process of suffering with another person to help in the healing of sickness, sorrow, stress, pain or brokenness, enabling the person to grow again.

Competence: a balance of knowledge, skills and attitudes.

Concern: an attitude of marked interest in serving the patient more than self, characterized by the giving of greater consideration to the needs of another person in community; the powerful process of becoming a servant, responding with individual consideration to the needs of others.

Confidence: the powerful process of believing in our Creator, ourselves and others, which inspires trust, respect, hope, courage and dignity as we see our worth as a person.

Conflict: the powerful process for change in a struggle/embrace relationship, arising from differing expectations, needs, wants, passions, powers, principles, priorities and purposes.

Conscience: stemming from two Latin words, *con* (with) and *science* (knowledge), this is inner awareness of our passions, perceptions, principles, priorities, purposes and the freedom to choose.

Controlling stress: managing the thoughts and circumstances which challenge us to adapt either positively and pro-adaptively, or negatively and maladaptively.

Control over practice: the powerful process of managing the science, art, attitudes and business in the practice of the medical profession.

Desire: the faculty of our imagination that creates a vision of our aspirations, dreams, wants and wishes for something of value.

Destiny: our vision of the end of life's journey.

Education: the powerful process of stimulating our physical, intellectual, social and spiritual growth, so we can become what we were meant to be.

Education: not stuffing our minds with facts, knowledge and technology, but rather discovering, challenging and nurturing our creative imagination with awareness and freedom...

> To think...to feel
> To image, desire...to purpose
> To prioritize...to choose
> To act...to persist
> To become response-able...to change
> To grow into our full potential.

Empathy: derived from Latin, *em* (in) and *pathos* (feelings), this is a deep inner feeling for another person, putting ourselves in their situation.

Ethical ecology: the moral climate, community conscience, and sum total of all forces outside of ourselves—good/evil or positive/negative—which impact our thoughts, behavior, character, growth, harmony, unity and balance in society and the individual.

Ethics: the community collaboration concerning the highest standards of human behavior and moral values; the highest good.

Evil: any force, thought, fantasy or attitude which violates the harmony, unity or balance in the family of man and our environment.

Excellence: the highest human standard of behavior, ethic, practice or thing achieved by superiority of character.

Family: a unity of persons—ideally father, mother and child (or children)—committed to each other in loving relationships for growth and sharing of common needs, purposes and values.

Feeling: the faculty of our mind that reacts or responds to stimuli or circumstances with emotions that energize our behaviors and thoughts, either positively or negatively.

Freedom: the quintessential inner nutrient of growth that liberates us to think, feel, desire, purpose, prioritize, choose, act, persist, become response-able, and change.

Habitude: an attitude in process of becoming a solidified habit.

Healing: the process of managing and mobilizing all the powers possible in our reaction or response to circumstances, sickness, sorrow, stress, pain or brokenness, mostly by changing our attitudes so we can grow again.

Holistic medicine: the discipline which seizes the unity of a person—his physical, intellectual, social and spiritual well-being—and his potential for growth.

Hope: defined by Dr. Robert Schuller as "Holding On, Praying Expectantly."

Humility: the virtue achieved by recognizing our own limitations and our need for assistance from others and from our Creator.

Humor: a uniquely human capacity of mind which expresses or reacts to something funny with smiles or laughter.

Life: the expression of movement, structure and processes in the phenomena of creative force, union, growth, birth, growth, struggle (forming identity and independence), growth, embrace (learning interdependence and partnering), growth, maturity, growth, productivity, growth, death and creative force.

Mediation: the process of resolving conflict with the aid of a neutral third party, with the goal of preserving the best possible working relationship and outcome among the participants.

Noma fascies apraxia: a Latin phrase meaning "an inability to put name and face together."

Partner: a unique person in relationship with one or more persons who are growing toward interdependence and unity of purpose and values.

Peace: not the absence of conflict, but rather a successful outcome of the processes of conflict resolution.

Persistence: a continuous commitment to action, urged on by a strong belief that the highest good will come, regardless of adversity and circumstance.

Prioritizing: the faculty of mind which sets our value systems and treasures of the soul for the highest good.

Pro-adaptive: a positive manner of adjusting to circumstances, responding rather than reacting.

Process: a system of "how to" advance in growth, expertise, excellence and productivity by continuous improvement over time.

Purpose: the faculty of mind that sets specific goals and plans which determine the direction of our destiny, giving meaning to life's aspirations.

Rapport: getting connected to the whole person rather than superficially paying attention only to words.

Religion: a system of values, traditions and spiritual practices which aspire to the highest good for man, inspired by the Creator of the universe.

Respect: defined by Webster as a sense of worth or excellence toward another person.

Response-ability: the ability to respond, not react, to stimuli or circumstances, so we become pro-adaptive rather than maladaptive.

Sensitivity: the degree or measure of our emotional response to human pain or hurt.

Sexual intimacy: a union of mind, heart and sexual expression through the process of pleasuring and sharing our deepest wishes, dreams, desires, thoughts, feelings, values and purposes.

Sin: any choice, attitude or action which violates a trusting, positive relationship between persons, our Creator, or our potential for growth.

Success: a journey of striving for excellence in living, serving and growing to our full potential.

Sympathy: Feeling (*pathos*) with (*sym*) another person.

Thinking: the faculty of our conscious mind that processes knowledge and experience by questioning, reasoning, problem-solving, assessing, analyzing, computing and compartmentalizing memories.

Truth: an absolutely dependable belief, word, fact, idea, perception, principle, value or way that stands the test of time and trial.

Value: a thing, ideal, person, idea, purpose or relationship that we treasure, prize and deem important.

Values: what a person (or institution) prizes, places as top worth, and prioritizes in order of importance.

Virtue: the culmination of excellent character traits that have been cultivated by the processes of striving for the growth of our thoughts, attitudes, actions and habits of excellence.

Wisdom: the treasury of truth which is accumulated by using the power of discernment to refine our knowledge and experience.

About the Author

Dr. Ed Hollenberg was born in India, the son of missionary parents, and he came to the U.S. at age one. He has been in family practice for more than 48 years, achieving several honors along the way: Diplomat of American Board of Family Practice; Associate Clinical Professor Family Practice Residency; member of Indiana Medical Licensing Board; and committee member of Federation of State Medical Licensing Boards.

Dr. Hollenberg and his wife, Jean, are the parents of six children: one teacher, three physicians, and two nurses. They have 18 grandchildren. In addition to his medical practice, Dr. Hollenberg enjoys gardening, tree farming, woodworking, photography and encouraging people to grow into their full potential. He is a lay leader of First United Methodist Church in Winamac, Indiana. For more information, visit his Web site at *www.powerfulpartnering13C.com.*